A BREATH OF FRESH AIR

A BREATH OF FRESH AIR

A balanced and informed perspective
on the unusual phenomena sweeping
the worldwide church

Mike Fearon

Eagle
Guildford, Surrey

The right of Mike Fearon to be identified as the author of this work has been asserted by him in accordance with the Copyright, Design and Patents Act 1988.

Copyright © 1994 Mike Fearon

British Library Cataloguing-in-Publication Data. A catalogue record for this book is available from the British Library

Published by Eagle, an imprint of Inter Publishing Services (IPS) Ltd, 59 Woodbridge Road, Guildford, Surrey GU1 4RF

All Scripture quotations, unless otherwise noted, are taken from the *Holy Bible, New International Version*. Copyright © 1973, 1978, 1984 by the International Bible Society. Used by permission of Hodder & Stoughton.

Typeset by The Electronic Book Factory Ltd., Fife, Scotland
Printed in the UK by HarperCollins Manufacturing, Glasgow

ISBN No. 0 86347139 0

Contents

Preface

The reader has every right to approach this book with grave suspicion.

Strange occurrences have been noted in churches across the world, during 1994. Laughing, crying, shaking and falling to the ground are the most obvious features, though it is clear that deeper work has been taking place too. Lives have been transformed, marriages restored, churches reinvigorated – and a good time has been had by many!

'Surely though,' queries the discerning reader, 'it is much too early for anyone to be writing a book about all of this.'

I willingly concede that any detailed, long-term assessment would be premature. But this book has a different purpose.

For many church-goers, 1994 has been a time of confusion and bewilderment. The Holy Spirit seemingly has turned churches upside down, and thrown into question many people's long-cherished views about religious life. Some claim that the fashionable phenomena has nothing to do with God, but is simply mass hysteria / demonic activity / a media hype. (Choose your own poison!)

For the man in the street, the Church seems to have finally awoken up after a long kip. Christians have been seen smiling for a change, and some of them actually seem to be happy! The best party in town seems unexpectedly to be happening in the most staid of congregations. Jesus Christ is suddenly a very attractive and trendy dude.

In such challenging times, *sound guidance* is urgently needed by individuals desperate to come to terms with the stress and turmoil that change brings with it. It's no use in five years time, when you needed it last week!

Some solid facts would make a useful starting point. A good clear description of the recent events. Throw in some background. Pin down the key people. Check for skeletons in the cupboard. Kill off the hyperbole and media invention.

Let's look at the possibilities. Assess strengths, weaknesses, opportunities and threats. Invite along some pundits to give their range of views. Then start to draw some provisional conclusions.

'All in double-quick time, please. And not too many long words either!'

Before long, you can start to sift the wheat from the chaff, and begin to form your own tentative opinions. More importantly, you can begin to work out the personal implications for yourself.

Simple enough?

Let's get cracking!

Mike Fearon
London
October 28th 1994

Chapter One

Laughing in the Aisles

They certainly know how to 'butter people up' at Holy Trinity Brompton!

I arrived one gorgeous July evening for a service at HTB, as it is affectionately known, to discover the place heaving at the gunnels. A steward politely took me around to the front to try to find me a vacant pew in the bulging choir stalls. People were sitting patiently and contented on the steps and floors around the proud stone sanctuary at the head of the nave, and within the sanctuary itself.

With no room to swing a cat, there seemed to be only one seat left in the house.

'Would you like to sit in the bishop's throne?' enquired the steward . . .

The Wine Press

There was a time when the only church-related news stories that were apt to make the national press ran along the lines of 'Gay Vicar runs off with Choir Master'.

In summer 1994, the newspapers were having a field day with a different type of religious story. No paper has yet run the headline 'Religious Nutters', but the style of reporting may often have suggested such a caption to many a hard-pressed sub-editor.

Take the *Daily Mail* story which ran on September 2nd 1994: 'This man has just been given the Toronto Blessing. What in God's name is going on?' I wondered that myself, since it was unclear whether the headline referred to the photo below it – of the man lying prostrate in the aisle during a HTB service – or to the picture of former topless model Samantha Fox beside it.

'It is, it must be said, a disquieting sight: the congregation fall where they stand, their eyes rolling wildly,' began Geoffrey Levy's article. 'Most are convulsed in near-hysterical laughter. Others weep uncontrollably. Many shake violently, as though having a fit. Visions of angels, huge figures, some with wings, bathed in orange light, swim before their eyes.

'This is the Toronto Blessing.'

Is it really? According to the people that I've seen and spoken to – it isn't!

1994 saw what might more accurately be described as 'a movement of the Holy Spirit' in many hundreds of Britain's 50,000 churches, and thousands more across the globe. It roughly followed a pattern which began in January at a tiny Canadian fellowship that meets in Toronto, hence the term 'Toronto Blessing'. When a church experiences the phenomena, the outward signs consist of most of the congregation raising their hands to receive from God, and feeling a great sense of peace. A minority – perhaps 10–25 per cent – experience stronger, physical manifestation.

For the moment, let's be neutral and call it 'an altered state of consciousness' in which their bodies often begin to shake violently; sometimes they speak – or sing – in strange languages; laughing or crying may occur; they may fall over, usually landing limply without hurting themselves (if they are not caught by willing hands on the way down); some, with eyes closed, begin marching or running on the spot; less frequently, people may roar and mimic the actions of a lion . . .

None of these are actually *new* occurrences. As we will see, they have happened in the Church – on and off – for 2,000 years. The significant factor is the sheer unprecedented scale on which these phenomena began to occur during 1994.

In an average pentecostal or charismatic church over the last few dozen years, a prophecy or two might be given at many meetings, a few times a year someone might fall to the floor in ecstacy, and several people might be relied upon to speak or sing in tongues at virtually every meeting. These gifts have been seen with very similar frequency within the house church movement – now perhaps better termed 'The New Churches' – since the seventies. Perhaps a few dozen churches of other denominations were also accustomed to seeing these gifts manifested. This used to be the norm.

The movement of the Holy Spirit which swept through British churches in 1994 led to these manifestations occurring in literally hundreds of churches where charismatic gifts had seldom, if ever, been present before; while those churches where charismatic gifts were a regular occurrence were staggered at the increased usage.

By autumn 1994, there were many thousands of churches worldwide where, on average, several people abruptly fall in ecstacy, 'slain in the Spirit' at every meeting; where speaking in tongues is always manifest, and often singing in tongues; where violent shaking occurs in a way seldom seen since the birth of the Quaker movement; where virtually unknown charismatic phenomena, such as people jumping up and down, marching on the spot, or roaring like lions, have become not infrequent items in the Holy Spirit's powerful arsenal of blessings.

So the new phenomonon is both one of *scale* – more churches affected, and more people in each church – and of *magnitude,* with phenoma previously seen infrequently becoming more commonplace, and having a far deeper and more lasting effect.

It is this *intensity* which has attracted the national press. In her feature in *The Times* (July 2nd 1994) Ruth Gledhill noted: 'People were dancing in the aisles, and the back of the young man in front of me had begun vibrating as the beginning of a progression to spiritual drunkenness that was to end in rigid, on-the-spot shaking and leaping.'

As she left the service, she glanced back 'beyond the empty chairs and bodies strewn over the floor to see many who were not affected chatting calmly over coffee as if nothing was happening, while bodies were splayed at their feet, bearing beatific smiles and looks of tremendous peace.'

The churches where these phenomena occur soon attracted many visitors from other churches, often seeking ways to introduce this fresh spiritual outpouring into their own fellowships. HTB, for example, was packed to bursting for many months after the blessing began to occur there, as hundreds of people flocked each week to witness and experience what God was doing in their midst.

At the time of writing, four months after the 'Toronto Blessing' made its unexpected but very welcome appearance, services there are so full that the choir stalls and chancel area behind the speaker have to be used as overflow areas, with scores of people standing in the gallery and around every doorway. Nearly 2,000 people pack into the building every Sunday.

Some people glibly dismiss the Toronto Blessing as dangerous fanaticism, or as an eerie occult manifestation. For others, churches like HTB are God's wine-presses, producing the fragrant new wine of God's kingdom on earth. They are the cutting edge of contemporary Christianity.

But who is right?

We could start by asking some of the people who have experienced this amazing blessing. Let's find out what it's like to be on the receiving end.

Come, Holy Spirit

'I didn't really see how lying on the floor was going to promote the kingdom of God,' remembers Ruth Meaden about a particularly vibrant and buzzing HTB service. 'But I had an incredible sense of God holding me and saying that he is my father and no man, organisation or church will ever be able to break that bond. I didn't understand what was going on but it didn't matter. I had never been so close to God.

'I had also never been so happy. I had a passion for God like I've never known, and instead of being angry at my old friends I found myself weeping for them to find what I have.

'I am no longer walking with God, I'm running, jumping, dancing and laughing. I don't know how long it will last, but I don't care either. I keep pinching myself in case I'm dreaming, but I'm not!' she told HTB's in-house newspaper.

Ashley Meaney remembers: 'It was as if I'd taken laughing gas. It was almost like Jesus was telling me jokes. It was as if Jesus was in the room and he just wanted to have some laughter and we started to laugh. Then I felt this desire to do this little dance . . .

'I enjoyed the feeling of letting go and just being *me* before God and *me* in front of people. I was out of control and it was fantastic. For me, it was so right

– a complete expression of wholeness and freedom in who I am in Christ.

'I have a much stronger sense of the presence of the Lord as a result of what has happened.'

Bill Cahusac remembers effervescently, 'I don't think I've ever laughed as much as I did that evening. I can't really describe what I was thinking exactly. It was just the most incredible sense of joy. You know that feeling when you're just so happy. It was as if something was going on inside and and the only thing that I could do was to laugh.

'I feel freer and more alive than I've ever felt in my life. I just feel more and more free, and more and more alive, and more and more in love with Jesus. All I want is to know Jesus more, and not *just* to know Jesus more but to give away the incredible blessing that he has given to me.

'I wasn't forced to the floor, but I did feel quite weak around the knees so I co-operated and just let myself go. I thought, "Well now I'm here, I'll stick around for a while and see what the Lord wants to do. And it was amazing, because the prayers [that people were saying for me] got slightly more specific and really touched me deep down in a lot of areas to do with fears and worry and anxiety. I then went into a time of crying – just sobbing – for about twenty minutes, just sobbing.'

Many members of HTB have experienced the love of God in some new way.

When Bob Read was prayed for at the church, because of what he had heard from others, he thought there was going to be great laughter and rejoicing, but it transpired that God had a much deeper work to perform. He began weeping. Then he moved into a deep mourning – a wailing, mourning feeling that he had never experienced before.

'I think God was finishing off a work that he's been

doing for years at different stages over my life, regarding my father who died when I was about thirteen. I thought I had released my father, but I think I had to have a time of deep mourning and a realisation of how I must have felt all those years ago. It was a wrenching and letting go,' he says regarding the therapeutic nature of his experience.

'I was on the floor by now, curled over and over holding my stomach. It was a new thing for me. But then God just showered his fatherhood and his love for me. Then I felt myself going into different places around London, where there is great suffering. I got a tiny touch of how it hurts God – the suffering and alienation.'

HTB's vicar, Sandy Millar, told me: 'We believe in the ministry of the Spirit, and if you say that, it inevitably takes you down paths you didn't expect.

'There seems to be a significant action of God to decrease emphasis on denominationalism; people are much more keen to describe themselves as simply Christians. There's so much of a hunger by so many people for God, I feel we ought to reach as many people as possible.

'We need a theology for everything we do, the beginnings of an understanding. Then we need a model; for us, the Vineyard have been immensely helpful. We have ministers meetings here every month. Once you've got your theology and your model, you just have to get stuck in. Our function is to keep up with God, and not to tell God what to do. As a church, I think we've been telling God what to do for quite a long time; and now he's decided to do something for himself, and we find that hard.

'More work still must be done to explain what has been happening, but the Christian life is lived on the ground, with disciplined Bible study and praying. We'll

see the fruit in due course. For me, it's important
simply to listen to the Spirit at this moment, though
with a number of people, the changes are demon-
strable. They have a new desire to read the Bible, a
greater love for Jesus, and a fresh desire to reach out to
other people. By any standards, that sounds like a work
of the Spirit of God. I've heard of relationships being
healed, and people sensing the need to be reconciled.'

When I had first visited HTB, back in 1989, I had
found a lively Anglican church with a strong social
ministry and good solid teaching. It was also a little
staid, and very upwardly mobile. But when I revisited
the church one evening some two months after the
Blessing had arrived, all the staidness had been blown
away like stale cobwebs. Like Cinderella transformed,
here was a congregation ready to go to the ball!

At a typical HTB meeting now, the teaching is still
there and the work with the homeless and outcast
continues apace, but the clear emphasis now rests on
'waiting for the Lord'. On that second visit, I saw nothing that I hadn't seen before, during the golden years
of charismatic renewal in the late seventies, though it
was apparent as I made my way around the building,
stepping over the prone bodies, that far more people
were smitten than I had ever seen affected in one place
before. Though not all had dropped to the floor, about
15 per cent of the congregation showed signs of being
in a state of profound spiritual exhuberance.

One striking feature, which had gone unreported in
all the press accounts, was the remarkable beauty of
the congregational singing. It possessed a guileless and
enchanting loveliness, as though angels were joining
in with the rich harmonies. Angelic figures, bathed
in orange light, were conspicuous by their absence,
however . . .

Subsequent visits, a few weeks later, found a church

struggling a little to come to terms with its newfound notoriety. The regular congregation took the prospect of having to arrive an hour early for evening service, if they were to stand any chance of getting a decent seat at their own service, in good humour.

A Fresh Pentecost

If HTB seemed to have become 'more pentecostal than the pentecostals', across town at Kensington Temple – an Elim pentecostal church – overt emotionalism was being kept on a tight rein.

'Here at KT, we were already in the charismatic swim of things; but what has happened here since June has been at a deeper level, and with a greater dimension,' senior pastor Colin Dye told me at the end of September 1994.

'I knew that other churches were being affected in the same way. It's unfortunate that the press picked out one or two churches, and I felt that we at Kensington Temple needed to back away. The last thing I wanted was to be caught up in some sort of impression of a bandwaggon. I was having the phone ringing every day, with journalists asking if anything was happening here. I felt that if this was something big and fresh from God, we should not be reporting it in the papers. We should be on our faces asking God, discerning it, and certainly not comparing church with church.

'Even with our emphasis on tongues, we have never chased phenomena, ever. That is *not* a test or a measure of spirituality, and it never was. Neither, though, do we shun phenomena. We encourage people to respond to the move of God and the Holy Spirit.

'For months, we waited on God, prayerfully seeking what we should do, and asking what he was saying to us as a church. It was relatively easy to minister in the Blessing, because the phenomena were present, but we didn't know how much place to give to them. Eventually we felt that by September 1994, once the holiday season was over, we had had time to pray the matter through and to seek God.

'We didn't feel it was right to cancel our Bible training programme in these times of refreshing. Training was not neglected. Evangelism continued as before, but we knew it couldn't simply be 'business as usual'. We knew there had to be fundamental changes in the way we opened up to the Holy Spirit and the way we responded to him as a church. Teaching, preaching and evangelism intensified, and the levels of dramatic conversions has been astonishing.'

At an executive council meeting, the Elim denomination found twenty to thirty churches in each of eight regions were being visited by phenomena. 'I would say between a third and a half of all our Elim churches were affected. I'm convinced that as many more were touched by the Spirit, without the manifestations being seen. We feel that God has revitalised the roots of pentecostalism, and is renewing our links with past revivals. People are looking back to the Great Awakening – which happened in America in the eighteenth century – but there are stronger parallels with the 1904 Welsh revival.

'I can see a new level of power at work, there's no doubt about it. You can't be on your back 365 days a year, yet the early fruits are much closer to New Testament Christianity than anything the Church has been offering day-by-day. I would be happy to dialogue on that point', said Dye.

'It's strange that many people who would not hold to a pentecostal theology or style are nevertheless arriving at a similar experience of God. The difference between, for example, Morris Cerullo and John

Wimber, is purely one of style. There are strengths
and weaknesses with each approach, but God is doing
the same thing with different people.'

God's Vineyard?

One Sunday evening, in the hall of Elliott School in
Putney where the South London Vineyard meets, I
discovered a conservative middle-class congregation of
about 150, attending a good but unspectacular service.
At the conclusion, everyone stood in silence to 'wait
upon God'. After about thirty seconds, the silence was
abruptly broken by spurts of fruity or embarrassed
giggling. Around me, a few people began shaking —
in a way that some might deem erotic. A single voice,
singing sweetly in some unknown tongue, rose into the
still air, powerfully charged with expectation.

It soon became apparent that the 'Blessing' that was
beginning to unfold before my eyes was far from identical to the phenomena I had witnessed at HTB. Here
there were far more people shaking, like eighteenth-
century Quakers, and far fewer people falling to the
floor. The atmosphere became exquisitely peaceful.

Some sat quietly, others prayed blissfully. A soloist
began to play quiet, worshipful songs, as a pastor
invited visitors to sit at one side if they desired prayer
and ministry. Someone brought welcome coffee round
for those now unmoved by the proceedings. Mostly,
people had collected spontaneously into small casual
groups, some bent over prone figures, some seated
and talking quietly. Many were energetically praying
for others, with an open hand held a couple of inches
above the person's head. In the interests of propriety,
men prayed with men, and women with women.

Suddenly, close to me, a young man began to lean
backwards at an angle of about ten degrees. With a

beatific look on his face, he made absurd mincing steps backward to try to regain his balance – like a character in a Tom and Jerry cartoon! – until welcome hands caught him and lowered him safely to the floor. He looked angelic as he lay enraptured on the carpeted ground.

At St Paul's, Onslow Square, a satellite church of HTB, the atmosphere and the style of blessing was closer, oddly, to that of the Vineyard than that of the parent church. Here, an accomplished rock band led us through contemporary worship songs, any teaching element was virtually non-existent, and the upwardly-mobile congregation was ready and willing to shake vibrantly.

'When the Holy Spirit hit St Paul's Onslow Square, SW7, on Sunday morning, I felt it through the floor,' reported Andrew Brown cynically, in *The Independent*. 'There were four heavy thuds as congregants fainted *(sic)* and then rapid drummings – like the noise that rabbits make to warn one another – when people began to shake uncontrollably and beat their feet against the floor.

'Towards the front a woman with short black hair was bouncing like a road mender's drill for about twenty minutes. Sometimes she laughed but mostly she just bounced against the hands that were laid on her from the sides. From somewhere came tremendous pantings and gaspings that were not quite sexual. The laughter was really strange. From three or four places in the church, you could hear this gut-busting abandoned giggle. It was not an adult sound at all. It was more like the laughter that you get by tickling a happy toddler; but it was coming from respectable women in their thirties. They sounded as if they had just been told the best joke in the world and it was going on and on and on.'

Nine days after my first visit, on September 6th, I returned to the Putney Vineyard to hear Marc Dupont, the associate pastor of the Toronto Airport Vineyard where this strange blessing had first erupted, just eight months earlier. This time, the hall was packed with perhaps three hundred people.

The twenty minutes of opening worship passed peacefully, then Marc Dupont took the stage. This confident American, who came to Christ as a result of the witness of a lively Baptist church, had moved from a Californian church to join the team at the Airport Vineyard in Toronto. Now, he spoke lucidly about the good things he had seen God doing in America, Europe and India.

'When transition hits, and the Spirit begins to move, sometimes people are taken by surprise by it.' He warned that people who are on the cutting edge of God's work can sometimes be subject to spiritual pride. They can delude themselves that God will accelerate what *they* are doing, when perhaps God actually wants them to be doing something different. Abandonment is needed.

Marc Dupont believes that the pace is going to accelerate, and that it is important that Christians enter into what God is doing now, not what he was doing ten years ago. Renewal is coming to traditional churches.

Dupont 'moved into prophetic ministry' in 1975. He speaks of a vision he claims God gave him – a picture of God taking away the four walls of a church building and replacing them with glass. He considers that, in the present time frame, God is releasing gifts and revelations to people who may not immediately understand what these are all about.

Within four months of arriving in Britain, the impact on British churches easily eclipsed anything happening in Canada. Marc estimated that people in 1,000–1,500 UK churches had experienced the 'Toronto Blessing' – though, of course, it is notoriously difficult to find accurate figures.

'God is giving revelation of his heart for the poor,' claims Marc Dupont. Elijah did not have a nice, polite message, and Dupont believes that God is giving a similarly unequivocal message in the present time. Troubles will come, but the Church must be ready for them.

It doesn't matter whether or not people go to Toronto looking for blessing. God is surely everywhere, though many of the 500 church leaders who – to that point – had visited the Toronto Vineyard, were perhaps unclear on that point of theology.

In the ministry time that followed Marc Dupont's talk, I witnessed by far the most stunningly powerful move of the Holy Spirit I had seen up to that moment. Well over a hundred people, nearly half of those present, were powerfully affected. At one point, I counted two dozen people lying comatose, and the final tally was probably twice that number.

Firstly, those pastors who needed encouragement came forward with their wives – and I wondered what their congregations would have made of the antics of this sober group of church leaders, when the Holy Spirit fell dynamically upon them. Many people shook, some bounced like road drills, one or two even resembled turkeys gobbling!

Then came those who had prayerfully petitioned God and wished to receive the gift of prophecy. As Marc prayed for them, I witnessed for the first time one of the more unusual phenomena connected with the Spirit's outpouring. Many of these would-be prophets began to make strange roaring sounds in the depths of their throats – the notorious lion noises.

Dupont continued to orchestrate the proceedings, shushing the roaring prophetic wannabees and calling out those with a burden for evangelism. I went forward peacefully, and as I stood, Marc received words of knowledge about various people who had come forward. As the Spirit came, I began to weep, but the tears soon dried and I was left with a profound sense of peace – a warm glow through my whole body, centring on my abdomen and thorax.

Those in need of personal renewal, and a hug from God, came forward at the end. I was introduced to Luke (no, not the Gospel writer!) who had been shaking in the Spirit, and asked him how it had felt. He described feeling like an onlooker, bemused at how his own body was behaving. Above all though, he said, it had felt like an awesome 'hit' with some potent spiritual narcotic. He was high as a kite.

Afterwards, I tried to arrange an interview with Marc Dupont, but he was sceptical, claiming that he had been quoted out of context too many times. I resisted making the obvious comment: 'If you're a prophet, aren't you supposed to know whether or not I'll misquote you?'

Baptists in the Spirit

Many Baptist churches experienced similar occurrences, during the summer of 1994. Rob Warner at Herne Hill Baptist Church fell to the floor 'under the weight of the glory of God'. He told the *Baptist Times*: 'The external manifestations are secondary to meeting with God. It frightens me, but I see God at work. I have never experienced such a profound outpouring of the Spirit, but this is not yet a revival.'

Quite independently, Bookham Baptist Church, Surrey, received a startling visit from the Holy Spirit early

in June. On the 10th, a few days after he had called
the church to prayer, Revd Ian McFarlane was in
his garden – planting petunias! – when he began to
shake and had to go inside to sit down. When the
church was being cleared after the service that Sunday
evening, he invited those present to stand and 'wait
upon the Lord'.

The Holy Spirit came with such power that McFarlane
fell off the platform and lay on the ground 'slain in the
Spirit' for twenty minutes. Though he could not move,
he was aware that similarly staggering occurances
were going on all around him. When he opened his
eyes, he saw others laughing, weeping, and praying for
each other. 'Teaching must go alongside experience,'
he says, downplaying the feel-good factor. He calls it
'a restoring of people's first love for God'.

For Revd Mike Wood at Lewin Road, Streatham, the
key word was 'refreshment'. Passionately committed
to reconciliation between racial minorities, and desiring to see a deeper hunger for God and the Bible, he
told *The Baptist Times*, 'The test will be in the fruit
– whether this leads to conversions and whether the
church is renewed'.

At Queen's Road Baptist Church – where we will be
returning later in the book – open meetings were held
for members of other churches to receive the Blessing,
and to 'take it back' to their own churches.

'We've had closed meetings for the church as well,
where we've begun with prayer, then blessing one
another till most were on the floor,' pastor Norman
Moss told me. 'Then there was an opportunity for
people to use a microphone to tell others of their
experience. The depth of earnestness in prayer was
striking; an added dimension was there.

'Subsequently, we've seen marriages helped, and
people have found a great sense of peace, as well as

more profound spiritual growth. Some people have
fallen when they had no expectation to do so. But it's
too early to make final judgement.'

In Focus

Peter Watherston is an elder at the Mayflower Family
Centre. In the four years I've known him, I've found
him to be easily one of the most controlled and least
emotional people I have ever met in my life. Worn down
by the pressures of inner city ministry in London's Can-
ning Town, he and his wife were in need of a refreshing rest when they booked onto Focus '94, a week-
long teaching holiday at Morecambe Bay, Lancashire,
hosted by HTB and its church plants.

'When I closed my eyes during worship the first
evening, it sounded as though I was in London Zoo or
the African jungle,' he remembers. Though he had been
'moving in a charismatic direction' for several years, he
is not a charismatic himself. 'People have talked of this
being a time of refreshing, and that sums it up. People
seem to be walking closer to God, and to have become
more active in evangelism through this Blessing.'

He had seen no evidence of physical healings, though
he willingly concedes that many emotional healings
may have occurred. Peter believes that 1994 has been
a time of preparation rather than an end in itself. 'It
felt good. Let's wait and see what happens next.'

Others at Focus '94, which took place at the end of
July 1994, began tentatively to piece together a more
complete picture of the Holy Spirit's fresh workings.

Mary Pytches felt that God was restoring again
authority and leadership to his Church. 'And, boy,
don't we need it? He's putting some backbone back
into our men. Praise God we are going to have some
fathers in God at last. People have met angels who

have said, "The trumpet is at the Lord's mouth." When the trumpet is sounded and the army is on its feet, then we'll all go out and there'll be a great conquest. Something wonderful is in store for us.'

On a more conservative note, Clive Calver, General Director of the Evangelical Alliance, cautioned, 'When God moves, it does not rest well with the religious establishment. God always rocks the boat. If this is an end in itself, I've got to confess to being slightly disappointed because I've spent the last twenty years waiting for God to turn society around.

'This is the beginning. God is after a people broken before him. God forgive those who've condemned this as a work of the Enemy. I believe that God starts with us, but we don't want it to finish here, do we? I like laughing, but I'd like our world to laugh too.

'God wants a people who will offer themselves so totally and completely that he can blow by his Spirit in a way that we have never seen before. This is just a beginning – and as God gets surrendered lives, he wants to take us out to make a difference.

'It's a call to repentance. It's a call to surrender ourselves. When we do that, we'll stop waiting for God and find that God is waiting for us. And when he's found us, I believe he's going to use us to change this nation in a way we haven't seen since the days of Wesley and Whitefield . . .'

It's been a long time coming!

Chapter Two

From Nine in the Morning

According to David Barratt in *The Twentieth Century Pentecostal*, there were, in 1988, 332 million charismatic or pentecostal Christians, making them the largest single movement within the worldwide Church – itself the single largest religion on the globe. More recent, but less reliable, estimates suggest that the figure could now be as high as half a billion – fully 10 per cent of the world's population!

Growth to this pinnacle position began in earnest only at the turn of the century, with the so-called 'Tongues Movement', more properly called the Pentecostal Movement. By the late 1980s, there were nearly 200,000,000 people in the rapidly growing pentecostal denominations. With missionary zeal, they went boldly to the poor and marginalised of the Third World, attracting adherents into a 'poor man's faith' whose followers strongly identified with the historical Jesus, the friend of the oppressed and the downtrodden.

In the 1960s, this army of love was joined by millions emerging from the more staid and traditional denominations. Some remained within their own denominations, like yeast within a loaf, seeking to revive and renew structures from the inside, though many left to form the house churches. This was called the Charismatic Movement, or 'the third force' alongside the Catholics and Protestants. (This is actually an

inaccurate designation, 'the fourth force' would be
more accurate, since the original schism was between
the Eastern and Western churches early in the Christian era, and the Protestants were actually the third
force.)

123 million strong, in Barratt's estimation, the charismatics emerged in the sixties, at the same time that
more liberal Christians were trying to be 'honest to
God' by pretending that he was dead . . .

In the 1980s, a 'third wave' crashed in from amongst
evangelicals who had theologically opposed both the
Pentecostal movement in the 1900s, and the Charismatic movement sixty years later. Barratt estimated
that this 'third wave' is growing by around nineteen
million members each year, though this figure will
need to be revised in view of the wind from Toronto.

The Church, under the Holy Spirit, has come a long
way since the first Pentecost! But what a long strange
trip it's been.

Pentecostal Fire

It all began at nine o'clock one morning in AD 30.

As the well-known passage in the second chapter of
Acts describes, the disciples of Christ were gathered
together in one house, when the sounds of a powerful
wind were heard. The remnants of Christ's followers
who would become the early Church witnessed a phenomenon that appeared like tongues of fire, separating
and coming to rest on the head of each person. At that
moment, they were filled with the Holy Spirit, and
began to speak in diverse tongues, as the Spirit gave
utterance.

Some liberal theologians still claim that the disciples were simple people who became quite emotional
and excited. When this happened, they made peculiar

sounds! These tongues have been 'explained away' down the years as hysteria, hypnosis or auto-suggestion. But the original Greek in which the Book of Acts was written, significantly makes no mention of the disciples being in a state of ecstacy or hysteria. The Bible simply says, in a matter-of-fact way, that 'All of them were filled with the Holy Spirit and began to speak in other tongues as the Spirit enabled them' (Acts 2:4).

It's difficult to support any claim that the disciples simply began gibbering like monkeys, making an incomprehensible noise, as sceptics might like us to believe. The Greek word *glossa* translated as 'tongues' is the same word used to mean 'languages'.

The context, too, demands that the disciples immediately began to speak expressively in recognisable languages. It's vaguely possible that some form of non-verbal telepathic communication was taking place between the disciples and their listeners – but to substitute one hard-to-take notion with another, equally unconventional, theory will get us nowhere.

Now there were staying in Jerusalem God-fearing Jews from every nation under heaven. When they heard this sound, a crowd came together in bewilderment, because each one heard them speaking in his own language. Utterly amazed, they asked: 'Are not all these men who are speaking Galileans? Then how is it that each of us hears them in his own native language? Parthians, Medes and Elamites; residents of Mosopotamia, Judea and Cappadocia, Pontus and Asia, Phrygia and Pamphylia, Egypt and the parts of Libya near Cyrene; visitors from Rome (both Jews and converts to Judaism); Cretans and Arabs – we hear them declaring the wonders of God in our own tongues!'

(Acts 2:5–11)

The clearest inference is that the Holy Spirit spoke

out declaratorily in other languages, using the bodies of the disciples as his consecrated and willing vehicles. This phenomenon of speaking in unlearned languages is evidently the most usual occurrence when an individual is filled with the Holy Spirit. There are several other occurrences in the book of Acts, at Ephesus for example: 'When Paul placed his hands on them, the Holy Spirit came on them, and they spoke in tongues and prophesied' (Acts 19:6,7).

It is apparent that this 'filling' by the Holy Spirit crucially was not a gradual occurrence. Over and over again, we read in the Bible of people receiving the Spirit *suddenly*; constantly we find the dogmatic statement that such-and-such a person was filled by the Spirit at a particular time. Now how could anyone have been so certain just *when* the event had taken place, unless something dramatic – such as the speaking in tongues – had taken place to *demonstrate*, beyond doubt, that it had occurred?

Tongues of the Spirit

The 1994 outpouring did not happen in isolation. Countless thousands have experienced the same phenomenon of speaking in tongues that is described in Acts.

Scientist Robert C. Frost, for example, describes his own experience in his book *Aglow with the Spirit*: 'As I read the book of Acts, I discovered men that were full of faith, wisdom, power and joy . . . Furthermore, their secret seemed to be related to the fullness of the Spirit, for repeatedly I found the above realities linked with the little phrase, "full of the Holy Ghost"' (Acts 6:3,5,8; 13:52) I was not content to read about something that was real some 2,000 years ago; I wanted to experience it now!

At that point, I stepped into the hallway and allowed the infilling Holy Spirit to magnify God through me in a divinely directed way just as I had read they did in the Book of Acts when the promise of the Father was possessed by faith ... God had answered my prayer and a whole new dimension in the Spirit-filled life began to unfold progressively.'

It's time that I too 'came clean'. In the summer of 1976, while living and working in the tiny village of Poynton, just outside Stockport, I lay on my bed one night, praying to be filled with the Holy Spirit as many of my friends had been filled. After two years of hammering on heaven's closed door in prayer, the iron doors opened and the Spirit came upon me – welling up, it seemed, from recesses of my inmost being. Slowly and hesitantly at first, I began to speak in tongues.

For about three years, I moved in charismatic circles. My college Christian Union at Huddersfield Polytechnic – now a university – seemed to have more than its fair share of Spirit-filled believers practising the gifts of the Holy Spirit. I saw others receive the Holy Spirit, and witnessed the apparent deliverance of people from demonic oppression – though this was far from the spectacular display that we read about in Scripture.

I soon learned, too, that the gifts of the Spirit are easily misunderstood. During one of our missions, a concert was staged in the common room of a hall of residence, while members of the CU kept a prayer vigil in a Christian student's room. Unfortunately, the overheard sounds of people praying in tongues freaked out students in neighbouring rooms. Soon, unfounded rumours were flying around the hall of residence that we were performing an exorcism in there!

My home church, Kirkheaton Parish Church, was firmly entrenched in the renewal movement, and began to experience the occasional use of the gifts of the

Spirit – usually in prayer meetings rather than during congregational worship.

I believe though, that God provides whatever gifts are needed at particular stages in a Christian's life. Moving to London in 1979, I became more concerned with the plight of the Church in the inner-city, and the needs of the poor. I became a 'closet charismatic', restricting the gifts to occasionally singing in tongues in my bathtub!

In Other Tongues

Being filled with the Spirit and speaking in tongues is a mystical phenomenon which has recurred in parts of the Christian Church continually down from Pentecost to the present day, specially in times of genuine revival. The great spiritual leader, Charles G. Finney, wrote that he had been filled with the Spirit in the autumn of 1812. It seems likely that D.L. Moody had a similar experience.

In the days of the apostles, Spirit-filled Christians spoke in unlearned languages, some of which seem to have been 'heavenly' tongues with no earthly equivalent, but many were recognised as being the languages of other countries and cultures. This is true of 'tongues' in the present day.

As Frost says in *Aglow with the Spirit*: 'My uncle spoke in the Chinese language when he was baptised in the Spirit. Chinese missionaries were present and recognised the words of praise as they were spoken. He subsequently became a missionary to the Chinese in Hong Kong. Although it was necessary for him to learn the language, this was acheived with great facility, even though he was an older person. He related to me how on some occasions the Chinese would praise God in English as they were baptised in the Holy Spirit.'

Ralph Wilkerson relates how, while at a conference, he met a man named Dr Tosh, who sought the powerful anointing of the Holy Spirit. When Wilkerson agreed to pray with Dr Tosh, three other men – one of whom was a translator for the United Nations – asked if they could be present. Dr Tosh 'sat in an easy chair with his eyes closed,' says Wilkerson. I slipped over and laid hands on him, saying simply 'Receive the Holy Spirit, *now,* in Jesus' name!' And he burst forth suddenly, but quietly, in a language of the Holy Spirit. The U.N. interpreter interrupted, 'Sir, it is rather unusual. You have spoken the identical phrase in three different languages – French, Italian and Spanish!'

Of course, that was in the now far-off days when God seemed to work far more sedately than he has done during the dynamic 1994 outpouring of his Spirit . . .

Some would argue that there is nothing unusual about the experiences described above, claiming that the people have simply remembered odd snatches of other languages, subconsciously, and regurgitated a few phrases. Dennis Bennett, in *The Holy Spirit and You,* debunks this theory with the story of Mrs Wendell Mason, a Christian from La Verne, California, who works with the deaf.

Mrs Mason says: 'I have seen and prayed with at least twenty deaf people to receive the Holy Spirit, and heard them speak fluently in a heavenly language to God, then return to their sign language when communicating with me. I have seen deaf-mute persons receive the Holy Spirit and speak in tongues!'

Clearly these are examples of people who have never heard *any* language which they could possibly have remembered subconsciously. Similar testimonies come from many others who have worked with the deaf. It would be totally impossible for these people to imitate

any language since they have never heard a word in
their lives!

Wetting the Baby's Head

It is, of course, possible that on these other occasions
in Acts, some other phenomena betrayed the presence
of the Holy Spirit. On Pentecost, the Church's day of
birth, it is clear that speaking in tongues was the
major, but not the *only* sign that the Holy Spirit
had come majestically into the hearts and lives of the
disciples.

Their extraordinary behaviour was such that some
bystanders poked fun at the disciples. 'They have had
too much wine!' said the mockers, according to Acts
2:13. They're drunk! The accusation is one that few
commentators have bothered to comment upon; the
allegations that someone has been 'on the bottle',
'down the boozer,' or 'gone on a bender' have seldom
been made about those who have received the anointing of the Holy Spirit in modern times, because the
blessing has usually been a comparatively sober and
orderly matter.

The 1994 outpouring, however, has been characterised by the original and authentic Pentecost phenomenon which Acts 2 records. Those who have received
the outpouring have often appeared to be intoxicated,
even though no alcohol has passed their lips. At several
meetings where the so-called Toronto Blessing has
been in evidence, I have seen very respectable church
leaders staggering about so legless they could hardly
stand up, lurching around for all the world like classic music hall drunks, merrily sozzled. These people
themselves have later confessed to feeling completely
inebriated. Take the 'confessions' of two people from
HTB who 'had a skinful' of the Holy Spirit:

'I spent over an hour rolling on the floor hysterically crying and laughing. When I left I was so drunk! I couldn't get into the car. I had to be put in.'

'I was trying to analyse what was going on and I tried to wipe the tears away and I couldn't move my arms up to my face. It was just amazing. I felt really drunk and I cried for about an hour and a half. God is working deeper.'

Former Elim pastor Adrian Hawkes told me about one man whose experience of the Holy Spirit left him so drunk that he was unable to climb into his car afterwards. It eventually required several friends to shoe-horn him into the passenger seat, while his wife drove him home. Unfortunately, the man was so heavy that his wife was unable to lift him out at the other end! In resignation, she simply left him in the car and went to bed. When the man sobered up a few hours later, he found that he couldn't open the car doors to get out – his wife had inadvertently double-locked them all. He ended up having to climb out through the sun roof!

Hawkes' colleague Paul Dakin told me of another man who frequently became 'drunk in the Spirit' whenever he prayed: 'He'd stagger around and say to me, "Oh, someone phoned for you, but I can't remember who it was. I'd been praying a lot!"'

The Toronto Airport Vineyard has a story of a woman who climbed into her car after receiving the undiluted 100 per cent proof Spirit, and began zig-zagging all over the freeway. A traffic policeman pulled her over and tried to breathalyse her. As she tried to blow into the breath tester, she fell to the ground laughing; at which point the policeman fell too, and they rolled around the freeway under the power of God. 'I don't know what you've got, lady, but I need it!' exclaimed the officer. He went to church the next week, and found Jesus!

Gifts of the Spirit

The Holy Spirit doesn't come simply so that people can
become 'pissed as newts' without having to go down
to the pub. God is not attempting simply to put public
houses, off licences and breweries out of business.

Most emphatically, the pouring out of the Holy
Spirit in Acts was to confer *power!* Christ had left
his disciples with an enormous task to perform –
a task found in Matthew's Gospel: 'Go and make
disciples of all nations, baptising them in the name
of the Father and of the Son and of the Holy Spirit,
and teaching them to obey everything I have commanded you. And surely, I am with you always, to
the very end of the age' (Matt 28:19–20). A considerable commission indeed, but one which the filling of
the Holy Spirit was intended to give them POWER
to fulfil.

During the period between Christ's resurrection and
his ascension, he gave them this command: 'Do not
leave Jerusalem, but wait for the gift my Father
promised, which you have heard me speak about. For
John baptised with water, but in a few days you will
be baptised with the Holy Spirit' (Acts 1:4–5).

In the light of these words from Christ's own lips, it
is strange therefore when some Christians claim that
baptism in Holy Spirit is unscriptural.

There was no question of first and second class
Christians here at this epoch-making moment, *all* were
filled with the Spirit. Jim Packer, in his commentary on
Acts, notes that the accompanying noise 'like a strong
wind', and the visible phenomena 'tongues like flames
of fire', are reminiscent of Old Testament references to
God's presence.

The supernatural abilities conferred by the Holy
Spirit are not confined to speaking in tongues (though

in the present day, tongues seem to be the most usual manifestation).

St Paul said: 'There are varieties of gifts, but the same Spirit. There are varieties of service, but the same Lord ... One man, through the Spirit, has the gift of wise speech, while another, by the power of the same Spirit, can put the deepest knowledge into words. Another, by the same Spirit, is granted faith; another, by the one Spirit, gifts of healing, and another miraculous powers; another has the gift of prophecy, and another ability to distinguish true spirits from false; yet another has the gift of ecstatic utterance of different kinds, and another the ability to interpret it.' *(1 Cor 12:4–5, 8-10 NEB)*

These nine gifts to which Paul alludes can be grouped as follows:

A) Inspirational or Fellowship gifts (The power to *say*)
   1. The gift of Tongues.
   2. The gift of Interpretation.
   3. The gift of Prophecy.
B) Gifts of Power (The power to *do*)
   4. The gift of Healing.
   5. The working of Miracles.
   6. The gift of Faith.
C) Gifts of Revelation (The power to *know*)
   7. Discerning of Spirits.
   8. The 'Word of Knowledge'.
   9. The 'Word of Wisdom'.

Tongues of Prophecy

Of the fellowship gifts, we have already considered the gift of tongues. The second gift – of interpretation –

follows on from the first. As Dennis Bennett puts it: 'The interpretation of tongues is bringing the meaning of what has been said through the gift of tongues at a public meeting. A person feels moved to speak or sing in tongues, and either he or another is given, by the Holy Spirit, the *meaning* of what has been said.

'He or she cannot *understand* the tongue. It is not a *translation* but an *interpretation*, giving the general meaning of what was said. The gift of interpretation may come directly into the person's mind, *in toto* or just a few beginning words may be given, and as the interpreter trusts the Lord and begins to speak, the rest of the mesage comes.'

Many individuals known to me personally could confirm the above assertion.

The interpretation does not appear to be subjective. I remember on one occasion at Kirkheaton, I gave a word from the Lord, in a language unknown to me. I prayed and waited for an interpretation to come. Suddenly, I felt words coming into my mind – 'and when you pass through the waters I will be with you.' Unaccustomed to receiving interpretations, I hesitated; and as I did so, someone else in the room – our curate Chris Edmondson – spoke out the same interpretation.

It was an interpretation similar to the words of Isaiah 43: 'Have no fear; for I have paid your ransom; I have called you by name and you are my own. When you pass through deep waters, I am with you, when you pass through rivers they will not sweep you away . . .' It is difficult to see how two of us could have had identical interpretations if the gift were not an *objective* phenomenon in this case – though I accept that on other occasions where only one person receives an inkling of the interpretation, it could be subjective.

The third gift – the gift of prophecy – appears to be similar in effect to a combination of tongues and interpretation used together. Both functions are combined in one message from one individual, in a language that those present can all understand. One difference is that, whereas tongues and interpretation together are usually meant as a sign to unbelievers, prophecy is claimed to be just the reverse. As St Paul said: 'Clearly then these "strange tongues" are not intended as a sign for believers, but for unbelievers, whereas prophecy is designed not for unbelievers but for those who hold the faith' (1 Cor 14:22 NEB).

I must make it clear that prophecy *per se*, as practised in the present day, is not the same as the prophecies found in Scripture. Scriptural prophecies are not simply *proclamations* of God's words, like modern day prophecies, but also contain a *predictive* element. Scriptural prophets combined prophecy with another gift, the Word of Knowledge. They were thus able to accurately foretell future events.

When these came to pass, the accuracy of the *prediction* was a measure by which people could know that the *proclamatory* element was genuinely of God. Today, there are few 'prophets' in the biblical sense, whose proclamations also contain accurate predictive material. It is far more common for prophecies to be simple proclamations – usually of words that are virtually paraphrases of Scripture verses. Whether that situation will change as a result of the 1994 outpouring remains to be seen.

History of the Spirit

The first reference in Scripture to the Holy Spirit does not come, as some might think, in the Gospels, and certainly not as late as the Acts of the Apostles. The Holy Spirit is mentioned at the very beginning of divine history:

'In the beginning God created the heavens and the earth. Now the earth was formless and empty, darkness was over the surface of the deep, and the Spirit of God was hovering over the waters' (Genesis 1:1–2).

It was as the Holy Spirit that God formed and shaped the world, and it is similarly as the organising Spirit that he has come into the lives of Christians down the centuries. No evangelical would dispute that the Spirit has been constantly active as personal guide, comforter and bestower of grace throughout history.

Some consider that the *gifts* of the Holy Spirit have been significantly absent in the Church since the times of the apostles, and made their reappearance only within the last hundred years – this is the *Latter Rains* theory. Whilst it seems true that the Spirit has been more prevalent and active in the lives of Christians, as a giver of gifts, during the twentieth century than at any time since the first century, crucially there are many references in the writings of the Church Fathers, and prominent Christian saints down the years, to disprove any notion that the gifts of the Spirit were absent for 1,800 years.

Powerful charismatic works of the Holy Spirit are described in the writings of Justin Martyr (c100–165), Irenaeus (140–203), Tertullian (c165–220), Hilarion (c291–371), Augustine (354–430), Francis of Assisi (1181–1221) and Teresa of Avila (1515–1582) to mention but a few.

For many reasons it is difficult to assess with any certainty how active the Spirit has been through Church history, in the sense of bestowing the pentecostal gifts. We must remember, that only in our own century has illiteracy been largely conquered, and the printed page become a familiar sight.

Previously, most Christians would not have been able to preserve records of charismatic experiences in

any written form at all; and even if they had been able,
the scarcity of affordable printing would have both
hampered any spread of written details, and increased
the chances of any single written source becoming
lost or destroyed. Major revivals in obscure parts of
the globe may be missing from the pages of history
simply because no written records have survived; the
dissolution of the monasteries under Henry VIII, in
particular, resulted in priceless ecclesiastical records
being lost for ever.

During the Dark Ages, when the clergy were treated
with reverence and awe, as the founts of received
wisdom (forgive my cynicism!) any spiritual experience
overtaking the laity was looked upon with grave suspicion. A layman becoming filled with the Holy Spirit,
speaking in tongues, and blessed with other gifts of the
Spirit, would have kept very quiet about it all, fearing
for his life in some trumped-up charge of sorcery or
blasphemy! It is a sober reminder that the Spirit is
often denied or quenched by the very people who ought
rightly to be fervent for God's anointing.

Many have compared the 1994 outpouring with the
great American Awakening, of the eighteenth century.
Jonathan Edwards had a remarkable experience of
God's absolute sovereignty in 1727, and his subsequent
preaching triggered, not merely a revival of God's
people, but a profound Awakening which transformed
American society. Edwards' wife was once in ecstasy
for seventeen days, unable to take care of her family,
make meals or welcome guests, yet she claimed to have
a delightful sense of the nearness and love of God.

Yet the recent wind from Toronto brought with it an
unfortunate tendency to quote details from previous
revivals without due regard for balance or context.
Though undoubtedly many genuine signs and wonders
marked Edwards' evangelistic ministry, he considered

many of the 'gifts of the Spirit' he witnessed to be counterfeit.

Birth of Pentecostalism

American Pentecostalism strictly began on New Year's Eve, 1899, in the closing moments of the nineteenth century, when Miss Agnes Ozman spoke in tongues at a healing service in Kansas. The revival which began in Azusa Street, Los Angeles, in 1906, brought the Pentecostal movement to prominence in America.

So much has been written about the development of Pentecostalism – the bibliographies list some 10,000 volumes – that nothing can be added, and little summary is needed. It was seen initially as a movement of uneducated hillbillies, rednecks and holy rollers, and changed its image only with the present generation. American Pentecostalism now controls a multi-million dollar television and publishing empire, yet its most characteristic feature remains the speaking in tongues – though a more accurate characteristic might be its sheer diversity.

The main Pentecostal denominations in Britain, where it spread in the 1920s are the Elim Pentecostal churches and the Assemblies of God, though there are literally hundreds of smaller denominations – some with only a single church.

'Even the formalised statements of belief and doctrine within Pentecostalism reflect amazing variety, containing not only the classical and common doctrines of the Christian church, usually amplified by various additions on Pentecostal doctrine – tongues, baptism in the Spirit and so forth – but also offer "articles of faith" on such topics as footwashing, church property, the usefulness of camp meetings, and membership of secret societies or labor unions', writes

Donald Dayton in *Theological Roots of Pentecostalism*.
'Such statements are not always to be trusted in the
search for a characteristic theological understanding
of Pentecostalism'. . .

British pioneer Smith Wigglesworth gives a better
idea of the flavour of the movement: 'Pentecost is
believing that after the Holy Ghost comes upon you,
you have the power. Do not be afraid to believe.
Believe that God makes you a partaker of the divine
nature through his grace and precious promises. His
own eternal power working in you will bring forth
a divine order that can never be surpassed by the
world.'

Some Pentecostals consider that *conversion, sanctification* and *enpowerment* by the Holy Spirit are three
distinct stages in the Christian life. Others collapse
the first two stages into one, while a third stream
– more in line with conservative evangelical theory
– sees all three functions as completed, or at least
begun, by Christ at the moment a person starts to
become his follower. The Christian is justified by grace,
through faith – not by adherence to a set of rules, or
by submission to man-made dogma.

The expression '*full* Gospel' – as in Full Gospel
Businessmen's Fellowship – is often bandied about to
mean that belief in physical healing and empowerment
with the other charismatic gifts is an essential part of
the message of salvation – i.e. you're not saved unless
you have the gifts, and are able to heal yourself and
others of all physical malady.

It requires, however, considerable distortion and
mutilation of the clear meaning of the Scriptures to
argue that salvation entails anything other than a
simple belief that Christ died in order that each believing individual can become a part of God's family.

This is not to deny that God *can*, and sometimes

does, perform real miracles, generously bestow healing, and empower Christians to speak in tongues
and/or prophesy as he wills it. But God cannot be
defined or constrained by human doctrines. He is
sovereign and acts as he wills.

In Britain, the reigning monarch is immune from
all the laws which Parliament enacts on his or her
behalf. None of them apply to the sovereign! When the
Queen recently consented to pay tax on her income, it
was an act of grace – not a submission to law. When
God behaves in a regular and orderly manner, it is
not because he is bound by tradition or procedure
which people take to be law, and then build doctrines
around. His sovereign authority can and does confound
attempts by theologians to *constrict* his behaviour in
any way.

Some have accused Pentecostals of having no theology. This is an unfair allegation in itself, though it may
be true that pentecostal theological emphasis is not a
matter with which many conservative evangelicals can
easily be in agreement. Four basic theological themes
to which pentecostal theology addresses itself – the
four gestalts of Pentecostalism – are salvation, the
Holy Spirit, healing and Christ's return.

Some evangelicals may lament that other issues
should have been lumped together with that of salvation, but it's been happening for far longer than
the 'Penties' have been around; the Council of Nicea
lumped the doctrine of salvation in with everything
else they believed to be essential to the Christian
faith, and called it the Nicene Creed. No one seriously
objects to this useful summary of basic Christian belief,
though it includes far more than three other principles
alongside salvation.

Pentecostal statements of faith are surely no worse
that the Church of England's Thirty-nine Articles, or

even the multiple clauses in the Evangelical Alliance's statement of faith!

Fruits of the Spirit

Charismatic gifts seem to have been dispensed comparatively rarely, even in the last hundred years or so for which we have reliable records. Many Christians in the more traditional denominations have therefore claimed persuasively that their use is not an essential part of Christian faith and practice.

The 'Latter Rain' movement accepted the rarity with which the gifts had been dispensed up until this century, and suggested that the explosion of gifts in the twentieth century has occurred because these are the last days, and Christ's return to earth is imminent.

A contributory factor for the surge of interest in God at the turn of the century was the rising expectation in many quarters, without biblical justification, that the end of the century would usher in a new era. Expectations are now even stronger as the fast-approaching AD 2000 will soon usher in, not simply a new century, but a new millenium. Many Christians suffered from PMT – *pre-millenial tension* – immediately before the year AD 1000 too, but they were disappointed. It is perhaps best not to raise one's hopes for events to which, as Christ said, the timetable is in God's hands alone.

Another explanation for the apparent increase in the use of gifts may lie in an elementary perusal of population statistics. The world's population is currently doubling roughly every forty years. There are probably more people alive now than have ever lived; consequently, there are more Christians on Earth today than there are in Heaven. The apparent increase of Holy Ghost activity today may simply be because there are more believing Christians around than ever before!

Many staunch Methodists comment that the high regard in which most Pentecostals hold John Wesley for his emphasis on the Holy Spirit may be a little misguided. An examination of Wesley's writings suggest that he was more interested in the *fruits* of the Spirit than the *gifts*.

The fruits of the Spirit are listed in Paul's letter to the Galatians: 'Love, joy, peace, patience, kindness, goodness, faithfulness, gentleness and self-control' (Gal 5:22–23). The first three relate to God; the second three to others; and the last three to ourselves. There are then, an equal number of *gifts* and *fruits*, though neither list may necessarily be complete. Christians often squabble about the gifts of the Spirit – power can be intoxicating – but are usually at one about the desirability of acquiring the fruits.

Fruit takes time to grow and mature, and it requires careful nurturing. The fruits of the outpouring of God's blessing will require time to ripen. 1994 saw only the blossom and, however lovely the fragrance, many will not be satisfied until they have tasted the choicest ripened fruits. Till then, the suggestion that certain Christians have become intoxicated with experience – and not with sound doctrine, biblical learning and sacrificial giving – will persist.

It was always thus:

'Then Peter stood up with the Eleven, raised his voice and addressed the crowd: "Fellow Jews and all of you who live in Jerusalem, let me explain this to you; listen carefully to what I say. These men are not drunk, as you suppose. It's only nine in the morning!' (Acts 2:14–15).

The pubs were not open yet!

Instead, he claimed, the Pentecost experience was the blessing proclaimed by the prophet Joel some 500 years years earlier:

In the last days, God says,
  I will pour out my Spirit on all people.
Your sons and daughters will prophesy,
  your young men will see visions,
  your old men will dream dreams.
Even on my servants, both men and women,
  I will pour out my Spirit in those days,
  and they will prophesy.
I will show wonders in the heavens above
  and signs on the earth below,
  blood and fire and billows of smoke.
The sun will be turned to darkness
  and the moon to blood
  before the coming of the great and glorious day of
    the Lord.
And everyone who calls
  on the name of the Lord will be saved.
(Acts 2:17–21 quoting Joel 2:28–32)

Only the first part of the prophecy was fulfilled at
Pentecost. Some would say optimistically that signs
in the heavens and the return of Jesus Christ on the
new-born wings of morning is, two thousand years
later, now just around the corner.

Chapter Three

One in the Spirit

D r Andrew Walker was born into the Elim Four-
square Gospel Church, and received a pentecostal
upbringing. In 1960, aged 14, Walker waited on the
Spirit as an Apostolic pastor laid hands on his young
head.

'I felt from his hands what these days a New Ager
might call "waves of energy", and then my tongue was
locked solid, and the Walker of the chat was struck
dumb. I tried to talk, but all I could manage was
a stammer of disconnected sounds. Then the sounds
connected, the tongues rushed out, and I felt good
but strange, and a little frightened,' he recalled in
Charismatic Renewal: The Search for a Theology.

Four years later, he had abandoned God altogether,
and he returned to the Church only in 1971. Clearly,
the anointing of the Holy Spirit was not the panacea
for all his ills, doubts, temptations or questions.

Tom Smail recalls, in the same book, his own introduction to charismatic expression, five years after
Walker's experience. When laying hands on a sick
member of his congregation led unexpectedly to healing, Smail was stunned. Of course, he believed that God
could heal, but to see that God *did* heal was another
matter altogether!

Later, while he was considering the implications, he
met the American pastor Dennis Bennett, who had

received baptism in the Holy Spirit, though he was
not a Pentecostal. Smail liked the man, but considered
that his theology was impossible:

'One of the reasons why nowadays I avoid describing
a renewal experience as "baptism in the Spirit" is that
baptism speaks of birth and beginning, the coming
into life of something that was not there before. The
Holy Spirit was in my life long before 1965, long
before I had any formulated awareness of charismatic
experiences and gifts, as indeed according to Paul he is
at work in the lives of all Christians who confess Jesus
as Lord.'

He now describes his own experience of the anointing
of the Holy Spirit as 'an entry into the good' of all
that he had previously believed. Tom Smail became
a leading light in what became known as the Charismatic movement. Just as an exceptional outpouring
of the Holy Spirit at the turn of the century led to the
founding of the Pentecostal movement, so a second
wave of outpouring sixty years later resulted in a sister
movement.

Semi-detached Suburban

Whereas Pentecostalism had attracted the working
classes, who liked it 'because it works' and often were
unconcerned about the theological niceties of what was
happening, charismatic renewal tended to appeal to
the more thoughtful middle-classes. Many remained
within their own churches, for a while at least, before
branching out courageously to form the fledgling house
church movement – though a few waifs found refuge in
the thriving Pentecostal churches.

If the Pentecostals expected that these brothers
in the Holy Ghost from other denominations would
either join them straight away – or at least come to

them for advice — they were often disappointed. The
Charismatic movement charted its own course, largely
independent of Pentecostal tradition. There were a few
shipwrecks along the way, and considerable storms
within the mainstream churches; a few mutinys arose;
and many charismatics were made to walk the plank by
churches that considered them a disruptive influence
— but considerable spiritual refreshment was enjoyed
along the way!

Adrian Hawkes recalls the expectation that Pentecostals had of the fledgling charismatics — expectation
that was never fulfilled: 'that these people would be
kicked out of traditional churches and swell the ranks
of the Pentecostals. But it didn't happen, they weren't
kicked out because there was a new atmosphere in the
country. A second expectation was that these people
would come to the Pentecostals for *advice*, but this
rarely happened.'

Hawkes remembers though, in the late sixties, receiving a call from some Catholic monks who wanted
to see him. It seems that they had been reading
about people being filled with the Holy Spirit during
their studies of Scripture. They had immediately laid
hands on each other and prayed for the anointing in
the Spirit, which they had duly received. 'Now what
should we do?' they wanted to know!

Many early charismatics made the same mistakes
and sank to the same excesses as some Pentecostals,
such as misuse of the gifts: for example, prophesying
that Mr So-and-so must go and marry Miss Whatsits.
Any genuine work of God soon finds itself subtly cor-
rupted with elements of the flesh and the devil, and
comparison with Scripture will often reveal startling
factual errors.

There's a story of an old lady who began to 'prophesy': 'This is the word of the Lord. You are very dear

to me, I hold nothing against you, *as far as I can remember ...*'

I remember one new Christian who told me he had been given 'a song from the Lord'. It certainly had a lovely tune, but I felt uneasy about the lyric which described Jesus picking flowers for his mum, and King Solomon *leading his mighty armies out for battle*.

Hawkes remembers a 'prophecy' which began: 'Thus saith the Lord, when *Noah* crossed the Red Sea ...' A bit later on, 'God' realised his error: 'Thus saith the Lord, I'm sorry I made a mistake, it was *Moses* and the Red Sea ...'

Not all criticisms of the Pentecostals and Charismatics were founded on such obvious errors. Sometimes the mistakes lay with the critics themselves, says Hawkes: 'One denominational magazine slammed charismatic Catholics, but when I talked with the author of the article, it turned out that he'd never even *met* a charismatic Catholic! Other churches made out that Pentecostals were totally illiterate and knew nothing about theology.'

I pray that the same beligerent attitude and senseless criticisms will not characterise the adversaries of the more recent move of the Holy Spirit.

The Charismatic Years

Some see the charismatic renewal as God's most dynamic activity in today's Church. Others believe it is a gigantic confidence trick, perpetuated by a group of theological cranks and charlatans. The polarity is so pronounced that a middle ground is often hard to find – but here goes!

In the early 1960s, men like Arthur Wallis, David Lillie, Eric Houfe, Charles Clarke and Philip Smith

(but why were there no women pioneers?) found charismatic renewal for themselves, and introduced it into
their various churches and denominations. Other early
charismatic pioneers went on to become both well-
known figures in the movement and figureheads for
renewal in the wider Church: David Watson, David
Pawson, John Noble, Michael Harper and Douglas
McBain, spring to mind.

Overseas, the charismatic movement affected Anglo-
Catholics in California, early in the 1960s. The South
African, David du Plessis, circulated statesman-like
amongst Protestants and Catholics alike, encouraging
and guiding. And a charismatic team of American Full
Gospel Businessmen – ably supported by the likes of
Derek Prince, Brother Andrew, Oral Roberts and Nicky
Cruz – held a convention at the London Hilton in 1965,
and evangelised on the streets of Soho. The launch
of *Renewal* magazine in 1966 gave the burgeoning
renewal movement its own in-house magazine.

Michael Harper resigned from his curacy under
John Stott to organise the Fountain Trust, a service agency to organise conferences and to stimulate
charismatic renewal. The US edition of *The Cross
and the Switchblade*, with its discreet mention of
charismatic gifts, was regarded as too racy by every
British religious publisher, and it became an unlikely
underground classic for a while.

'In the late sixties and early seventies, God touched
many people. We were baptised in the Holy Spirit and
we knew that there was no way that we could stay
in our old churches with the gifts of the Spirit and
function as we wished,' reflects Gerald Coates. 'Most
of us were not the church leaders – if we were, it might
have been different. Some of us were asked to go – as
I was – whilst others felt obliged to leave.'

Charismatics who felt rejected by traditional churches

often founded churches in their own homes, the so-
called house churches which have now grown much
too large to meet in anyone's home – unless you
happen to live in Buckingham Palace. Dave Tomlinson
established a strong house church in Middlesbrough,
later moving to London. John Noble founded a church
in his Ilford home in 1967, while Bryn Jones led the
Bradford New Covenant Church in 1969. Terry Virgo
followed suit in Hove, Gerald Coates in Surrey, and
Roger Forster in South London. Before long, these
burgeoning communities of like-minded believers were
hiring school halls and community centres for their
joyful meetings.

Tom Lee's Post Green Community in Dorset, and
the Pulkingham's Cathedral of the Isles, Cumbrae,
developed charismatic living in more rural surroundings. Colin Urquhart headed up the Bethany Fellowship. The charismatic pioneers' non-religious approach
to Christianity – their dislike of churchy jargon for
example – progressively evolved in homes up and down
the British Isles. They rejected the dead formalism of
traditional religion.

God seemed to be doing all things new in all sorts of
unlikely places, with all sorts of unlikely people!

'There were about a dozen churches, each with half
a dozen members,' remembers Coates. 'They seemed
to be of no importance whatsoever, but when you look
now at events like the *March for Jesus* – 10 million
Christians involved, all over the world – ACET, the
largest AIDS initiative in the UK in 1994, and a wide
range of other ventures both local and national, they all
came from about half a dozen people like myself . . .'

Still, some charismatics managed to remain within
their denominations; David Watson is perhaps the
most famous example. The Church of Scotland and
the Methodist Church both gave official support to

their charismatic members in the early 1970s. Frank
Wilson was perhaps the first Baptist to receive baptism
in Holy Spirit, but David Pawson – in Chalfont St
Peter, then Guildford – became the denomination's
most celebrated charismatic.

As a whole, the Baptists responded better than the
other denominations to the charismatic renewal. Jim
Graham, Bob Roxburgh and many others soon came to
the fore. In the URC, Tom Smail and Bob Gordon were
leading lights. Charismatic renewal gradually became
accepted in traditional pentecostal churches.

'The *Nationwide Festival of Light* marked an important stage in the movement's growth,' believes Coates.
'It meant that Christians who were charismatics were
expressing a care for the world in which we live, albeit
with a very narrow and limited agenda. Many of us who
were involved were charismatic evangelicals.' This, of
course, was the origin of the organisation that has now
become CARE.

'Then there was the musical *Come Together*, a significant and historic tour that was Christ-centred and
which brought Christians together, emphasising the
body of Christ.' Without *Come Together*, this book
would never have been written, because it played a
significant part in my own conversion.

By 1972, there were twenty-seven charismatic groups
in the UK. A year later, David Watson moved his
congregation from tiny St Cuthbert's, York, to the more
spacious St Michael-le-Belfrey, close by York Minster.
The songs and playing of The Fisherfolk stimulated
distinctivly charismatic worship. The Dales and Downs
Bible weeks were born a few years later, and Don
Double's Good News Crusade joined the Fountain
Trust in sponsoring charismatic conferences.

Who could forget the boisterous and flamboyant Arthur
Blessitt, dragging a full-sized cross – with a wheel on

the back end! – from Trafalgar Square to Edinburgh. Whenever anyone came up to him with the obvious question – 'Excuse me, but why are you carrying that cross?' – he lovingly pointed them towards Jesus.

Towards a Theology

'In the 1960s neo-Pentecostals were content to take over Pentecostal theology in large measure and give speaking in tongues a Pentecostal prominence,' says James Dunn in *The History of Christianity*. 'But the widening of the charismatic movement since the 1960s had brought with it a questioning of the classic Pentecostal categories, a desire to formulate the theology of the Pentecostal experience more carefully, and a renewed concern to let the life of the Spirit be expressed in new forms of community.'

In Jim Packer's words, the charismatic renewal has been 'a movement looking for a theology'. One was clearly needed if only to differentiate between the genuine and the counterfeit. Many charismatics might have decried the use of 'tying God down' in theology – they wanted to *experience* God, not talk about him – yet they soon *had* a theology, albeit one they had picked up piecemeal. It was like a curate's egg – good in parts.

The genuineness of a subjective encounter with God's Spirit in no way authenticates the theology that stems from attempts to explain the encounter. Only objective conformity with God's revealed word in the Scriptures would guarantee trustworthy doctrine.

A reliable theology would also have to be true to God's perfect revelation through the life of Christ. In practice, some charismatics down to the present day, sadly take little notice of the incarnation and atoning death of Jesus Christ, because they are too busy looking to the Holy Spirit. But the way to Pentecost is through Calvary, and the Spirit was sent from the cross.

In charismatic theory, we often find that 'to enter into Pentecost is to pass beyond the Cross into a new supernatural world in which centre stage is held not by the incarnate, crucified and risen Lord, but by the Spirit and the dramatic manifestation of his triumphant power,' says Smail.

We should not look to the Holy Spirit to overcome evil for us, like some supernatural disinfectant. Jesus Christ overcame it maturely, by letting it do its worst to him, then rising triumphantly from death itself. Glorification of the Spirit should be avoided; Christ is the triumphant Lord, who conquered death and rose victorious from the grave.

Out of the Shell

In the 1970s, Christians in general were often divided over the work of the Holy Spirit, and many preferred to stick with their old ways.

> Like a mighty tortoise moves the Church of God.
> Brothers we are treading where we've always
>   trod.

Yet there was clearly a problem of relevance – or, rather, the lack of it. Many recognised an obvious impatience with the organised Church; a feverish activity to reorganise the Church; an alarming rise in occultism outside the Church; and a steady growth in traditional Pentecostalism.

The Holy Spirit was once the forgotten person of the Trinity, now Christ was in danger of being forgotten by some, as charismatics strove to plead spiritual gifts from God's Spirit, as though he were merely a cosmic Santa Claus. The Holy Spirit's symbols of fire, wind, water and dove were embroidered on banners and altar cloths across the globe.

The movement of the Holy Spirit affects thought, speech, feelings and actions; it creates life, glorifies Jesus and unites all believers. The song *We Are One in the Spirit* became an anthem for a whole generation of charismatics in the late sixties and through the seventies.

The Spirit convicts of sin, causes new birth, works in sanctification, and witnesses to the believer's relationship with Christ. He provides revelation and illumination that is beyond normal human facility.

It's clear from Scripture (John 14:16 for example) that the Holy Spirit is a person, not a thing. Nevertheless, as recently as 1973, David Watson found it necessary to reiterate in his classic book *One In The Spirit* that the Holy Spirit is the third person of the Trinity; that he is indeed God. It's strange to think how but a generation ago so many Christians were theologically naive about the Holy Spirit!

Watson's milestone book went on to explain progressively how God leads his people through circumstances, through other Christians, through the Bible, and through a believer's prayer life. Through the Holy Spirit, God bestows many wonderful fruits and gifts. Most charismatics now know the lists off by heart.

Now, there is little need for preachers to reiterate how the Holy Spirit is Comforter, Counsellor, the Spirit of truth, misunderstood by the world. If you explain that now in most churches, the congregation will say, 'We know that already. Tell us something we don't yet understand!'

Baptism in Holy Spirit

A major source of disagreement amongst Christians
this century – who don't always demonstrate the spiritual fruits – concerns the notion of the baptism in
Holy Spirit. Watson asked the rhetorical questions, 'Is
every believer "baptised in the Holy Spirit?" Does it
happen automatically at regeneration? Is it a universal
blessing for all members of the new covenant?' Watson
was able to quote two well-respected expositors who
disagreed like chalk and cheese on this matter:

'According to scripture, we have been baptised with
the spirit because we have repented and believed,'
affirmed John Stott, at that time still Rector of All
Souls, Langham Place. It seemed clear from scriptures
such as John 3:1–8; Romans 8:9; and 1 Cor 2:10–14
that no one could be a Christian without having the
Holy Spirit. 'I would appeal to you not to urge upon
people a baptism with the Spirit as a second and subsequent experience entirely distinct from conversion, for
this cannot be proved from scripture.' Nearly a quarter
of a century later, many conservative evangelicals
still held to that view. They rejected the charismatic
movement virtually out of hand, believing that it has
no adequate theology.

'I am convinced that there are large numbers of
Christian people who are quenching the Spirit uncon-
sciously by denying the possibility in their very under-
standing of the doctrine of the Spirit', said Dr Martyn
Lloyd-Jones, a short walk away at Westminster Chapel.
'There is nothing, I am convinced, that so quenches the
Spirit as the teaching which identifies the baptism of
the Holy Ghost with regeneration.'

It must be agreed, said Watson, that all Christians
have the Holy Spirit: 'Any attempt to drive a wedge
between the Spirit of Christ and the Spirit of God is to

plunge straight into dangerous heresy.' Yet not every Christian is *filled* with the Holy Spirit: 'The command "Be filled with the Spirit" is a present imperative: "Go on and on being filled" is the force of it.'

There are few subjects over which Christians become as steamed up as the expression 'baptism in the Spirit'. Good cases can be made from Scripture for at least two positions: i) it happens at the moment of conversion, or ii) it is a subsequent event.

Water baptism is linked with Christian initiation, and is seen in many cultures as the ultimate demonstration of public faith. It is a rich word, meaning to plunge, sink, drown, drench or overwhelm. The word 'baptism' speaks both of an initiation and an overwhelming.

The early Pentecostals chose the expression 'baptised in the Holy Spirit' to describe their experiences, seeing their own power encounter with the dynamic Spirit as parallel to the accounts in Acts. The expression occurs only *seven* times in the whole of Scripture, and each time, the original Greek text clearly says 'baptism *in* Holy Spirit'. (For no apparent reason, the translators generally render the expression 'baptism *with the* Holy Spirit'.)

The first occurrence is found in Matthew's Gospel, where John the Baptist says to the Pharisees, Sadducees and, apparently, everyone else in earshot: 'I baptise you with water for repentance. But after me will come one who is more powerful than I, whose sandals I am not fit to carry. He will baptise you with the Holy Spirit and with fire' (Matt 3:11). The next three occurrences of the expression are found in Mark 1:8; Luke 3:16; and John 1:33, and all three times, virtually identical words are found again on the lips of John the Baptist. It is unclear whether all four Gospels are referring to the same one-off exclamation, or whether the saying was a regular part of his preaching. In Luke, John is talking to 'the people', but neither of the other two Gospels give any indication of context.

'John baptised with water but in a few days, you will be baptised with the Holy Spirit' (Acts 1:5). These are Christ's words, spoken to the apostles a few moments before he ascended into heaven.

The sixth time we find the expression, it is from Peter's mouth, quoting this same occurrence of the expression. Some critics argue that the expression 'baptism in Holy Spirit' referred *only* to the one-off event on the day of Pentecost, but I do not find that the evidence above bears this out. Indeed, in this sixth use of the expression, Peter particularly likens a *subsequent* event he witnessed at Cornelius's house (described in detail in Acts 10:44–46) to the events on the day of Pentecost.

Though 'baptism in Holy Spirit' is a biblical expression, elsewhere, the Spirit is described as coming (Acts 19:6), being poured out (Acts 10:45), or falling (Acts 10:44). The most common expression is 'filled with the Holy Spirit', favoured by Luke, even to describe the original Pentecost event (Luke 1:41,67; 4:1; Acts 2:4; 4:8; 6:5; 7:55; 9:17; 11:24; 13:52 et al.). Luke uses the word *pletho* for 'fill', and this is the same Greek word used in Matt 27:48 and John 19:29 for filling a sponge with vinegar; it means filled in the sense of being immersed. Each time, he is speaking of individual Christians at specific times, and it is nowhere suggested that *all* Christians are *filled* with the Spirit, all the time.

Only from the *seventh* occurrence of the expression 'baptism in Holy Spirit' can we detect that *all* Christians have clearly *received* the Spirit: 'For we were all baptised by one Spirit into one body – whether Jews or

Greeks, slave or free – and we were all given the one
Spirit to drink' (1 Cor 12:13). Yet here Paul is clearly
speaking of the body of Christ, a metaphor for the
Church. He clearly means that the Church has been
baptised in the Spirit, which is quite different from
saying that every believer has been thus deluged. A
metaphor can only metaphorically be baptised!

The Christian *has* the Holy Spirit from the very
beginning of the walk with God, but a cautious believer
might be likened to a sail boat skimming the water's
surface, with only its keel submerged. With Holy Spirit
baptism, the call is to allow one's very nature to change,
and to become, as it were, a submarine, filling our
ballast tanks with the Spirit, and becoming totally
submerged in God, with nothing of ourselves showing
on the surface. A Christian 'becomes a submarine' by
repenting, obeying, thirsting and asking. 'Ask and it
will be given; seek and you will find.'

As Watson says, 'In the final analysis, it is the love
and power and reality of the Spirit that counts, not
the phrase.' Still, though, many conservative evangelicals rejected the Charismatic movement out of
hand, because it still seemed to them to have no valid
theology of the Holy Spirit. That would not begin to
come until the eighties.

Trouble at the Mill

The expectations that the Charismatic movement im-
plicitly loaded on its members were often impossible
to fulfil. You can't live up to such a theologically
loose series of expectations where nebulous 'inner
conviction' and contrived proof texts often take the
place of systematic theology.

There were pragmatic problems too, Gerald Coates
recalls: 'In 1976 there was a well-documented split

between Bryn Jones and Arthur Wallis on the one hand, and John Noble and myself on the other, relating to adultery by one of the leaders of the movement. We expected him to be disciplined, and a much lesser discipline was imposed.' On the other hand, the Coates/Noble camp was far less legalistic in many other aspects. Coates describes it as 'a great split forward', because it allowed him to develop all manner of different models for the Church.

Boundaries were still being pushed back. I vividly recall Pentecost 1978 at York Minster, where my church gave a multi-media presentation. I remember some of the younger members having to be disuaded, during rehearsals, from putting their lunch on the high altar!

The old wineskins of traditional denominations still found it difficult to contain the potent 'new' wine of the charismatics – it had actually been in the vats for 2,000 years and was an excellent vintage. Some local churches were able to keep their old traditions and to cultivate the new work of the Spirit. St Michael-le-Belfrey, Millmead Baptist and Gold Hill Baptist spring to mind, but there were many others like HTB and St Luke's, Hackney. Generally though, the charismatic renewal led maturely to the wholesale formation of new churches, fellowships and networks.

There were many para-church organisations, too; often viewed with suspicion by the traditional churches. The Full Gospel Businessmen's Fellowship was one, growing from just five UK branches in 1976 to 232 by 1986. 'Their formula was simple and direct: show love by inviting your acquaintances to a meal, tell them what God is now doing in people's lives, invite them to come to Christ and pray for their personal needs, financial, medical and mental,' says Gervais Angel in *Delusion or Dynamite?* 'At a time when

male unemployment was beginning to take effect, the
message that God uses males and gives them dignity,
was a magnet.'

By about 1979 or 1980, the momentum began to
slow. Pundits like Eddie Gibbs, the Bible Society's
church growth guru, began to wonder whether charismatic renewal would continue to be an effective media
for growth. I have fond memories of working a few
feet from Eddie in London Bible House around that
time, and finding him to be a very approachable but
cautious man.

Distinctive music continued to emerge from renewal
groups and songwriters. As in the 1970s, the new decade saw books, tapes and – now – videos continue to be
widely influential in spreading ministries. The distinctives of charismatic renewal, though, were beginning to
blur as their most striking innovations – contemporary
worship and home groups – were adapted wholesale by
Christians of all persuasions.

Apart from the Church of England, the Catholic
Church had been more affected by the charismatic
renewal that any other denomination. By 1986, the
Roman Catholics had 1,000 charismatic prayer groups
in Britain; more than 12,000 Methodists were committed to charismatic renewal, many within the Dunamis
Renewal Fellowship; the house churches had 40–45,000
members, though many felt the growth rate was far
poorer than they had expected; and numerically the traditional Pentecostal denominations went from strength
to strength. The Assemblies of God reported in 1984
that their membership had increased by 71 per cent in
the previous ten years.

Yet there were many charismatics who were still
becoming increasingly disillusioned. Perhaps some had
expected to see greater miracles – people walking
on water or rising from the dead, perhaps – and

were unprepared for the hard realities of constant prayer, culturally-relevant evangelism and attention to Bible study, leading to an undramatic but steady growth. Many were suffering from the lack of vision, which Gerald Coates terms 'post-charismatic depression'. They despaired of the gulf between the claims being made for charismatic ministries and the realities of the poor and oppressed, the sick and the unsaved.

'Under the influence of charismatic teaching people learn to trust in ecstatic experiences, impulses, coincidences, and a host of other subjective influences,' Masters and Whitcomb cautioned sagely in *The Charismatic Phenomenon*. 'They quickly come to trust impulses as the direct guidance of God, and many progress to receive all their guidance through dreams and visions . . .

'Ex-charismatics have spoken of the disillusionment over the lack of real concern for righteousness and holiness. They have found that the baptism of the Spirit formula for sanctification did not really touch their lives and bring them power over their sin. Many have singled out for criticism the characteristic style of worship, with its emphasis on emotional abandonment.'

Many wise charismatics are ready to acknowledge the mistakes of the past, and to urge discernment in the future. I know of no charismatics who would be happy with the notion of dreams and visions replacing Scripture as their major source of guidance, as Masters and Whitcomb seemed to fear.

Unfortunately, these authors occasionally exposed their gaping ignorance of the real views of charismatics: 'The overwhelming majority of charismatic leaders still hope for a world-wide ecumenical church under the leadership of the Pope.'

Do they really?

Others were more belligerent, like C.S. Butler in *Test*

the Spirits, ridiculing what they didn't understand, tilting pathetically at windmills like latter-day Don Quixotes: 'What are we to make of a group whose claims of miracles are exaggerated, many of whose healings are at best psychological, whose tongues are gibberish and not languages, and whose behaviour is often excessive and extreme?'

Some were able eloquently to express genuine concerns and fears: When Jesus cast out demons, people did not dispute the fact that he had healed demoniacs. What his critics questioned was his right to claim the authority of God for what he was doing (Mark 3:22).

Our question about the reality of the charismatic renewal is of a similar kind. There are behaviour changes in people who claim to be baptised in the Spirit. The mental, emotional and physical conditions of people have been altered under the ministry of charismatic gifts ... But what most concerns critics is whether this has anything to do with Christ.

Similar changes do take place, as we shall see, in non-Christian contexts. In order to decide whether or not we are dealing with God or delusion here, Christians must turn to the Bible for enlightenment.

For some, there were deeper problems, too ...

Charismatic Reality?

American, Neil Babcox, is one former charismatic, a pastor whose honest desire to be true to God led him close to despair, when he came to believe that certain spiritual gifts he had been displaying – speaking in tongues and prophecy – were not authentic.

In his honest book *My Search for Charismatic Reality,* Babcox relates how in the early 1970s, his sister-in-law introduced him to a prayer meeting that 'featured' speaking in tongues as its 'star' attraction. The hostess at whose house the group met, he later discovered, was a spiritualist. The featured speaker, Brother Bernardi, looked grave. During the evening, the lights were dimmed.

'Everyone crowded around me in a circle. They placed their hands on me and prayed in tongues. Brother Bernardi urged me to speak out by faith. But I just couldn't bring myself to do it – which isn't surprising when you consider that I wasn't a Christian, not to mention that I hadn't the dimmest notion of what was going on.'

The whole fiasco seems to have borne greater similarity to a fairground seance than a genuine charismatic meeting. It would be difficult to envisage a more inept approach to the conferring of the gift of tongues.

Later, one of the Jesus People at Southern Illinois University invited him to a more orthodox Bible study, and he eventually became a follower of Christ. His spiritual life was like a roller coaster ride until, at another prayer meeting, he was prayed over that he might receive the gift of tongues.

He did receive it, though he was very uneasy about the experience. A college professor convinced a couple of his friends that they didn't have this gift at all. Neil was confused.

As a young pastor, Neil encountered many books that were sarcastic and scathing in their arguments against the authenticity of speaking in tongues. Psychological arguments were raised, but the same arguments would as well have been used to 'discredit' conversion, regeneration and answered prayer – in which all conservative evangelicals believe. It was difficult to see why charismatic gifts should have been singled out for particular criticism.

Others considered that gifts of the Spirit went out with the early Church; that only pagans now speak in 'tongues'; that 'tongues' is simply gibberish and not a real language at all. Some arguments are ludicrous, such as the claim that when St Paul says, 'I thank God that I speak in tongues more than all of you' (1 Cor 14:18), he was referring to foreign languages he had learned through study, during his travels!

'Though some good points were made in those books, on the whole their biblical arguments were unsatisfactory to me,' Neil says. 'Too often, instead of presenting the facts in the light of Scripture taken as a whole, proof texts were cited that didn't prove anything.' His faith in the gifts remained intact, though he found a theological immaturity in the charismatic movement.

Though prophetic messages were quite common at Pastor Babcox's church, these were exhortive, rather than predictive. Occasionally, something was said that was contradictory to the Bible, and this was dismissed as 'the overzealous attempts of a misguided saint'. Neil Babcox occasionally prophesied himself, and he gives a good description of the sensations that preceded his 'supernatural utterances': 'When prophetic pressure mounts within your soul, there are certain tell-tale signs that a prophecy is about to be born. These signs are varied, and of course everyone has their own idiosyncrasies. But generally speaking, you can expect your prophetic message to be preceded by such phenomena as a rapid pulse, sweaty palms, and a diverse mixture of chills and tingling sensations. But finally, duty whispers an ultimatum in your ear: Now or never! – So you speak!'

Many will confirm the above.

Babcox soon began to realise, however, that the 'prophecies' he gave in church were very poor relatives indeed of the majestic utterances found in the Bible. He began to fear that these modern prophecies were too intuitional and subjective. In biblical times, false

prophecies were punishable by death. If this were
still the case, then there might be more silence in
charismatic meetings!

Crisis Point

It was good that the prophetic gifts could be nurtured, and allowances made for human error – people
incorrectly grasping the subtle whispers of the Holy
Spirit. And yet, the situation never seemed to improve
over the years. Neither Pastor Babcox nor the other
'prophets' within his congregation ever managed to
produce genuinely predictive utterances, or anything
other than bland platitudes and vague paraphrases of
pieces of Scripture. The problem seems global; nowhere
do there appear to be hesitant prophets in the 1970s
maturing to toss out effortless utterances of great
precision in the 1990s.

Neil Babcox became ashamed to hear the words,
'thus saith the Lord' applied to banal greeting card
rhetoric a million miles removed from the Bible's
sublime revelations. The glory of Christ has been
fully revealed in the Gospels, so what of any major
significance can be added? It seemed, too, that perhaps
the predictive nature of biblical prophecy was the only
real guide that these were genuine. Without such accurate foretelling of future events in modern prophecy,
these often superficial and superfluous ramblings were
essentially valueless. What was he to do? He resolved
never again to open his mouth in prophecy.

He became increasingly concerned that his 'tongues',
too, were not a definable language. It was, he concluded, something that he had learned through rep-
etition, guided by the peer pressure of his Christian
friends. (Perhaps, though, 'tongues' was not intended
to be a language, but rather the inarticulate soul

struggling to express through bubbling syllables something of the effervescence it felt, as it struggled to
evoke the mysteries of God as a form of sublime
spiritual release.) I too, know of disenchanted ex-
charismatics who now dismiss their gifts as delu-
sions, or works of psychological origin. Pastor Babcox
renounced the validity of his own experiences of speaking in tongues.

Instead, Neil Babcox placed his faith firmly in the
Bible, without bitterness, fully believing that the charismatic movement was from God, yet aware that the
gifts were not – it seemed – right for him. He was glad
that charismatics had regained the joy in the Lord
that he read about in the psalms, but aware too that
theological aberrations were not unknown amongst
charismatics. At least one leader is now believed to
have fabricated his testimony. The scandal of Jim and
Tammy Bakker, and the disgrace of Jimmy Swaggart,
suggest that not all Spirit-filled Christians live morally
upstanding lives.

Neil Babcox discovered that his church's most note-
able 'prophet' was relieved by the conclusions at which
he had arrived, and had similar misgivings herself.
Perhaps her gift had once been genuine, but she was
now pleased that she was no longer expected to bring
forth God's revelations virtually to order, on a weekly
basis.

Others in his church whose 'tongues' had long ceased
to convince them they were a real language, were
relieved when they no longer had to feel guilty for
not 'making greater use of their prayer language'.
One person confessed that the pleasant feelings she
had received when 'praying in tongues' were identical
to those she had felt when chanting mantras as a TM
student before she became a Christian . . .

'So much that I had believed in, so much that I

had cherished, so much of my past spiritual life was shattered. The transition from shadow to substance is natural and wholesome. But to reverse the process, to discover that so much that you thought was substance is a shadow – a mere mirage – is devastating.'

Neil Babcox retained his faith and his effective ministry, and he is now a sadder but wiser man. Many conservative evangelicals fear that the Toronto Blessing will produce the same bitter fruit.

Chapter Four

Riding the Third Wave

In the early eighties, at Fuller Theological Seminary, Eddie Gibbs introduced David Watson to a local pastor – a former rock musician who had once played keyboards for the Righteous Brothers – named John Wimber.

A former seminary lecturer himself, Wimber had returned to the pastorate to explore whether God would work in affluent California in the way he had evidently worked in Third World countries – *through signs and wonders.*

Wimber passionately believed that God wanted to perform powerful miracles in today's Church. His infectious enthusiasm led to David Watson, by now dying of cancer, to ask John Wimber to pray for his recovery. In a much-publicised ministry week, prayer and laying on of hands took place, evidently to no avail. Soon David Watson, to many *the* figurehead of the British charismatic movement, was dead.

Signs and wonders had failed.

Or they had been misunderstood.

Either way, it was perhaps the watershed moment for charismatic renewal.

Resurrection

'The new churches still continued to grow. If every other church in Britain had continued to grow at the same rate, we would have had revival on our hands, make no mistake about that,' Gerald Coates says adamantly and – some would say – triumphally.

Defeat was soon to turn to victory; at least, that's one interpretation of the events that followed. In 1984, Mission England attracted an audience of 1.25 million, with a staggering 100,000 going forward for counselling. When, in October 1984, Wimber brought a team to minister in London, triumph filled the air. An ill-advised reference by a member of Wimber's team, to Watson's death at the hands of 'The Enemy', did little to stem Wimber's acclaim and rise to prominence. Like Elisha from Elijah, it seemed to some that Wimber had inherited Watson's mantle.

The next summer, Dr Billy Graham attracted 257,700 to meetings at Mission Sheffield, and around 25,000 registered a response. When, that autumn, Wimber returned for a hat-trick of conferences at Brighton, Wembley and Sheffield, his style of ministry began to be copied by British charismatics – albeit with many of the unsuitable Americanisms removed – particularly at St Andrews, Chorleywood, under the vibrant leadership of David Pytches and Barry Kissell.

The grand slam came with two best-selling books, *Power Evangelism* and *Power Healing,* and a major European conference, Acts 86. The John Wimber bandwaggon was well and truly on the move.

In America, Wimber's power base had grown from one congregation affiliated to conservative evangelical Chuck Smith's California-based Calvary Chapel, in 1977. Wimber's charismatic emphasis sat uneasily with Smith, so he joined up with Ken Gulliksen's Vineyard movement, at that point only seven churches strong. When Gulliksen went off to Boston to plant another church, he turned his Vineyard over to Wimber. In 1983, Wimber moved his congregation to Anaheim, California.

A network of affiliated Vineyard churches sprang up, subscribing to Wimber's characteristic emphasis on signs and wonders as symbols of God's power; on healing; and on 'power encounters' with the forces of darkness. It's clear that most of the Vineyard's growth has been transfer growth – achieved by Christians coming to Wimber from other congregations – rather than through the scale of conversions that should have followed had Wimber's power evangelism theology been justified by practise.

The 'equipping of the saints' with the teaching to follow in Wimber's footsteps was another major emphasis. Charismatic Vineyard meetings became noted for people occasionally trembling, falling, weeping, laughing, and falling into peaceful trance-like states, leading to release and refreshment. This was the direct progenitor of the 'Toronto Blessing'.

Wimber's theology was very much the theology of the eighties. Here was a 'third wave', coming hard on the heels of the earlier Pentecostal and Charismatic movements. The controversial expression 'baptism in the Spirit' gradually gave way to the more acceptable word 'anointing', along with other subtle shifts in phrasing and theology.

'Gifts of the Spirit were not limited in number and not the possession of the individual, rather they were dynamically given according to situation and need,' asserts Wright of third wave theology in *Charismatic Renewal: The Search for a Theology*. 'The focus was placed upon the intimacy of the believer's relationship with the Spirit who enables, rather than proof of ownership of gifts.'

The gifts of the Spirit were no longer seen virtually as 'super powers' possessed by God's super-hero saints. There was no longer a sense that the good charismatic was expected to collect 'the full set', as though they

were wine glasses given free by petrol stations as
a special offer. Clumsy theological descriptions gave
way to a fresh understanding of the work of the Holy
Spirit, which integrated more closely with conservative
evangelical theology. The third wave brought a dignity
and elegance to charismatic theology, moving beyond
dead-locked debates into warmer and more pragmatic
territory. And it was a neat piece of marketing!

Wimber's major contribution to the twentieth century Church was to think through the connections
between the Holy Spirit, miracles, and evangelism; and
to begin to establish a workable theology of signs and
wonders. Whereas previous outpourings of the Holy
Spirit had often led people into a purely experiential faith, Wimber's teaching began to integrate the
miraculous into a theoretic framework.

Wimber the Theologian?

For many years as a pastor and seminary lecturer,
John Wimber had believed that the gifts of the Holy
Spirit were no longer available. The books of Peter
Wagner, Donald Gee and Morton Kelsey made him
think again. These authors, and particularly Kelsey,
offered fascinating psychological insights into the outworkings of the Christian faith. The complex interplay
of the psychological and the spiritual is a topic which
we must address briefly later in this book.

'Slowly I began to realise that my ability to know
people's concerns and when they were ready to convert
to Christ – what previously I thought were merely
psychological insights – were possibly spiritual gifts
like a word of knowledge or a word of wisdom,' he
says in *Power Evangelism*, a book that has sold more
than 250,000 copies worldwide.

Wimber realised that Christ had always combined

his preaching of the kingdom of God with signs and wonders – it's pretty obvious if you read the synoptic Gospels thoroughly. 'The spiritual gifts took on new meaning for me. Scripture indicated that they authenticated the Gospel, cutting through people's resistance and drawing attention to the good news of Jesus Christ.'

In the 1960s, conservative evangelicals were taught not to focus too much on the Holy Spirit for fear of falling into the 'excesses' of the Pentecostals. Yet the gospel is 'the power of God for the salvation of everyone who believes' (Rom 1:16). Charismatics pose the question: Where is this power to come from, if not from the Holy Spirit? Wimber sees signs and wonders as manifestations of the kingdom – the source of power for healing and evangelism.

The biblical concept of this kingdom extends beyond the mere physical realm – the Kingdom of God is not simply a country or dominion. Christ was a divine invader, come to reclaim the spiritual kingdom that was rightfully his, and to set the world to rights. Under Vineyard theology, the book of Acts – a major text for Pentecostals and Charismatics alike – loses its supremacy to the synoptic Gospels and their stories of kingdom power and authority. The house churches had also been placing emphasis on this so-called 'kingdom theology'.

Wimber sees Christ's ministry as twofold. First was the call to repentance and the invitation to be a part of God's kingdom by coming under his divine authority. Then came the miracles, to prove that he was 'the presence of the kingdom, the Anointed One'. But some would argue that the miracles were signs of grace, rather than proof of authority.

'The kingdom of God created the Church at Pentecost through the outpouring of the Holy Spirit,' says Wimber, but was the Holy Spirit passive in the outpouring he warns.

'The Church is the primary (though not exclusive) residence of God's dynamic rule. This means the Church witnesses to the King and his kingdom, but it does not have authority in itself to build the kingdom. Only God has that authority.

When the Church is confused with the kingdom, leaders assume that God's authority is coextensive with the office they hold, that *they* are the rule of God. Authoritarianism and even cultishness can be the unfortunate result of this kind of thinking.'

In the Great Commission at the close of Matthew's Gospel, the disciples were commanded, not merely to bring converts into the Church, but to disciple them into obedience to God's written word, the laws of the kingdom. The Church can thus be seen as a shop window or a doorway into the kingdom, but not as the final destination in itself. Yet the Church is the 'body of Christ', and such a view could be injurious to the body.

Wimber's critics have attacked him on several fronts. John Goodwin – pastor of Calvary Chapel, San Jose – for example, writing in *Media Spotlight* in 1990, said: 'The primary indicator of heresy in the teachings of John Wimber is his departure from Scripture and will-ingness to go beyond the word of God for truth . . . [and his] apostolic mindset, combined with a lack of account-ability to the word, results in paranormal actions and teachings which are dangerously unchecked.'

Goodwin also criticises Wimber's 'have-experience-will-travel' mentality; his apparent lack of discernment regarding various occult-tinged techniques he employs; and his strong emphasis on fighting demonic powers.

Personally, I find much of Goodwin's criticism boils down to a knee-jerk response to Wimber's willingness

to find a contemporary context for his teaching – which
I do not consider to be heretical. I find Goodwin's own
statement that God 'has defined himself for us through
doctrinal systems' to be easily as objectionable as any
accusation he lays at Wimber's door. This usually
means that a person has worked out their own theology
with reference to Scripture, and therefore considers it
to have the same inerrant qualitiy as Scripture itself.
God is God, and to consider that he can be tied down
and restricted by human theological interpretation is
an unwarranted assumption to which we will return
in chapter nine.

Wimber's books are not written by him alone, but
penned largely by his colleague Kevin Springer, based
upon Wimber's seminars and sermons. Wimber appears
seldom to read the manuscripts adequately, or in
detail before publication; contradictory ideas sometimes trickle through, though this may be due to
Wimber changing his mind and refining his theology
as he goes along.

Of course, other theologians have also entertained
mutually contradictory or paradoxical ideas: there is
often a tension between the universal and the particular. Bible stories such as Abraham's pleas for Sodom
and Gomorrah suggests that God can change his plans
in response to the petitions of the faithful. God does
not continually impose his will, but allows us freedom
of choice in many aspects and areas of life.

Pundits have piped up to criticise virtually every
aspect of Wimber's controversial ministry, but he has
also attracted many friends and supporters. In his
Foreword to Wimber's book *The Dynamics of Spiritual
Growth*, Michael Green writes: 'I believe John Wimber
is frequently and unnecessarily misunderstood. He is
thought of as "Mr Signs and Wonders", and his two
books *Power Evangelism* and *Power Healing* might be

construed as reinforcing that image. But Wimber is not a systematic theologian: he is a Christian leader who has hitherto brought his main artillery to bear against one of the most damaging weaknesses in Western Christianity, our deep-seated scepticism about the supernatural. He has attempted, with considerable success, to open our eyes to the seriousness of this crippling heresy.'

It is against this background that the events which began in North America, and spread to Britain in 1994, must be set.

Power in Action

'Power Evangelism is flourishing in non-technological countries,' Wimber asserts. 'People living in these countries are often animist. That is, they believe there are actual spirits that hold people in bondage, and the supernatural power of the Holy Spirit is needed to break their hold.'

Every missionary returning from the Third World has stories to tell about God's wonder-working powers. It seems as though the rationalist mindset of many Westerners prevents them from believing that God really *can* still perform wonders today.

While visiting India in the autumn of 1993, I personally saw ample evidence of God's wonder working power. Sitting in the living room of his modest home in Mussourie, Northern India, Pastor Peter Singh told me about the spiritual opposition he detected from the gurus, and from the more superstitious forms of Hindu faith. Some people feel that, if they go near a dead body, spirits may enter their own bodies. Others knowingly invite evil spirits into themselves.

I met a girl of about twelve from whom Peter had cast several demons. The girl's father had come to him, bringing the girl, and asking if there was any possibility that he could do something about her condition; the only other alternative the father had in mind was to take her to a Hindu witchdoctor.

'God is powerful. I delivered her in the name of Jesus Christ, just two months ago,' Singh told me. 'Eight months previously, she was a Hindu. When she gave her heart to Jesus she was the first girl in her family to do so.'

With the help of a translator, I heard the girl's story from her own lips: 'I went to a cottage at the outskirts of my village in Andhra Pradesh. Some evil influence came and entered into my body. I could get no sleep, I was in pain, and I kept getting dirty thoughts. I was brought to Peter Singh and he prayed for me in the name of Jesus. As he laid his hands on me, the demons came out, and went away in the name of Jesus. But later they came back.' The spirits had not been bound, or ordered to report to Jesus for judgement.

'Next day, I went to college, but I couldn't concentrate on my studies. Peter came down to pray, and the demon came out again, this time explaining that someone had made some black magic on me, to kill me.'

Peter Singh explained how the demon had told him that five people had given a tribal witchdoctor 15,000 rupees, to put a spell on the girl and to kill her: 'The witch doctors had made a mud ball, to which they made *puja* (worship) and recited some *mantras* (incantations) so that demons would make her sick. Her grandmother had left her some property, and three of her aunts had become very jealous. That's why the witchcraft was put on her. The witchdoctor sent terrible pains to her chest, joints and stomach. When I cast out the demon, it went back to the witchdoctor, who was not able to withstand it when the pain was reversed.

'I brought her with my wife and I, 2,000 kilometres here to Mussourie, to get her away from the witch-doctor. But he joined up with other sorcerors and continued to send spells to cause the girl pain. She saw a vision of a serpent; the serpent was split into two and spoiled. After two days, she saw that the snake was dead, and her pain was gone. She said "Praise the Lord" for her deliverance. "Now I am free".'

'God is always powerful, but sometimes the Christian needs more power. When the disciples asked Jesus why they were not able to cast out certain devils, their Lord replied that some devils require prayer and fasting before they can be cast out. You need to be patient, and to take time and pray and fight the tempter. Sometimes we don't pray enough; we just tell the demons to go, and they will not go. Therefore, by the power of God's Holy Spirit we have to rebuke them, then they will go. If Jesus Christ cannot deliver you, nothing in the world can set you free,' reflected one of Singh's Christian colleagues, on his own finds and experiences. 'The evil spell, the power of the mantras, resides in the joints of the body. Demonic spirits enter into a person through the nose and mind, often driving the person to suicide.'

There is, of course, a danger of cultural stereotyping – considering the Third World to be full of superstitious people ready to mis-attribute anything out of the ordinary to the work of spirits and demons. In my experience, this is a false notion; the 'noble savage' is a concept that rightly went out with the colonial era, and the peoples of the developing countries are quite able to distinguish between the psychiatric and the psychic.

Deliverance, and other works of power, are found in Christian communities across the globe – though perhaps not with the regularity that Wimber might like to suppose. This may begin to change, through the waves of the Holy Spirit that recently flooded the global Church.

Wimber is clearly called to a specific ministry of power evangelism; but not every believer is similarly called. Each has a unique part to play within the body of Christ: 'The body is a unit, though it is made up of many parts; and though all its parts are many, they form one body. So it is with Christ. For we were all baptised by one Spirit into one body ... and we were all given the one Spirit to drink.

Now the body is not made up of one part but of many. If the foot should say, "Because I am not a hand, I do not belong to the body," it would not for that reason cease to be part of the body ... If the whole body were an eye, where would the sense of hearing be? If the whole body were an ear, where would the sense of smell be? But in fact, God has arranged the parts of the body, every one of them, just as he wanted them to be.'
(1 Cor 12:12–14;17–18)

It can be disastrous to emulate someone else's area of ministry when God may have a very different plan for your own life. Emphasis on spiritual warfare is offensive to many evangelicals, and its insensitive propagation can only cause splits and divisions within the body.

Though mavericks like him are very welcome, I think it unlikely that God wants to clone an entire army of John Wimbers!

Gift of Healing

It is unfortunate that a good—evil dualism had slipped on board Wimber's theology as a stowaway, almost unnoticed at first. This tended to exaggerate Satan's importance in God's plan; in the long term, this emphasis on spiritual warfare could only be counter-productive.

Wimber tends to see sickness as often caused by Satan, rather than taking the more evangelical view that sickness and death are inevitable consequences of the Fall which came when Adam and Eve disobeyed God in the Garden of Eden.

'God is a healing God, but he tends to be selective in whom he heals,' according to Wimber's theology. He is glad to 'help God out' with a spot of Jungian psychology, and some of Agnes Sanford's inner healing techniques. But still, healing is never guaranteed. Wimber recommends that sick people should receive prayer regardless of whether or not God heals them. As long as a sick person is not cruelly given false hope, even if only one in a thousand receive any tangible benefit, praying is a worthwhile action. It is difficult to argue with this approach.

Only the Divine Healing Movement considers that salvation and sanctification should destroy, not simply the *consequence* of sin – as the price is then borne by Christ on the cross – but also the *effects* of sin, which lead to sickness and death. It should, perhaps, have been obvious when members of the Divine Healing Movement were not automatically healed of all their infirmities, and continued to die when their time came, that this pernicious doctrine was not all it was cracked up to be.

When Jesus Christ healed a man with a withered arm, by asking him to stretch it out, the healing must have necessitated the reconnection of nerve endings and the restoration of withered muscle tissue. It was a far cry from any healings that have been seen during the charismatic renewal!

Evangelicals do not believe that healing is automatically included in the atonement; for a start, Scripture is totally silent about such a possibility. The Divine Healing Movement blames the fact that people continue to get sick, and to die, because of their lack of faith; an assertion that is harmful to Christian unity and derogatory towards the sick individual. Christ never blamed a sick person for lack of faith, only the person who was praying for them. For Wimber too, the faith of the person doing the praying is seen as more important than the faith of the sick person for whom the praying is done.

Often sickness is the body's way of slowing a person down, when their lifestyle, lack of exercise, lack of sleep or other deficiency is resulting in long-term health problems. Pain is the body's way of warning the brain that damage is being done. It isn't necessarily a good thing to cure all sickness and pain instantaneously, because the consequences might be worse than the initial illness. It's pointless to cure symptoms alone if an underlying malady remains.

Any GP will say that something like 70 per cent of all the patients he sees will get better anyway, perhaps 20 per cent are incurable, and there is only a narrow band of people in the middle who can actually be treated. Yet if a Christian prays for the sick and only a few per cent seem to improve, then cynics will shake their heads – even though prayer may have been as effective as medication!

In recent times, Jennifer Rees Larcombe and Julie Sheldon have each written books about their remarkable healings from encephalitis and dystonia respectively. In 1986, I wrote a feature story for *Christian Family* about Lesley Bottomley's surprising cure from multiple sclerosis, diagnosed by three doctors, after receiving prayer from a colleague of Colin Urquhart

– I even took photos of her leaping about! For some, such as Susan James and Joni Eareckson-Tada, the only healing has been internal – receiving the spiritual and emotional strength to live with paralysis.

'People accept that God *could* heal, but not that he *does* heal. They write off prayer as a placebo effect,' said Gerald Coates sadly. 'If you're unwell and on medication that will cure you anyway within a few weeks, but you are prayed for in our church and are well the next day, then I say be thankful to God.'

Gifts of Power

Healing is just one of the three spiritual gifts of power. The other two are miracles and faith.

Miracles are far too broad a category to consider here. It's perhaps worth pointing out, however, that most biblical miracles come into one of two categories. The first comprises objects – be they bread, coins, fish, oil, angels or people – appearing and disappearing as though from some unseen doorway to another dimension. The second consists of matter and energy – be it fire, lightning, animals, body tissue, wind or waves – mentally controlled and directed by will. I have an enormous amount to say on the topic, but it deserves a book to itself.

The gift of faith seems closely associated with healing and miracles. 'Faith gives substance to our hopes, and makes us certain of realities we do not see' (Heb 11:1 NEB). The gift of faith seems somehow to be the *means* by which miraculous signs and wonders are brought into being. An absence of faith or an overly-doubting mind seem to *prevent* God from working through an individual. No one can work a miracle in God's name without implicit faith in him, but not all miracles are dependent upon God. Pharaoh's magicians were able to duplicate most of the feats that Moses performed.

Instead of asking 'how do miracles happen?' Lawrence Le Shan asks instead, 'What is going on between the miracle worker and the rest of reality at the moment the paranormal occurrence takes place?' He concludes that there are 'different ways of being in the world.' One way is the normal everyday life, but there are – he argues – other ways. One is a state of extreme thoughtfulness and contemplation, which he calls the clairvoyant reality. In this state, he considers, the mind is somehow able to 'import' unusual phenomena into the everyday world. Colin Wilson, his definitive study of the paranormal, calls it Faculty X; a better term since the state seems to facilitate a far broader range of phenomena than mere clairvoyance.

If there is such a latent natural ability, it would explain why Eastern gurus like Sai Baba are able to produce staggering miracles; but when a Christian performs a miracle, how does the Holy Spirit come into it? The answer seems to be that the Holy Spirit *releases* the untapped natural potential, and enables a person to become the supernatural being that he or she was always capable of becoming. But, additionally, the Holy Spirit enables the recipient to *pray in faith*, and prayer is the most powerful means of change, as well as an agency through which supernatural events become possible.

As Archbishop William Temple realised: 'When I pray, coincidences start to happen. When I don't pray, they don't happen.'

Praying with the gift of faith has a twofold purpose. It is a genuine and deep concern for others; and also an offering of oneself and one's capabilities as a channel through which God may operate. These capabilities may well include natural abilities, but

it will be the power of prayer – through the gift of
faith – which really opens up a channel for effective
supernatural action.

Return to Kansas

In the third wave, prophecy and words of knowledge
acquired a greater role in the charismatic movement,
fuelling a growing belief that God wants to address the
nations as well as the Church. 1985 saw the launch
of *Prophecy Today* which, though unconnected with
Wimber, showed a similar openness to accept that God
had a powerful message to give out.

Indeed, both David Pawson and Clifford Hill had
moved in prophetic ministry for some time. Prophecy
seems to have been tagged on to Wimber's ministry
as a comparatively late thought, perhaps consequent
to his meeting with the prophet Paul Cain in 1988.

Cain, at that time, was connected with the Kansas
City Fellowship, led by Mike Bickle. In 1982, Bickle
had felt a clear call from God to move from his comfortable church in St Louis, to found a new fellowship
in Kansas – where the Pentecostal movement had
started more than eight decades earlier – and to begin
a work that would be characterised by prayer, holiness,
unwavering faith, and sacrificial giving to the poor.

Bickle was initially sceptical when both Bob Jones
and Agustine Alcala had come to him claiming to be
prophets, foretelling that thousands would rally to
Bickle, that 'in days to come there would be a full
manifestation of the gifts of the Spirit, but it will only
be for an appointed time.' Also, there would be a false
prophet to watch out for, and major resistance from
many people, according to David Pytches in his book
Some Said It Thundered.

Bob Jones was raised in the backwaters of Arkansas

in the 1930s, and he received his first supernatural
visitation at the age of nine. The prophet's credentials
– astonishingly accurate revelations, predictions and
words of knowledge – soon melted Bickle's initial
scepticism, and convinced him that Jones was truly a
prophet of the Lord. For several years, Jones received
powerful words of prophecy which came to pass, more
or less as he had been shown in advance. Soon other
prophets gathered to the fledgling Kansas City Fellowship. By the end of the decade, thousands had indeed
flocked to Bickle, who was taking meetings across the
States and in the UK, and a time of great wonders
seemed very close at hand.

Yet the KCF's methodology attracted its share of
criticism. Ernest Gruen, pastor of Full Faith Church
of Love, in Kansas City, compiled a 233 page dos-
sier on KCF's techniques. These included a veritable
spiritual 'protection racket', offering leadership to
other churches in Kansas City, prophesying that other
churches should disband and join the KCF, and pro-
nouncing judgement on dissenters!

When KCF became part of Wimber's Vineyard network, Wimber admitted that Bob Jones had made
'unwise but not unbiblical' statements, and in July 1990,
Mike Bickle publically recanted his elitist statements.

For some pundits, KCF sailed close to the wind
of heretical doctrine, taking on board much of the
unorthodox teaching of the 'Latter Rain' movement,
and its offshoot, The Manifest Sons of God. Though
KCF followed Manifest Sons teaching regarding the
restoration of the offices of apostle and prophet, a call
for radical holiness, a ministry of signs and wonders,
defeat of demonic spirits, and an expected outbreak
of worldwide revival, none of these is demonstrably
unbiblical *per se*.

Neither KCF nor the Vineyard have gone to the

extremes of the cultish Manifest Sons teaching – rooted
in occult teaching and methodology – which espouses
a veritable godhood-on-earth, prophets and apostles
becoming immortal, the second coming of Jesus in and
through the Church, the Church ruling the nations in
Christ's place, and draconian shepherding of church
members.

While visiting Kansas City, David Pytches asked a
group of prophets about the way they received their
prophecies, whether through the *psyche* (soul) or the
pneuma (spirit). The consensus seemed to be that
'the psyche was involved in their visions. They were
clearly neither embarrassed nor threatened in any
way by our description of their gifts as psychic in
the pure sense.' This, of course, is the same way in
which occultists claim to receive similar visions and
predictions.

'Who among those who might object to Christians
using the term can prove in fact that occultists themselves really do operate through the psyche? Or who
will argue that because spiritualists profess to operate
through the spirit world, we Christians must avoid the
use of the word *spirit* in our religious experience or
theology?' asked David Pytches in his book.

'The human spirit is a channel which picks up
spiritual transmissions from God or from the powers of
darkness and these are reflected onto the screen of the
soul. The same TV channel can carry beastly cruelty,
pornography or breathtaking beauty. The responsibility for the subject matter lies not in the channel itself
but in the source of transmission, or the choice of the
person tuning into the programme.'

According to Paul Cain, 'The psychic person is born
with the ability, but uses it to draw attention to themselves, rather than to Christ. The prophetic person
is under God, but the clairvoyant isn't.' For him,

awesome incidents where he rattles off prophecies
relating to major international events are few and
far between. More commonly, he receives expressions
or impressions, which have become more accurate the
more he has learned to discern God's voice. 'You know
that you know,' he says of the ineffable and awesome
moments – but he believes that God often speaks to him
too through visions and dreams.

Mike Bickle has summarised other ways in which
Cain receives his revelations: by mental impression;
by physical symptoms (pains in his body corresponding to where someone is afflicted); the angel of the
Lord standing by him invisibly and speaking to him;
different hues, each with a different significance; and
hearing voices, internally or audibly.

Discernment is needed to 'taste that the Lord is
good.' Prophecy should be weighed (1 Cor 14:29) and
peace of heart is a further confirmation (Col 3:15). Paul
seems to list prophecy as a natural talent in Romans
12:6–8, but one which must be correctly exercised and
used for the common good.

Citizen Cain

It's not everyday one gets to meet a real, live prophet.
What would it be like? I wondered. Would he place his
arm pastorally around my shoulder and suggest we
talk about the hard times in my life? Would he come
on like the Barnum-esque showman I'd seen captivate
a 7,000 strong audience at London's Docklands Arena
in 1991? Would he ramble and digress, losing track of
his thoughts, as he had that night? Would I end up
shaking with apprehension?

When it came to the crunch, the only part that
shook was my hand as he greeted me. Immaculately
dressed, and not a bit like Charlton Heston in *The Ten*

Commandments, I met a man very different from any popular images.

Born in the year of the Wall Street Crash, there are few Christian leaders in the world as colourful as the tall, white-haired Paul Cain. Renowned, or perhaps notorious, as one of the so-called Kansas City Prophets – despite the fact that he is actually a Texan – Cain seems loved or hated in equal measures by different elements within the UK Church.

To many of his admirers, he is a thundering Elijah figure giving prophetic utterance; whilst his detractors deride his ministry as all noise and no substance, seeing him as a glib American evangelist at best, and a con man at worst. Everyone seems to have a view about him, though seldom based on more than hearsay, or anecdotes taken out of context.

The decision of Spring Harvest, the evangelical holiday and teaching event held each spring, to invite such a controversial figure as Paul Cain to their 1992 jamboree, attracted discussion and dispute amongst many evangelicals.

The magazine *Evangelicals Now* fired an opening salvo by claiming editorially that: 'Spring Harvest is making it impossible for some of the best and most biblical and vibrant evangelicals to consider participating in Spring Harvest. They gladly recognise many charismatics as fellow-believers, but the kind of teaching represented by these men is, as the phrase goes, "something else".'

David Roberts, editor of the evangelical magazine *Alpha* believed there were some evangelicals who felt the invitation to Paul Cain to participate 'goes beyond the pale of evangelical dialogue'.

Rev Clive Calver – who was both a member of the Spring Harvest executive, and Executive Director of the Evangelical Alliance – responded: 'Spring

Harvest is not able to endorse all the views of its 440 speakers at each year's events. Each sector of the Church has its characters and mavericks, and evangelicals are no exception. The danger comes when we seek to marginalise or ignore our controversial figures, instead of listening to their contribution and giving it the careful assessment which it merits – hence the invitation to Paul Cain.'

For others, the problem lay not with the constraints of dialogue, but rather with the source of Paul Cain's prophecies. Their argument ran that, in the Bible, when prophets spoke for God the words were fulfilled, but Cain's 'prophecies' had demonstrably been proved wrong.

In an interview at the time, Calver told me it is dangerous to assume that Old Testament prophecy and that which occurs in the Church today should be accorded equivalent authority and respect. Contemporary prophecy is an attempt to interpret the word of God, but it is not direct dictation, and is therefore fallible. 'I am encouraged to note that Paul Cain is very casual and tentative. Like many who claim a prophetic ministry, he hates saying "The Lord says".'

Nevertheless, even Cain's supporter and colleague, the controversial John Wimber, affirmed in his in-house magazine *Equipping the Saints*, that – in July 1990, in front of 1,000 church leaders at Holy Trinity Brompton – Cain stated: 'Thus saith the Lord: Revival will be released in England in October of 1990 . . . Tokens of revival will come in October 1990.'

Considerable concern was expressed by Wimber that Cain's prophecy had proved to be considerably overstated. Wimber's concern was picked up in Britain by *Renewal* magazine and by myself, writing in the *Church Times*. Subsequently, in material published only in the States, Wimber has retracted his view and

apologised – and Cain is adamant that he predicted
only *tokens* of revival in the Lord's name.

Though Wimber stated that 'revival is a term that
Christians understand in different ways,' many leading evangelicals were unconvinced by his explanation
that the 'tokens' to which Cain referred was internal
revival – that 'the Church was touched by the Spirit of
God, and individuals and congregations were revived'.

It is clear from his writings that Wimber sees from
an American perspective – where Church attendance
frequently is largely cultural, and where faith might
often be deepened by internal revival – rather than
the British perspective, where attendance at evangelical churches implies much deeper commitment from
the outset.

'Cain was invited, not to the normal family weeks
of Spring Harvest, but to a Spring Harvest high risk
week,' Calver told me. 'This is an opportunity to hear
people of different perspectives from within the evangelical fold, in a situation where they will face cross-
examination and critique. Cain will be ministering
alongside people such as R. T. Kendall, from the
opposite end of the evangelical spectrum.'

The whole issue of prophetic ministry had become
a very big talking point amongst evangelicals. One
leading evangelical told me at the time – off the
record – that Wimber was changing his position. To
me, it was clear that many other senior evangelicals,
too, were shifting their ground and being forced to take
a more neutral stance.

That was when I resolved to meet Cain for myself.

A Prophetable Encounter

Sitting beside him on the black leather settee in R. T.
Kendall's study at Westminister Chapel, I discovered

how inaccurate many of the stories about him are: for
example, the tale that he'd left John Wimber's Vineyard Fellowship and joined the Westminster Chapel
congregation.

'I've never been a member of the Vineyard church.
John Wimber and I have taken conferences together,
and John has shared his platform with me. We had a
friendly disengagement as from December 31st 1991.
He has his vision and I have mine. His is to "equip
the saints", and mine is to teach holiness and revival,
which is easier without conference-type situations,'
Cain explained to me, slowly and deliberately.

He had now submitted his ministry to Westminster
Chapel, with Dr Kendall and his deacons overseeing
Cain's work. 'Dr Kendall and I have been friends now
for about eighteen months. I look to him to speak into
my ministry and my life.'

Cain intended spending considerable time ministering
in Britain in the future, and felt it right to come under
the authority of a British church. As a London centre
for reformed theology with a long reputation for defend-
ing the Protestant faith, particularly under former
pastor Dr. Martyn Lloyd-Jones, Westminster Chapel
has been seen by many as an unusual choice for such
a charismatic figure popularly perceived as something
of a maverick. Yet the popular misconception seems to
have largely come undeserved. Cain is adamant about
his commitment to Scripture. 'I've always had a love
for the word.'

The endorsement of such a conservative bastion
of respectability doubtless increased his credibility
and authority with those who might have been worried by his connections with John Wimber's often
controversial signs and wonders approach to Church
ministry. Yet any suspicion that Cain might have
been using Westminster Chapel's reputation simply

as a convenient cover were dispelled for me by Cain's obvious respect for R. T. Kendall, who was present during our interview. On several occasions, Paul Cain deferred to Dr Kendall, who interrupted him whenever he felt the Texan was being unclear on points of Scripture.

'I've always been accountable to a church and to a pastor. I started out in the Southern Baptist church, and I'm an evangelical more than anything else. I've never been totally accepted by charismatics because of it. A lot of things I've done which seem very radical are not as they appear.

'My relationship with Mike Bickle, leader of the Kansas City Fellowship – it's now a Vineyard – is this: I have been speaking in recent years at a leadership conference sponsored by his fellowship. I occasionally see him at other conferences, but not often.' Cain was not keen on being referred to as one of the Kansas City Prophets.

Much information about Cain's life can be found in Bishop David Pytches book *Some Said It Thundered,* but this needs to be treated with some caution: 'I didn't know that David Pytches was writing a book. He was in one of our meetings in Kansas and he also heard some tapes, and collected information from Mike Bickle.'

Pytches' sources for his writing about Cain's early life were second and third hand. This need not have mattered, since he sent a copy of his completed manu-script to Kansas, with the aim of having Cain make any necessary corrections. Inadvertently, and due to administrative mishap, neither did Cain see the manu-script, nor was Pytches made aware that Cain had not seen it. Consequently, when Hodders published the book, it contained many errors about Cain's life – errors which were corrected in time for the American edition, three days before it went to press, but which still flaw the version on sale in British bookshops.

'It's no reflection on Pytches at all,' said Cain diplomatically. Nevertheless, much of the information about Cain in Britain is woefully inaccurate, and paints a picture of him which is inconsistent, often outlandish, and a source of bad press.

'There was a story told to Pytches about how the angel of the Lord appeared to me in the front seat of my car, dressed in a black monk's habit – but the event didn't happen that way at all. Another incident relating to my call to celibacy is so private that it's not an incident I ever wanted to see in a book. The people who told Pytches the stories failed to realise that some things are too personal and private for me to want divulged.'

Cain told me that he had found Spring Harvest an exhausting but rewarding experience, where many came up to him to apologise for the wrong views they had held of him. Such a 'coming to terms' with the prophetic ministry was perhaps an encouraging sign for the British Church, at a time when differences of opinion between charismatics and non-charismatics threaten to be worsened by conflicts over prophetic ministry.

Some modern 'prophets' seem to receive more 'prophetic words' in a single evening's ministry than the Old Testament prophets received in entire ministries, as they rattle off prophetic word after prophetic word in an alarming way which seems to have more in common with trance mediumship than Christian ministry.

Ways and Means

What might appear to be spontaneous words of knowledge that have come to Cain while he is speaking,

are often words that he has received in advance of
the meeting. Prophecy does not always occur spontaneously as he begins to speak; often these insights
come to him beforehand, and he marshalls them into
order as he gives his talk.

Cain is careful never to use prophetic gifts in a *con-
trolling* way. 'Everything the Lord has ever revealed to
me has been subject to the oversight of Church leaders.
I never give a "Thus saith the Lord" telling someone
whom they should marry, or telling a couple that they
should have a baby. A prophetic person is not someone
who goes around telling people what to do, though they
might give a confirming message once a decision had
been made.'

Cain's advocates have stressed that Cain is a man
of prayer, often spending hours in prayer before a
meeting. 'There have been times when I have not left
my room during the day when I have had to minister
that evening. It was *assumed* that I was spending
many hours in prayer when, actually, I spent hours
before the Lord making myself available for fellowship
with God, in study, and in preparation for the evening
meeting.

'I became known as a recluse, for staying shut-in,
waiting to hear from God. More people would hear
from God if they simply made themselves available,
alone with the Lord. I find it a model that the Lord
has given me for my life to learn to get alone with
Him and disavow my own ideas, vain traditions and
knowledge, to sit at the feet of Jesus and be available
for God to use.'

In shutting himself away, he also preserves his integ-
rity. He seeks to avoid the possibility of accidentally
learning things which God might want to reveal to him
to share as edification.

At the end of Wimber's Holiness Conference, held

at London's Docklands Arena in October 1990, at which Cain shared the platform, Cain claimed that God wanted to heal twenty-seven people of heart disease, and an undisclosed number of others from cancer. Participants duly came forward and prayer took place; yet the conference organisers had seemed unconcerned with clinical diagnosis, or with any follow-up which would prove that such healings had actually happened. Vagueness had seemed the order of the day.

'At the Wimber conferences there are questionnaires and testimony forms for people to fill out,' Cain told me patiently, though obviously bemused. He had little time for the notion that God's workings should be thoroughly tested or methodically proven.

'There were an unusual number of people at that conference who claimed to have been healed, and occasionally there are documented healings, though most doctors are not willing to attribute healings to God. Recently, a young girl was healed of multiple sclerosis and her doctor, finding her healed, asked the girl's parents to what the healing should be ascribed. When they explained that she had been prayed for, the doctor said this explanation was as good as any.

'I don't feel that I have anything to prove. My mission in life is to seek to show compassion. Jesus healed people out of compassion, and I pray for people because Jesus was compassionate. It's not up to me to see if they will be healed; I just do what the Lord has told me to do, and the rest is up to him.'

Paul Cain and Dr Kendall teamed up in October 1992 for a meeting at Wembley Conference Centre, based on Matthew 22:29, where Jesus says 'You do not know the Scriptures or the power of God'.

Cain and Kendall were set to make a formidable team — and one which sought to build a few bridges across the theological divides which pose a threat to Christian unity.

'I believe there will one day be a merger between the refined power of God in the Scriptures, and the raw power of God in signs and wonders,' said Cain. 'Some have raw power but no Scripture knowledge or right theology, and others have right theology and all Scriptures, without raw power. It's pitiful that we settle for one or the other, not knowing that we can have both.'

Amen!

Chapter Five

The Toronto Experience

'British Airways flight number 092 took off from Toronto Airport on Tuesday evening just as the Holy Spirit was landing on a small building a hundred yards from the end of the runway.'

So commenced Fred Langan's account in the *Sunday Telegraph* of phenomena which many considered to be a major new outpouring of the Holy Spirit. Some claimed it to be the beginning of worldwide revival, and others the work of the devil.

The Airport Vineyard church in Toronto is a very ordinary little fellowship, meeting in a down-at-heel office block on the end of a runway. It takes about ten minutes from the end of the checkout to reach this most comically-improbable building. Don't blink or you'll miss it. When you get there, the only indication that you have indeed arrived at the correct destination is a paper sign in the window.

The rock band which plays for the worship, in that unlikely venue for the commencement of global awakening, is quite undistinguished. There is nothing in the services themselves that is in any way out of the ordinary; it's a typical piece of modern evangelical worship. Nor is there anything exceptional about the pastor, John Arnott.

Yet the Toronto Airport Vineyard has become a veritable shrine of pilgrimage for church leaders from across the globe, singly and in groups, as they converged for a few days each throughout 1994.

Then they returned to their home churches and similar phenomena began to occur in their own congregations!

Birth of Blessing

South African evangelist Rodney Howard-Browne, possibly the spiritual heir of his fellow South African, David du Plessis, is perhaps the original spark that fired the 'Toronto Blessing'. A former associate of Ray MacCauley at his enormous Rhema church in Johannesburg, Howard-Browne moved his ministry to the USA in 1987. This dynamic evangelist at the heart of a worldwide move of God has prayed with Terry Virgo, supremo of the New Frontiers network of fellowships, and many American pastors.

Howard-Browne drew large crowds when he toured the States in 1993, mesmerising them with manifestations and anointings. 'He would only have to blow on the audience for whole sections to fall down. Rodney's speciality, however, is to have those who fall down begin to laugh uncontrollably, supposedly with the joy of the Lord,' commented Clifford Hill in *Prophecy Today*. 'Many of those who fall down shake uncontrollably and cry out with various sounds. A major feature of these meetings, which have taken many congregations in the charismatic sector in the USA by storm, is that they are orchestrated by the man who is in control of the meeting. Often those who fall down are unable to get up, and afterwards describe the feeling as being "like a block of cement". This is remarkably similar to the Hindu practice of using group laughter as a means of control, to bring worshippers under the power of the guru, and underlines the danger of manipulation by the leadership.'

The magazine *Charisma* reported on charismatic renewal in the Boston area, based on the Christian Teaching and Worship Center. 'All those who experienced this new jolt of Holy Spirit power at CTWC, including the leaders Paul and Mona Johnian, said they were initially sceptical of the spontaneous, boisterous laughter that interrupted their worship services in the autumn of 1993.'

Mona Johnian's doubts began to recede when her own pastor, Bill Ligon – the 'epitome of dignity' – was overcome by the Spirit. In her book *Fresh Blessing,* she describes the moment her own husband was anointed: 'On stage at a conference, Rodney Howard-Browne, Bill Ligon and Sid Roth were standing beside my husband Paul when he had just finished playing his violin. Rodney walked over and laid hands on him, praying for a fresh anointing to touch him. Paul felt no particular sensation at the time, yet when we returned to our church the same unique manifestations that had occurred at the conference began happening in our congregation. People fell to the floor when Pastor Paul laid hands on them.

Laughter and joy began to bubble up all over the congregation. Tears began to fall and stony hearts began to soften. From that day until now, the same things have been occurring in our services. There was definitely power given through this fresh anointing which had been transferred by faith and the laying on of hands.'

The manifestations, of course, were far from unique – they appear to have broken out in many places that Howard-Browne visited that eventful year. Johnian comments that a lady who attended one of her own conferences seemed to take the same phenomena back with her to a New Hampshire church. The Blessing was spreading across the USA like wildfire, *several months before the outbreak in Toronto.*

The Second Strand

1993 was a hard year for St Louis Vineyard pastor Randy Clark, who was near to burnout, and longed to experience God's fatherly touch. A friend encouraged Clark to attend a meeting by Rodney Howard-Browne in Tulsa, Oklahoma, and was greatly helped. This anointing was one that had enormous consequences for Canada and Britain.

Toronto Airport Vineyard pastor John Arnott heard about the spiritual boost that Clark, and several others, had received from Howard-Browne, at a Vineyard pastor's grapevine conference. He contacted Clark, and scheduled a series of meetings at the Airport Vineyard, commencing on January 20th, 1994. The revival train was beginning to pick up a good head of steam.

In 1993, Arnott also attended a conference for North American pastors, staged by a trio of Argentinian pastors, Ed Silvoso, Hector Jiminez, and Claudio Freidzon. The latter prayed with John Arnott at the conference, and in November 1993, Arnott visited Argentina. Since a powerful revival was underway there, some pundits consider that it was *this* time of prayer that was the key factor behind the radical change in Arnott's ministry.

Freidzon is a former theological professor, currently pastoring the King of Kings (Assemblies of God) church. He had been prayed over by flamboyant evangelist Benny Hinn – whose meetings Arnott had also attended – in Florida, in 1992. After Hinn prophesied over him, Freidzon's ministry moved up a gear; he was able to fill a 65,000 seater stadium, and his regular congregation ballooned to 4,000 strong. He began to hold additional meetings at his church, because the usual services couldn't accommodate the swarms of church leaders turning up for a taste of the blessing.

Freidzon gave the glory to God: 'The anointing

comes through the praise and worship. God's presence descends as we immerse ourselves in adoring him.' His critics, however, describe it as emotional manipulation. Laughter, of course, was the distinctive feature of his meetings.

'The emphasis on holiness, the desire of the people to praise and worship, and the increase in concern for reaching others is genuine,' said *Redemption* magazine, coming to his defence. 'A hallmark of this revival is the emphasis on worship and praise. Missionaries report that the *Shekinah* glory of the Lord seems to descend on the meetings.'

When Freidzon visited Germany at Pentecost 1994, the anointing of joy, laughter and rejoicing accompanied his meetings for up to seven hours. Dramatic healings seemingly were in evidence. 'One woman who had planned to commit suicide instead just bubbled over with joy,' according to Gerhard Bially, cited in the charismatic Catholic magazine *Good News*: 'Chronic headaches, back-pains, heart conditions and phobias were reported healed, and hundreds of people gave their lives to Christ.'

About 600 Christian leaders, mainly from the house churches, met in Berlin, for their annual pastors' meeting. Here some of the participants shared about the new move of the Spirit they had experienced since Claudio Freidzon had visited their churches, with the accompanying laughter, resting in the Spirit, tears, etc. Following this, similar phenomena swept through the meeting affecting the rest of the pastors. A major refreshing began to sweep through European churches, through channels which seemed to have bypassed Toronto.

When the January conference began at the Toronto Airport Vineyard, the two speakers, Clark and Arnott himself, had in turn been prayed for by Freidzon and

Howard-Browne respectively – contact with either of
whom had been shown to lead to spiritual manifestations virtually of epidemic proportions.

Moreover, Canada was a country ripe for revival.
Phil Gazley is familiar with the spiritual climate of the
country from his work as an Area YWAM co-ordinator
in Alberta, for eight years until the end of 1993. Now
a Vineyard worship leader in Croydon, South London,
Gazley told me: 'When I left Canada, there was very
much an atmosphere of anticipation, which had come
about through unity. People looked at certain cities
and said "something is bubbling, something's going to
happen" in certain places, because of the prayer and
intercession that had been birthed out of the depth
of unity.

'Church growth specialist Peter Wagner has exam-
ined the situation in Argentina and looked at places
like Calgary, San Antonio, Colorado Springs and Port-
land, where there have been massive prayer movements as a result of the unity. Different parts of
the body of Christ have come together without their
charismatic, conservative or evangelical tags, and said,
"We're going to accept that – whatever our other
disagreements – we can pray and worship together in
the name of Jesus." Pastors of different denominations
have come together to pray for revival. In Canada,
there was a feeling amongst Christians that something
was going to burst out, and no one cared just where.'

It seems little wonder that something spectacular
was about to happen.

Lift Off!

The Spirit moved in such a powerful way at Clark and
Arnott's meetings that the Toronto Airport Vineyard
was turned upside down. The signs and wonders were

more powerful, affected more people, went deeper, and lasted longer than anything they had previously experience. Hundreds of people heard about the occurrences and came along to see for themselves.

Soon, the fellowship was having to stage meetings six nights per week to cope with the demand. The church grew from 150 to over 1,000 in four months, with an average of two people – but as many as thirty on occasions – making commitments to Christ each night.

John Arnott's associate pastor, Mark Dupont, told *Alpha* magazine that Clark 'Took a team up to Toronto and everything began to break out. We have often seen falling, shaking, deliverances and healings so the phenomena wasn't new to us. But what was new was that it was going on and on. Often, after a conference, it's back to busines as usual. This was much more intense. There were far more people getting drunk in the Spirit, far more people overcome with laughter – which we haven't seen much of. That was rather new to us.

'The meetings aren't the most powerful things I have ever seen, but the sense of the presence of God is so strong. What is so overwhelming about it is not the physical phenomena, but the phenomenal hunger for the Lord, expressed in worship.

'We've talked to people weeks or months later, and asked what changes, if any, have there been. They talk about reading their Bible more; praying more; a new boldness for witnessing; and a stronger awareness of the Father's love.'

Arnott himself told Gerhard Bially's *Charisma* magazine, in a rare interview, that he was fully aware:

'That revival movements often are accompanied by "tares" or negative by-products. But he has learned that to uproot tares can sometimes kill the positive results as well. There's always going to be some fleshly enthusiasm as well, I would rather contend with a little fleshly zeal than carnal resistance.'

Unfortunately, some of the fleshly zeal has serious spiritual overtones concealed within it.

The Visitors

Bishop David Pytches, of St Andrews, Chorleywood, was one of the first visitors to witness the extrordinary events that were occurring in that modest little Toronto church. He missed most of the first evening's service when he was 'slain in the Spirit' very early on; and the press were quick to pick up that, filled with the Spirit, he roared like a lion!

Meanwhile, his wife, Mary Pytches, was praying for some of the laughter, a bite of the fruit, more gifting and anointing, and plenty of righteousness and holiness – in short, more of Jesus!

'On the first evening, I sort of went down in the Spirit in an "OK" sort of way. I didn't flap around too much,' she told a meeting at Focus '94. 'But what I did do was start to wail, and this really did disturb me. This was not what I went for. In fact, I felt that I had perhaps asked for a bicycle and got a sewing machine. I thought, No, I came for laughter, I didn't come for this, Lord.

'People were being anointed in all sorts of ways out there. It was just incredible. They were jerking and shaking and doing all those sort of things – and there was this incredible roaring.' Her husband was really getting into the swing of things!

Many consider that the roaring is acceptable because it is related to prophecy: '"They will follow the LORD; he will roar like a lion. When he roars, his children will come trembling from the west. They will come trembling like birds from Egypt, like doves from Assyria.

I will settle them in their homes," declares the LORD' (Hosea 11:10–11).

Some consider that it reflects Christ in his aspect of the Lion of Judah, and encourage those who roar to then immediately prophesy. The Toronto Vineyard claims that roaring people are usually intercessors involved in promoting unity. Cynics, however, might point to another passage of Scripture which describes Satan as a roaring lion. The Bible must be handled very carefully.

Mary Pytches: 'One night there was a German girl just overcome by the Spirit, and she was thrashing around. And then I was suddenly aware of a sound and I thought, "O God, O God". What I was hearing was the sound of an army marching. I thought of Ezekiel 37 when those dry bones came together. God breathed into them. Flesh came on them and then they stood on their feet like a mighty army.'

John Arnott invited her to the front, in the electric atmosphere, to describe the awesome sound of a mighty army that she was hearing clairvoyantly, in the Spirit. She heard the noise once more during her stay in Toronto, and others have heard it again since.

Not all the reports that have come from Toronto have been as favourable. One British charismatic writing in *Evangelism Today* (July 1994) about a visit to the Toronto Airport Vineyard on 18th June, commented: 'I observed a number of women who from the start were arm and/or hand waving and/or shaking, rapidly, even violently, and continuously. This looked very much self-induced and did not seem to be for any purpose.

'As various people, all of whom seemed to be known to the man in charge, were invited forward, we were treated to a performance of uncontrollable laughing, jerking and shaking. Each was interviewed but little

was said that I could describe as glorifying the Lord –
indeed some were virtually unable to speak intelligibly
due to the jerking, shaking and laughing. When one of
the team, a female, was asked to pray over one of the
men, she came out jerking so violently that it appeared
as if she could have been plugged into an electricity
supply.'

The performance became increasingly disturbing, as
people fell over one another, drunk in the Spirit.
Nothing was said that could be construed as glorifying
to Jesus, nor was anything seen that would indicate
that the Spirit was in fact present. There was talk that
hinted at revival, but no manifestation of repentance.
Men roared like lions, uncontrollable laughter greeted
the reading of Scripture, and the 'in' phrase seemed to
be, 'I'm a jerk for Jesus.'

Cathy Stayne, writing in *Good News* magazine, is
more positive: 'The format of each evening is very
simple. Praise and worship (much of which we already
know), testimonies, input or teaching, and then ministry for forty hours! (*sic*) What I really liked was the
relaxed atmosphere. They had their own cafe area
where you could get a drink and a muffin or a hot
dog, and then go back in for some ministry!

'Also, the people ministering were not burnt out
heaps – they were people who had been blessed themselves, who were part of that Vineyard, who now
desired to give it away. They were so positive. The
meetings were much like one would witness at a
Wimber conference . . .

'I was able to experience peace at a much deeper level
by the end, than at the beginning. Over there, they
liken it to Ezekiel walking deeper into the water. I
think that also for me I could relax more because I
was out of my normal situation and I didn't have my
usual responsibilities.'

Charismatic stalwart Michael Harper has written in the *Church of England Newspaper* of his own initial reservations: 'The noise of aircraft taking off and landing was incessant. It was also a very hot evening, the temperature was in the 90s, and the room where the meetings are held only had a few rather tired fans operating. The meeting room gradually filled up, until there was standing room only. The background music when we arrived was modern, the kind I dislike!

'There followed songs that I did not know, with words I could not see, and uninspiring music. The band was average. The preacher went on far too long, and didn't seem to be saying very much. What was all the fuss about.'

Yet Harper confesses, 'From the moment I stepped inside the door I knew God was there, and the rest didn't really seem to matter. Whether it is right to call it "revival" is debatable; what was clear to me from the first minute was that something extraordinary was happening, and that this was due not to the human factors, but to the divine presence and power.'

These events have been unsettling for many people, who feel they have no grid for evaluation, and no map to guide them. It is hard even to reconcile the various accounts as pertaining to the same church, or the same phenomena.

The single visit most influential to the British Church was surely Eleanor Mumford's two-day trip towards the end of May. The wife of a South London Vineyard leader, she described her experiences in two talks given at HTB on 29th May 1994. Tapes of the meetings have received wide circulation – it was probably the most bootlegged church service in history! Her infectious delivery and guileless sense of wonder did much to spread interest in the Toronto Airport Vineyard, to the exclusion of churches in

Europe and the USA where similar phenomena are
also taking place.

A Landmark Visit

'You may say, "What made you go to this funny little
place in Toronto?" Well, I went because I've never been
slow to go to a party! I heard that there were things
going on and I was mad to get there and to see. I just
have never been one to sit on the edge. I wanted to go
and to get into the middle,' she explained lyrically, in
her plummy cut-glass voice.

Eleanor had felt a spiritual bankruptcy, and went
to Toronto with a spirit of great expectation, badly
needing her Lord's touch. She was not the only one.

'There was a young Chinese pastor who arrived in
Toronto from Vancouver, where he was pastoring,
and he came fasting. The darling man looked as if
he had spent his whole life fasting, and he was the
most wonderful and godly man. And as he arrived at
the church, the Lord spoke to him clearly and said,
"You can forget about your fasting. This is a time for
celebration." And so, indeed, it was.

'I was reminded when I went in there of how the
people in the crowd at Pentecost said, "Are not these
Galileans?" Are these not just terribly ordinary people?

'As the worship leader strummed his rather tuneless
guitar, he stood up and said, "What have you come
for?" And we all said, "We've come for the Lord. We've
come for more of God." And he said, "Well, if you've
come for God, you'll not be disappointed!" And from
that moment on, that was the truth.

'The truth is that this whole move of the Lord is all
about Jesus. I was there for only forty-eight hours, and
I never heard anybody talk about the devil. I never
heard anybody talk about spiritual warfare. I never

heard a power or a principality mentioned. There was no space for talk of the opposition, because there was just a growing passion for the name of Jesus, and for the beauty of his presence among his people.'

One of the visiting pastors went back to his Californian church and asked God, 'Why have you been so kind to me? Why have you done these wonderful things? Why are you pouring out your Spirit on your churches in these days?' And the Lord answered him, 'So that my church will get excited about my Son.'

'I went scurrying back to church history, and to the Scriptures. It's all happened before, and there is nothing that I saw – however strange or unusual – that I have not since been able to read about in the Bible.

'During the time that I was there, I saw all sorts of people coming and going. There were so many very weary pastors who turned up with their even more weary wives, and they were so anointed by the Lord. There was one very sensible middle-aged man who'd been in pastoral ministry for years, and when he spoke to us after several days, he was just behaving like an old drunk. It was terribly funny.

'And once, he stood up and talked about the intimacy he'd gained with Jesus; then the pastor said to him, "Well thank you Wayne for telling us about this. May we now pray for you?" And he said, "I'd be glad for you to pray for me." They prayed for him and down he went! He was rolling on the floor for the next two hours and no one took any notice. He just continued to commune with his God.'

Mumford spoke of another, younger pastor: 'He was a very "all together" young man – quite serious minded and godly; thrilled with everything, but very much in control. He just watched, and he just soaked, and he just basked in the presence of the Lord. Then, after a day or two, he started to twitch, and he was a

little embarrassed. And then he began to shake, and
he was *very* embarrassed. After a while of shaking,
and laughing in the presence of the Lord, he decided,
"Who gives a rip? Who cares what people say?"'

Another young pastor was so overtaken by the gladness of the Lord that his wife made him sleep on
the couch because he was shaking and twitching so
violently:

'But he had a sense of responsibility and felt, 'I've
got to keep my church on the road." So he decided
that the obvious thing to do was to go into the office
and to type out the church bulletin, the news sheet.
"Someone's got to keep a grip round here," he said to
himself. So he went to type out the bulletin, and as he
got to announcing a seminar, he typed the title *Come,
Holy Spirit,* and fell under the power of God!'

Mumford explained that, as she was writing up the
story on the plane coming home, when she wrote
'Come, Holy Spirit', she too was overcome by the
Spirit!

'He's pouring his Spirit out upon us. He's sending us
his joy and he's refreshing our spirits just because he
loves us. I'm not sure that he's equipping us. I'm not
even sure it's about being better this, better that, better
ministers. I think it's just his love for us. It's about his
nearness to me, and my dearness to him . . .

'There was a story about a young woman who'd lain
on the floor and laughed for two hours, and then she
got up and she decided that she was peckish, and
went off to a very nasty restaurant, for which one
needs grace just to enter the door. She sat down
and, opposite, she saw a whole family sitting at a
table and, completely out of character, she went over
to them and she said, "Would you like to be saved?"
And they all said "Yes!" The whole family were led
to Christ.

'The children in the schools in Toronto are being sent home for shaking! Several of them have been sent with notes saying, "Dear Mrs So-and-so, would you please have this child tested for epilepsy." The children are rocking and rolling, and shaking and laughing!

'For my own self, there is a greater love for Jesus than I've ever known, a greater excitement about the kingdom than I ever thought possible, a greater sense that these are glorious, glorious days in which to be alive, I'm thrilled about Scripture, and going back to the word and finding it's all been there from the very beginning.'

The overwhelming majority of Christians who have been to visit the Toronto Airport Vineyard have returned with similarly favourable reports. Yet how is one to account for the negative experiences, the 'tares' amongst the crop, to which John Arnott refers? Perhaps the fellowship was simply having an 'off night'. Or maybe the people who came away disillusioned were simply unaccustomed to the particular worship style found there.

Yet there may be a more sinister reason for the occasional dissatisfaction and sense of unease.

Health and Wealth

Firstly, we've seen that John Arnott had attended meetings with Benny Hinn, and that the second key figure in the Toronto outpouring, Randy Clark, had received prayer from an Argentinian evangelist who had, in turn, been prayed for by Benny Hinn.

Secondly, when Randy Clark set out to receive the ministry of Rodney Howard-Browne, he was at first troubled to learn that Howard-Browne's next meetings were to take place in Kenneth Hagin Jr's Rhema Bible church, in Tulsa: A church with whose teachings Clark had doctrinal disagreements. Clark believed that God disapproved of his own smug, denominational attitudes. He went along and received ministry, in spite of his theological reservations.

The straight line connecting these two points is the heretical and cultish Faith Movement. Kenneth Hagin Sr is the veritable 'founding father' of the Faith Movement. Benny Hinn has tried subsequently to distance himself from the movement. Yet, as recently as Morris Cerrullo's Mission to London meetings in August 1994, at which Hinn spoke, his teaching has leaned heavily on the wealth and prosperity teaching which characterise the Faith Movement. As conservative evangelical Stephen Sizer puts it, the two men behind the Toronto Blessing, Clark and Arnott 'went in search of spiritual blessings from men whose teaching has been exposed as heretical and cultic . . .'

The unscriptural ideas of the Faith Movement gurus Kenneth Hagin and Kenneth Copeland, his 'heir apparent', have been taken on board in many parts of the charismatic movement, without adequate testing of their validity.

Dave Tomlinson, in his Foreword to *The Promise of Health and Wealth* by Dan McConnell writes: 'Numerous charismatic preachers and teachers, some within mainstream denominations and some in the new church sector, are presenting Faith Movement teaching, or at least echoing it, in one form or another. There are those here in the UK, and there are more than just a few, who proclaim that material prosperity is part and parcel of God's victory through the Cross. I have listened to a well-known charismatic teacher announcing spiritual and material prosperity, alongside healing and forgiveness, as the inclusive package of atonement.'

A triumphalist message of success issues from the
Faith Movement, which seeks to deny that the Christian life should be one of selfless giving to others, and
not one in which believers proudly collect trophies
for themselves. Dave Tomlinson has counselled many
sick people who have been afraid to admit – even
to themselves – that they are ill and in need of
treatment, so thoroughly have they been indoctrinated
with the notion that sickness is a sign of spiritual
inadequacy and lack of faith. Guilt, paranoias and
self-recrimination are the bitter fruits of the Faith
Movement.

Dan McConnell, in his book, explains why he believes
that nothing less than the doctrinal orthodoxy of the
charismatic movement is at stake. The attractive
health and wealth doctrines, though are the keys –
not to personal prosperity – but to spiritual poverty,
heresy and, perhaps, eternal damnation.

The Faith Movement teachings do not stem historically from the Holiness/Pentecostal traditions, but
rather from the heretical Christian Science school. The
Faith Movement's founder, Kenneth Hagin, plagiarised
the bulk of his theory from E.W. Kenyon, according to
McConnell – who gives several pages of examples in
which Hagin has demonstrably copied entire passages
word-for-word from Kenyon without crediting him. The
movement's fivefold distinctives – on revelation knowledge, identification, faith, healing, and prosperity –
were devised by Kenyon.

Kenyon's theories can, in turn, be traced back to
the metaphysical cults of both Christian Science and
New Thought. He was also well-versed in the writings
of the nineteenth-century American Transcendental
Movement – which in turn borrowed heavily from
ancient Hindu texts.

False Teaching

A quote apiece from Hagin and Copeland illustrate the strong strands of Eastern mysticism present in their teachings; the same mysticism that fuels much of the New Age Movement's ideology: 'Faith is a power force ... it is this force of faith which makes the laws of the spirit world function ... God cannot do anything for you apart or seperate from faith.' (Kenneth Copeland).

Hagin advocates Eastern monism, which sees God and man as being of the same essential nature: 'Man was created on terms of equality with God, and he could stand in God's presence without any consciousness of inferiority ... He made us the same class of being that He is Himself ... Man lived in the realm of God. He lived on equal terms with God ... The believer is called Christ ... that's who we are; we're Christ.'

Much of Benny Hinn's teaching is completely Christian, but his reliance on charismatic gifts over the word of God had led him to produce wildly unconventional statements such as: 'Man, I feel revelation knowledge coming on me here ... See, God the Father is a person, God the Son is a person, God the Holy Spirit is a person. But each of them is a triune being by Himself. If I can shock you – and maybe I should – there's nine of them ... You said, 'I never heard that'. Well, you think you're in this church to hear things you've heard for fifty years?'

In his book *The Anointing*, Hinn asks with all the zeal of a direct-mail sales letter: 'How would you like to receive not only the anointing of the Holy Spirit on your life, but also a double portion of that anointing? Think about it: the presence of the Spirit each day of your life and a double measure of the power.'

There is no biblical basis for anyone receiving a 'double portion' of the Holy Spirit, like some spiritual Oliver Twist. Indeed, if you have the Holy Spirit in your life, you have the infinite power of God working through you; how can you possibly have a double portion of something that is infinite?

(Hinn seems to have misunderstood the reference in 2 Kings 2:9 of Elisha asking for a double portion of Elijah's spirit. In ancient Israel, a 'double portion' was simply a way of designating an heir, and Elisha is simply asking Elijah to appoint him as his spiritual successor.)

The supernatural element in both Kenyon and Hagin's work stems – not from traditional Pentecostalism – but nakedly from the occult. Their theology is basically *deist*, seeing God as a pawn who must dance to the piper's tune, played by mortal men who seek to manipulate the laws of the universe!

This is the very basis of witchcraft. In one of its earliest forms, the brahmin priests of India (ca 800 BC) performed rites believed not simply to placate the demon gods, but to *control* the powerful spiritual forces that they represented. The rituals they used, preserved in the *Brahmanas* and the spellbinding *Atharva Veda*, influenced the American Transcendental Movement, and through it Kenyon and Hagin.

Their view of Christ is of a person filled with the 'satanic nature' who must be born again in hell. Their heretical notion of salvation deifies humans and spiritualises the atonement, subverting the truly Christian view that Christ's physical death alone atones for sin.

Many of the movement's practices – positive confession

for example, with its emphasis on positive thinking —
has more to do with psychology than religion.

As McConnell says: 'Many regard this as a healthy
practice, emphasising the psychological benefit of positive thinking and speaking. What this fails to consider is the historical fact that those who first taught
PMA/positive confession – the New Thought metaphy-
sicians – attributed its power to cosmic principalities
and occultic deities. Though the Bible does emphasise
the importance of a pure mind and holy speech, it
nowhere states that a person can alter physical reality through mental means, and it certainly does not
encourage verbal confession of the divine Name and
Word as means of manipulating God's will. In fact,
Scripture strictly prohibits both.'

Graham Cray was a former colleague of David
Watson, and is a charismatic evangelical of nearly
thirty years standing: 'I am profoundly suspicious of
the Faith teaching. The moment you link together faith
as a sort of entity that exists by itself, with phenomena
as "things that come as a consequence of your faith",
I think we are closer to the New Age than we are to
orthodox Christianity.

'I worry when people who are gifted with prophecy
turn themselves into Bible teachers and do extremely
strange things with Bible texts! I won't wear these
strange and unsustainable exegeses. I profoundly believe in the ministry of prophets, but we mustn't
let them take over the job of teachers,' Cray told
me.

Along with health, many evangelists have made
a wreck of their ministry through promising *wealth*
as a natural consequence of following Christ. At a
major London crusade during summer 1994, the Faith
Movement influence could strongly be detected in the
extraordinary length of time spent in trying to part

the audience from its money, on the grounds that God would make them richer if they were generous givers.

At one meeting I attended, there was little preaching of the Gospel, but a strong element of prayer warfare. The congregation were encouraged to 'stamp on Satan's head' by drumming their feet – a form of 'dominionist' prayer which owes much to the Manifest Sons of God, as well as to the Faith Movement. When we were led in a prayer during which we were all expected to claim for ourselves 'the treasures of Abraham', for which there is no biblical warrant, I could stomach no more, and I left. Since there was very little manifestation of spiritual gifts, despite the pentecostal fervour, I suspect that the Holy Spirit may have left too.

Mixed Blessing

Arnott and Clark may have been unwise in their choice of spiritual mentors, and the mentors themselves have perhaps displayed too much emotionalism and not enough discernment. It is probably the Toronto Vineyard's proximity to unbiblical notions and doctrinal error that has watered down the Spirit's anointing at times, and led to some erratic ministry. I suspect, however, that much of the problem lies in human error – and lack of discernment – rather than in beings of supernatural origin.

Yet, it would be unwise to 'throw the baby out with the bathwater'. Gerald Coates for one, has sprung to the Toronto Airport Vineyard's defence: 'Many key biblical characters were less than perfect. King David and the Apostle Peter are examples. God used them nevertheless.'

An even better example might be Samson: 'a rude instrument for a rude age'. If God can use even a man

whose first stop on arriving in a village tended to be
the local whore house, then all is not lost! As someone
once said, 'Let he who is without sin cast the first
stone . . .'

Whilst the Bible certainly makes no promises of
health and wealth to believers *as a right,* there are
undoubtedly those whom God made very wealthy:
Solomon is the most obvious example. I have no doubt
that the Lord could choose, in his divine grace, to
make healthy and wealthy people of those today who
continue to seek first the kingdom of God. He could also
announce that he was doing this through prophecy. It
is only the general proclamation that both are available
by right, that is wrong!

It would be wrong, too, to see the Bible's authentic
teaching on health and wealth as purely a form of
socialism. God has often thrown down the mighty, and
built a kingdom of equality from the bottom up, raising
up hosts of insignificant people in a 'right on' way that
would make even Karl Marx green with envy. But it is
also totally scriptural for God to raise up a few selected
individuals – *disproportionately empowered* with the
gifts of the Spirit – through whose ministry many are
to be blessed. The Bible is full of such people!

This way may be more akin to capitalism – nay,
Thatcherism! – but if God chooses to use certain people
as his instruments, and not others, that is his divine
prerogative. If God chooses to listen to the prayers
of some more than others, when all are calling for
the Holy Spirit, that is his sovereign right. But the
people he specially calls to be his channels – men
like Hinn, Freidzon and Howard-Browne – are only
human, and are not spiritually immunised against
errors and mistakes. They deserve prayer and support,
but should also be open to constructive criticism and
stern discipline.

'Men and women who take risks are going to get into trouble. That doesn't mean that we should write them off. Neither does anointing and power mean that we abandon our critical or intuitive faculties,' says Coates.

The Blessing may well be authentically of God – I'm personally convinced that it is – but I am deeply suspicious of some teaching associated with it. Many are gaining good mileage from it to prosper their own careers – and bank balances. Rather like the kidnap of Helen of Troy, the 'Toronto Blessing' has launched a thousand ministries; and, like the wooden horse, it is not always what it seems to be.

There are too many rich preachers – spouting their own ideas instead of expositing authentic scriptural revelations – who are hitching a ride on Christ's cross.

Chapter Six

Footprints on the Water

T he story of the Toronto Experience's trip across the Atlantic has been told so many times, in so many places, that it has now reached mythical proportions! Like myths, however, the core of truth has been distorted and misrepresented through transmission.

The generally accepted version starts on Tuesday morning, May 24th, 1994.

Eleanor Mumford had just returned to Britain after her eventful trip to the Toronto Airport Vineyard. At 11.30 am, she spoke briefly to several church leaders, including HTB curate Nicky Gumbel and his wife Pippa, at the Mumford's Kingston home.

'She prayed for us to be filled with the Holy Spirit,' says Nicky Gumbel. 'Everyone present was affected in a remarkable way, and the session continued unabated throughout lunch.'

When Gumbel returned to HTB at 2.00 pm, he found the lunchtime staff meeting he had been due to attend was just breaking up, and he offered both his apologies and his explanation for his absence. Though everyone was in a desperate hurry to get back to their work, they were intrigued by his story, and asked him to say a closing prayer for them.

He prayed that the Holy Spirit would fill everyone in the room in preparation for the busy afternoon ahead. As it happens, no one got any work done that afternoon, because the Spirit fell upon them all and the effect was instantaneous!

'People fell to the ground again and again. There were remarkable scenes as the Holy Spirit touched all those present in ways few had experienced or seen. Staff members walking past the room were also affected.'

Staff member Emmy Wilson recalls: 'When Nicky Gumbel prayed, the Spirit came in power on all of us. I just felt I was falling in love with the Lord all over again. Then of course, there was some leg tapping and some really excited sort of crying out to Jesus. One minute I was laughing, and the next minute I was just weeping and weeping before the Lord.'

The Dynamic Spirit

HTB Rector Sandy Millar was ensconced in an important Evangelical Alliance meeting at Whitefield House at the time. The telephone rang and Clive Calver picked it up.

'It's for you,' said Calver, passing the phone to Millar. 'It's urgent.'

The apologetic voice on the other end was Glenda, Millar's secretary: 'I'm sorry to interrupt the meeting, but I thought you ought to know that the entire staff is slain in the Spirit, and lying on the floor . . .'

The meeting came to a halt. Solemn men and women were watching, hoping this urgent call wasn't going to be too serious, and Millar took it all in his stride: 'Is that a good thing?' he quizzed his secretary. She replied in the affirmative.

'Then what are you doing on the telephone to me?' he enquired.

'I have crawled to the telephone on my hands and knees!' she protested, mildly hurt.

Millar tried to remain as serious as possible in the circumstances: 'Thank you very much, I'll try to get back as soon as I can.' That satisfied the people in the room, and the meeting continued – oblivious to the extraordinary events that were beginning to unfold.

Back at HTB, some two hours later, some of those present went to tell others in different offices and prayed with them where they found them. They too were powerfully affected by the Holy Spirit – many of them falling to the ground. Prayer was still continuing at 5.00 pm.

From that day onwards, so the story goes, both HTB and the South London Vineyard were transformed. The following Sunday, Elli Mumford spoke at both the morning and evening services at HTB, and said:

'In the course of the past week, our church has gone to pieces and the people are getting healed. We've got people who have gone down on the floor and got healed. Nobody even knew they were sick, and they got better without us even naming the words.

'I talked yesterday with a woman who has been mightily affected by the laughter of the Lord in the course of the last week. She was brought up during the war and she said, "I always had what I needed, but I never had sweets; I never had party dresses; I never knew joy. And Jesus has given me joy in the last week which has made up for all my childhood."

'It's such a sweet thing. She said, "All my life I've longed to be naughty." She lay on the floor at a meeting we had on Thursday, she rolled around like a drunk woman, and she was wonderful.'

At the close of the morning service, Mumford prayed for the Holy Spirit to come. There was a time of silence, then slowly but surely, some members of the congregation began to cry quietly, while others began to laugh joyfully. As these signs began to occur, she requested people to come forward if they required prayer. Many did, and Mumford's team began to pray for them; as they did so, they began to tumble over and lay on the floor, resting in the Spirit.

Soon the whole church was affected with scenes that few could remember having seen before. Even the children, returning from their own groups, began to pray with each other. It was glorious!

Though prayer continued till 1.30 pm, that didn't stop people from returning for another dose in the evening. Elli Mumford spoke again, telling a slightly longer version of the tale she had recounted during the morning. Again, after she had concluded, she asked the Holy Spirit to come.

Wham!

It was a repeat performance of the morning spectacle! When those who were not HTB members were requested to come forward for prayer, more than a hundred came to the front. As the Spirit fell in greater power, people fell limply to the ground in beatific joy. Many rows of chairs had to be cleared to make room for them all to lie on their own stretch of carpet. You could have played both halves of a football match during the lengthy time of prayer, which concluded after 9.30.

Two days later, Sandy Millar set out with staff member Jeremy Jennings across the Atlantic to check out how the Toronto Airport Vineyard had learned to cope with the Holy Spirit blessing, spreading like wild bushfire. That evening in Toronto, they witnessed incredible sights. Next morning at HTB, the Holy Spirit fell in power upon several staff members during a routine morning prayer time.

Repeat Performance

The Sunday after, Sandy Millar spoke at both HTB services. In the morning, he invited other members of

the congregation to come up and share how they had
been touched by God a week earlier.

'I know now with a surety that God loves me as a
father,' said one. 'It was the most wonderful experience
I have ever had. I have never been so calm,' said
another. Many were gripped by the power and majesty
of the Holy Spirit – God himself moving amongst them
as an unseen but omnipotent visitor. The planned
Communion Service could not take place, such were
the repercussions seemingly of the Spirit's awesome
impact upon the waiting people.

An estimated 1,200 people packed the evening service for a similar visitation. One young AIDS sufferer,
who was a recent visitor to the church, explained that
he had never before experienced the love he had found
at HTB in recent weeks. Again, the chairs had to be
removed to cope with those prostrate in blissful rest.
More than 100 Christians were still praying in the
church beyond 10.00 pm.

The next week, journalist Nicholas Monson was in
the church for the morning service, and his cynical
report – part of the first national press coverage –
appeared in the austere pages of the *Sunday Telegraph*
a week later. It reads like a murder scene, crossed with
Dante's *Inferno*!

'Mr Millar touched the man's forehead and then
bam! Right on cue, his eyelids fluttered, his knees
buckled and he was lowered to the floor where he
started to gibber. Soon there were four bodies on the
floor, two giggling, one gibbering and one silent. Then
curates (*sic*) began passing down the aisles praying
and touching the congregation, which was now falling
about me.

'To my right, a young man in shorts was in hysterics
rolling around the floor holding the head of another
who joined him in a fit of spiritual merriment. A

grinning girl sat over this scene almost in a trance with
both her hands shaking out in front of her. Alarmed,
I moved away from my seat towards the back of the
church but my exit was blocked by a large plump lady
lying face down in the aisle, being prayed over by six
people. She seemed in distress and was moaning, 'No,
no, no.' She made a move to get up but one of the
six praying over her promptly pushed her down . . . A
curate (sic) appeared at my side.

'She has been practising black magic and she needs
strong Christians around her to help her,' he said. 'Of
course,' I replied, nodding gratefully and stepped back
over the now comatose Sloane Ranger.'

Ah, HTB! To see yourselves as others see you!

Still, it's a dodgy piece of reportage that restricts
itself to the writer's own perspective, and makes no
effort to understand how others – particularly the
joyful participants – perceive the same events.

The day the article appeared, a representative from
Prophecy Today was sitting in the balcony with three
colleagues for the evening service: 'After a while, first
one colleague then the other – one on each side of
me – began shaking and laughing. Both members
were lowered to their seats by members of the HTB
ministry team.

'I have quite often ministered to the demonised, but
I had no sense whatever of anything demonic about
what was happening on each side of me. Indeed, I had
a strong sense that it was entirely good and healthy.
I, too, felt the Lord's presence weighing heavily on me
and fell to my knees in rather tearful adoration. My
male colleague and I recovered rather sooner than our
companion who, for about thirty-five to forty minutes
alternately rested peacefully or laughed loudly, stamp-
ing her feet and waving her arms.

'By this time, around seventy-five to one hundred

people out of – I would guess – 1,500 present, were receiving ministry. Some were laughing, others were weeping, others showed signs of demonic manifestations of the kind which I would associate with effective deliverance.'

That very much sums up my own impressions from the various visits I have made myself to HTB.

These services saw the commencement of a pattern that has continued ever since. By August 28th, hundreds of people – some from as far afield as East Anglia, Lancashire and the West Country – were patiently queueing around the church site at 5.35 pm, nearly an hour before the service began. In September, a ticket system was introduced in order that church members could stand a chance of getting into their own services!

And all this had begun that historic Tuesday morning when Nicky Gumbel went across to Kingston to hear Elli Mumford talk about her Toronto trip. Or did it?

Had the Holy Spirit really hidden in her luggage, tucked snugly between the neatly folded clothing, as her plane swept crossed the Altantic? Did the Third Person of the Trinity really slip into Britain unnoticed through the green customs channel, passport at the ready, leaving international air space with nothing to declare?

Did Eleanor Mumford really bring the Toronto Blessing back to Britain with her?

Pioneers in the Spirit

In the study of Gerald Coates' Esher home, I sat – cassette recorder whirring – slipping in my questions between Gerald's lucid answers, as the legendary house-church supremo held forth at length. He's awesome when he gets going!

'Over the twenty years of the Pioneer network we
have seen at various times, people on their knees,
we've seen prostrations, in a wide range of situations,
frequent and infrequent, and we simply regard this as
a reaction to the presence of God. So, when in April,
May and June, I saw in Geneva, Dublin, Sweden and
Frankfurt – and a few places in the UK – these
extraordinary manifestations, I wasn't too worried.

'In Dublin, people were laughing; in Geneva they
were weeping; and in Frankfurt there was laughter
and people weeping prostrate on the floor – all with
confessions of sin. In Geneva I had a terrific sense of
God's Spirit. I thought: Fine, that's what God is doing
in Geneva. In Dublin, when I heard the uproarious
laughter, and people collapsed in the Spirit in droves,
it was all fine by me.

'The trouble with travelling is that you have no grid,
no way of knowing what has gone on before you arrived.
I just thought: This probably happens every week; in
fact, perhaps more happens when I'm not here! I just
had no framework to assess the manifestations or the
fruit that followed – particularly the fruit . . .'

Coates is anxious not to convey that this sort of thing
was happening every half hour, when it was probably
more like once or twice a month.

'I was carrying on with many regular meetings, some
with manifestations – but it was the laughter in Dublin
and the tears/prostrations in Geneva and Frankfurt
that stood out – and I would mention these to my
wife when I came back. I told a friend of mine about
these things, too; he said that I should watch a video of
Rodney Howard-Browne – of whom I'd never heard.

'Then, around that time, I spoke at the Vineyard in
South London. It was a good morning, great response,
tears, laughter, shaking, repentance – a good meeting.
It was only when John Mumford took me out to lunch

and said, "We've never seen such power on a Sunday morning," that the penny finally dropped!

'I'd been seeing some of these things happening on and off over twenty years – and a lot more of it recently – but as soon as John spoke, I saw a pattern emerging. I knew something was happening. I went back home and watched the Rodney Howard-Browne video.

'In it, he gives his story. He was baptised at the age of eight, moved to America at the age of thirty-five in 1987. For five years these things had been happening in his ministry. In 1992 he shot to national prominence. In Florida, thousands of people fell into convulsive laughter under his ministry.

'In Fort Worth, Texas, too, I discovered when I viewed the video for myself. It was shot at a massive rally, on May 8th 1993, at which Howard-Browne shared the platform with none other than Faith Movement stalwart Kenneth Copeland! During the hour or so of live ministry, there is no teaching whatsoever – that part of the meeting may well have been edited out of the recording. Instead, the congregation was treated to the duo "hamming it up" like a pair of slapstick comics in burlesque. Their "tongues" sounded totally unconvincing, and the American style was an embarrassing echo of all that is worst in banal tele-evangelism.

'Then Howard-Browne began to "work" the audience, and literally dozens of people laughed and fell. Only a handful failed to fall when Howard-Browne touched them, one or two looked possibly to have been pushed, and some seemed to fall down because it was "expected" of them. Yet the majority of people seemed to have been genuinely "slain in the Spirit" in a spontaneous manner – in spite of Copeland's suspect theology, and Howard-Browne's unwise association with the Faith Movement's heir apparent. I had no doubt that

I was watching genuine spiritual activity at work, despite the "punch line" where Copeland touched Howard-Browne, and the stocky evangelist himself hit the deck!'

Signs Following

'On the video, I saw the drunkenness, people thrown to the floor, outrageous laughter and tears, and I knew that this was exactly what I had been seeing – though this was in a much greater depth that I was seeing,' Coates admits.

Then Elli Mumford came back from Toronto, and we know the rest of the story. It's important to note, however, that she was still in Toronto when the powerful signs manifested for the first time at the South London Vineyard under Gerald Coates' ministry. Coates had not even heard of the Toronto happenings when he spoke there:

'I would say that she *did* bring something back to that church, though clearly something was underway before she arrived back. And clearly she brought something to HTB. I've spoken at HTB and had people respond with tears, but it is the *intensity* and the *compulsive laughter* which marks out the recent occurrences there as being quite different.'

We see, then, that the Holy Spirit had put in an appearance of dynamic import at the South London Vineyard – complete with signs and wonders – on May 22nd, a full week before the much-publicised manifestations at HTB . . .

'HTB is a fashionable Anglican church,' added Coates, 'and the press aren't terribly interested in independent churches where odd and strange things go on anyway. That's how it got written up. The press have continued to run with HTB, though there are very special things happening in Woodham, Brighton, Aldershot, and my own church – with barely a mention.

'Reporting in the national press has been surprisingly warm, surprisingly fair, and surprisingly objective – given the fact that the writers have not had the first clue what they are really writing about, or any understanding of what has been going on!'

Pioneer shortened their normal worship to allow a time of waiting on God at the end: 'There has been lots of laughter, lots of tears,' continued Coates, 'and we've literally had to carry people out because they have been so drunk in the Spirit.

'I've never had more letters of apology, more confessions of sin, or more acts of kindness from church members. There is far greater warmth in the church. Because of our network and our close relationships, this has shot throughout the network. Some are seeing remarkable manifestations, with others it has been much quieter – and that's not to say there is any greater value in one than the other. My biggest concern is that we don't end up with an unintentional ministry of manifestations.'

'Manifestations, of course, provide no indication of the spiritual value of the work. At every meeting I have personally attended where signs and wonders were manifest, just about everybody seems to have derived some benefit, even when the physical symptoms in most individuals were unspectacular. A sign is just the way that God gets your attention; it's the effect that follows on the individual believer's relationship with the divine that is important.

'At a meeting I attended in Portsmouth with Pioneer network churches and an Elim church, out of the 500 people present, perhaps 400 were physically affected. Whereas at another meeting, probably *only* 25 per cent were noticeably affected.'

New Frontiers

Coates chairs the rather pompously-named Apostolic Team Leaders' Forum, comprising key leaders of the main new churches in the UK. He discovered at this forum that, in some UK churches, the phenomena had commenced back in January 1994, but the press had not picked up on it.

During a telephone conversation with New Frontiers leader David Holden, I heard the full and remarkable story of how God was moving through the New Frontiers network. The network's overall leader, house-church pioneer Terry Virgo, moved to the USA in the winter of 1992–3, to lead a depressed 1,000-strong church in Columbia. The first year had been an uphill struggle with little to show for his efforts. Then Virgo went to South Africa for three weeks, in April 1994, returning to find his struggling church transformed beyond all recognition.

While Virgo had been away, church members had made regular two-hour drives to St Louis, where Rodney Howard-Browne had been holding revival meetings. David Holden happened to be in the States himself at the time and, intrigued, he turned up at the last of Howard-Browne's four-week run of meetings.

'I disagreed with about half of what Howard-Browne said, and I was totally unimpressed with his exegesis,' Holden remembered. 'Yet when he prayed for me, I felt a tremendous exhilaration. Everywhere I went afterwards, manifestations seemed to be breaking out.'

Two weeks later, both Holden and Virgo returned to Britain to join all of New Frontiers' 250 leaders for a two-day retreat. When the leaders returned to their seperate fellowships, exactly the same signs broke out in their congregations. Many arranged special 'receiving meetings' for those who wanted prayer

that the Holy Spirit would come upon them. 14,000
people experienced remarkable moves of the Spirit at
Stoneleigh Bible Week.

'It didn't seem to affect my private devotions at all,
but the moment I went to meetings: *Boom!* It all happened!' Holden told me, though he knew of others who
had been enpowered by the Spirit during their private
devotional times. There was a gentle lull over August
1994, when many people were away on holiday, then it
picked up again – but now Holden began to see *inward*
rather than purely *outward* signs.

'Initially, I was personally troubled. I started to
realise that the falling over wasn't important, it was
the fruit that mattered. The fruit I was looking for were
a passion for Jesus; a sense of the presence of God; love;
unity; evangelism; and changed lives.'

Then the first fruits began to appear: 'People started
to realise that the experience could be life-changing.
We're more loving now than ever before; leaders from
different denominations have been holding hands;
people I've been counselling for years have changed
beyond recognition; and we are seeing more converts than before, though the increase isn't spectacular,' Holden told me when we spoke in October
1994.

On October 1st, during a Prayer for the Nations
rally at Westminster Central Hall, I'd witnessed a
spectacular display of unity, with Holden, Coates,
Forster, Millar, Dye and a host of leaders from mainstream denominations – but no obvious manifestations
of the Holy Spirit, aside from some lacklustre singing in tongues. But during the afternoon, some 400
London church leaders had been 'powerfully blessed',
according to Holden. I found it reassuring that not
every major rally had to be converted into a 'receiving
meeting'.

Holden confirmed that evangelicals and charismatics seemed to be growing together: 'Evangelicals are being powerfully affected by this renewal in the Spirit. It's God's way of getting more people who are open to moves of the Spirit to engage in dialogue. At fraternals, evangelical leaders have sheepishly been asking charismatics what is happening. I must have prayed for more Anglican vicars than ever before.'

Theologically, Holden believed that it all represented a time of God refreshing his people: 'I think it's a time of preparation – an equipping or empowerment. I'm responding to a sovereign move – but I have no hankering to go to Toronto!'

Fresh Breath

A few miles from the Pioneer heartland in Surrey, and only a stone's throw from Wimbledon football ground, Queen's Road Baptist Church has seen its own share of startling manifestations of the Holy Spirit.

The minister, Norman Moss, traces its beginning to a service held on May 8th 1994, when he noticed a girl in his congregation sobbing buckets in repentance. She claimed to have been given a vision in which she witnessed the whole church prostrate in repentance before God, and then joining hands together in a chain around the church.

Moss drew the congregation's attention to the vision, and they joined hands to pray after the service. Others who had gone home after the service caught wind of what had happened and returned to the church later in the evening.

The following week, Moss flew to Toronto. Since the Airport Vineyard had been experiencing the phenomena for four months, Moss figured that they had four

months more experience, from which he was anxious
to benefit: 'Now, when people say they are going to
go to Toronto, my advice is usually "Fine, if you can
afford it, go."'

From May 22nd, Queen's Road Baptist was packed
to the gunnels, and services sometimes continued past
midnight. The usual culprits had been rounded up –
laughing, sobbing, shaking and falling. At one point
200 people lay resting in the Spirit receiving prayer –
some of them for several hours.

A small weekly meeting of local pastors grew from
literally a handful to forty, then eighty, finally peaking
with about 200 – of whom about half were there for
the first time. There were several hundred – perhaps
a thousand – pastors who came to receive blessing over
the space of a few months.

Within a month, around 100 lapsed Christians had
reaffirmed their faith, and several had made their
first commitment to Christ. Many sensible people
experienced unusual phenomena: a senior social work
lecturer reported hearing angels singing, and a respectable Christian policeman could not stand because he
was so drunk with the Spirit!

When I first visited the church, incognito, I found
some of the falling to be very suspicious. I saw one
woman readjusting her skirt while she was on the
floor, but generally I detected no sense of vanity or
pride amongst these people who simply wanted a new
experience of God.

Moss agreed there were rare cases of people being
physically knocked down, and a much more common
phenomenon of people allowing themselves to slip
down: 'There have been cases where deep trauma or
malevolent spiritual influence has manifested; when
confronted, sudden falls have occurred, as though the
person was thrown to the floor. I wouldn't like to

suggest, though, that everyone who feels thrown to the floor has a demonic problem!'

Historically, the church has been charismatic since the late seventies, and has seen periods of tremendous growth. 'We are strong on body ministry,' continued Moss, 'there has long been opportunity for people to bring prophecy and words of knowledge. But we had rarely seen someone fall down.

'Now, with only one disappointing exception, people have come forward at every meeting to commit themselves to Christ. Not all are first-time commitments, some are re-commitments. There have been enormous demands for counselling,' Moss told me when I interviewed him, during my second visit, at the end of September.

'We've had open meetings on Sundays (after normal service) plus Wednesday open meetings and Tuesday pastors' meetings. We will continue to provide these for as long as there is a need, but we are not seeking to profit from them. We're still wondering where it is all leading.

'The essence of the experience is a deepening of the relationship with Jesus; a refreshing of people who are dried up; and people mature in Jesus experiencing more. I would like to see people receive power to be witnesses to Jesus. Evangelistically, we're seeing more conversions than usual, though not all have been added to our own congregation – some have gone with other churches.'

Moss continued to preach at every meeting. The 7.30 pm meeting I attended one Wednesday began with a time of worship – with a touch of singing in tongues as the only charismatic phenomenon displayed. After a testimony or two, Moss preached evangelistically, seeing several people make commitments/rededications. The service had been going on for some 100 minutes before the ministry team began to pray for people, who quickly began to form a peaceful acquaintance with the carpet . . .

It's fascinating that the Queen's Road Baptist blessings commenced on the same date as the South London Vineyard experiences – and the date that Elli Mumford was receiving by far the most constructive and positive opinion of anyone yet to report back from Toronto . . .

The date was May 22nd which, according to liturgical calendars, was for 1994 designated as Pentecost Sunday.

Ichthus

'We've had a lot of different experiences flowing in,' Roger Forster, leader of Ichthus Christian Fellowship, told me in September '94. 'Though it's convenient to talk about "The Toronto Blessing" as most people do, we first began to be aware of unusual manifestations when a group of our folk came back from a prayer and spiritual warfare conference in Argentina, with Carlos Anocondria, Ed Silvoso and some of those guys, then we had Ed over to see us.' (Silvoso is a colleague of Freidzen, whose ministry took off after prayer from Benny Hinn, as described in the previous chapter.)

'One of the team began to get these manifestations of "travailing" when praying and interceding. *This was back in November 1993*. We had one or two unusual things happening; though I should say that all the things we've seen happen, we'd seen before – but not in such profusion or with such intensity as we were having through 1994.

'Faith, my wife, was speaking up in Liverpool early in the year, and we witnessed the laughing. As soon as the so-called Toronto Blessing came to Sandy Millar's church, and to Terry Virgo's New Frontiers, we had

meetings with Sandy Millar in Westminster Chapel,
and laughter began again. From that time onwards,
it's just multiplied.

'During the first phase we had fifty-eight meetings in a row – every night except Saturdays – with
about 300 people at each meeting. We pushed all the
chairs back and had an open space. We began to
cut back the extra meetings each week, till we're
now down to our normal church programme, plus
two "receiving meetings". In the normal meetings,
manifestations sometimes still take place,' Forster
added.

At many of his meetings, the congregation bounced
around with an abundance of energy; while at other
times, an aura of peace and tranquillity persisted,
sweet and gentle. Persistence proved a virtue, with
Christians prepared to spend a long time praying
for others – then to come back the next night and
continue.

As Foster continued: 'It's not as though people said,
"I've spoken in tongues, so now I've finished", or "I've
been slain in the Spirit once, I've had my dose". They
realise that there is much more of God available to
them. There have been dreams, visions, prophecies and
manifestations affecting many people. One meeting can
be very different from another.

'Each meeting seems to have a slightly different
emphasis; different things happen. Sometimes more
laughter; sometimes more crying; sometimes more ges-
ticulations, and so forth. Sometimes we home in on
an actual theological point – ageism, anointing, or
intercession. One night the meeting may be very quiet
with people resting in the Spirit; another time it can
be noisy, with roaring, travailing and intercession.

'We are praying and trying to find a way to use
all the energy for intercession and world evangelism.

We've seen a trickle of converts – over and above the norm, though we want to see a lot more. Secondly, we keep monitoring any fruit. Those who have been clearly and strongly affected by the manifestations have also exhibited good character response and change. As a pastor, that's something I'm very concerned about, and for which I keep my eyes open.'

People with emotional traumas going back several years have been able to bring these up into the open for God to deal with therapeutically through his Spirit. They've 'got things out of their system' and begun to live freer lives.

'The hunger for God shown by people turning up to meetings – not just for the sensationalism, but spending hours in God's presence – is wonderful!'

But what of the *fruit* of the Spirit?

'Yes, they're there! There's a lady who was in a position of responsibility, who went down to the floor with a great crash. When she fell, I was frightened that she was going to break her back on a pillar behind her, but she missed it in a remarkable way. She was unconscious throughout the whole meeting and, coming to at the end, went up to put her arms around my wife, apologising for an incident that had happened some time ago. We'd forgotten the incident long ago, but it had clearly remained deep within her, and now it had come out – a release.

'There have been some very clear changes. A lad who dabbled with drugs and had a poor relationship with his father, came right back to God in one of our meetings, and the relationship with his father was repaired. This is the sort of fruit we have seen.'

It is becoming clear that, not only does the 1994 British outpouring of the Spirit have little to do with the Toronto Airport Vineyard – that connection seems to have been a convenient media story – but even the word 'blessing' (singular) is inappropriate. There was not a singular 'bog standard' Blessing being outpoured, but a host of different blessings, each Spirit-made for the recipient, producing specific fruit appropriate to each person's life!

There was a veritable rainbow of gifts and fruit showered on God's people, with a startling fresh intensity beginning in 1993, with wave peaks in January 1994, and at Pentecost 1994. Another of the churches affected – a part of the Pioneer network – is lead by former Elim pastor Adrian Hawkes.

Over the Rainbow

There's no yellow-brick road winding its way to the door of Adrian Hawkes' Rainbow Church (though Elton John has sung his hit *Goodbye Yellow Brick Road* within its historic auditorium), but rather a snarled congested artery – the Seven Sisters Road, churning past its period entrance hall, complete with indoor fountain. If they didn't get mugged first, the seven sisters would probably get knocked down if they tried to cross!

Even a brainless scarecrow could realise the potential the legendary Rainbow Theatre held for Christian outreach to the deprived inner-city jungle sprawling for miles around the building. You'd have to be a heartless tin man not to give Hawkes credit for his daring in snapping up the lease on this celebrated venue, believing it to be a heaven-sent opportunity to house his growing congregation. He's no cowardly lion. It was within the historic building's auditorium – where the church meets for Sunday celebrations – that the Holy Spirit topped the bill during 1994.

Yet, none of the remarkable phenomena that the Spirit produced in 1994 was different from the signs and wonders Hawkes has witnessed throughout the rest of his ministry:

'In terms of phenomena, I've seen them all before. I personally had the experience of bursting out laughing in my own living room twenty-five years ago! I'd come home from a church meeting feeling very discouraged. I thought I ought to pray, but I really didn't feel like it. Within minutes I was rolling around the carpet in hysterics. I started at midnight, and I was still laughing at six the next morning!

'The only thing that's been different in 1994, is that it is happening to *more* people. As a church leader, you get to know individuals and their traits. I've noticed that the people who laugh are the people who *need* to laugh; the people who cry could do with a good cry ... The phenomena may *appear* disconnected, but it's often very connected *with the needs of the particular individual*.

'Too much Christianity is cerebral. We cross our "t"s and dot our "i"s and make everything theologically correct; but our application leaves a lot to be desired. We don't perform our Christianity very well in practice. Acts of God are not necessarily rational, nor irrational, but *supra-rational*. They may sometimes seem weird, but they're not totally illogical. We sometimes need to think a bit laterally to understand what is happening. If you *know* the people to whom strange occurrences are happening, you can see a certain logic to the situation.

'One guy in my church was always po-going and getting excited. When someone prayed for him, he stood stock still – transfixed to the same spot for two hours. People were shouting and falling over around him, but he didn't budge. I'd never seen the guy stand still before, ever. God had done something which made him the total opposite of the way he normally behaves.

He received what he needed, and he needed to stand still peacefully,' concluded Hawkes.

Some Christians are disappointed that *others* went down in the Spirit when *they* remained standing. It must be remembered that God is dealing with *individuals*; he doesn't say, 'Oh, I'm going to choose a random 23 per cent of this congregation to slay in the Spirit!' The Spirit does not act capriciously, or at random. God is not interested in percentages; instead, he's passionately concerned with each individual. The people who are slain, or who shake, or cry, are the ones for whom such activity is appropriate at that time. Nothing more. What we see is the sum total of many separate individuals with whom God is dealing.

Yet God is also concerned with the whole body of Christ, which is the Church. If say 20 per cent are touched as individuals, it should have an effect on the whole body – everybody gets something!

God's gifts are always apt, and appropriate. If you're a man and someone presents your wife with a bouquet of roses at a function, you will be very pleased for her. But if the man is given a big bunch of flowers too, he'll probably be a little embarrassed about it! Some gifts are simply not appropriate for everybody.

I know of one couple who were both very hurt when the husband bought his wife a chip pan as a Christmas present. She was so distressed at being given such an unthoughtful present, that she hit him with it!

Not every gift is appropriate for every person, and not every occasion is an apt occasion for any particular gift. Yet Christians often desire presents from God that are inappropriate for them to receive at that time.

Spirit in Motion

Roger Forster comments: 'Each manifestation seems
to have a clear interpretation. People resting in the
Spirit have got to learn that, come Monday morning,
they have to come to God and rest, so that all their
work flows out from God. It's like a didactic thing, like
a set of visual aids.

'Manifestation could be underlining our television
and visually orientated society, because it is putting
the theology straight in front of people. Someone who
finds a lot of energy and who runs around the building
under the Spirit's power is perhaps someone who
needs to have their life activated. The laughter is
the joy of the Lord. Every manifestation has some
practical theological connotation, and that's a quick
way of teaching people.

'Ideally, we should live in the experience of being
filled moment by moment. But we don't actually live in
that mode, so God needs to step in,' Hawkes believes.

'It's the spiritually thirsty people who have been
refreshed. The less interested people – the ones who
seem to rush away at the end of a service – are not
necessarily being satisfied. It's those who don't care
about being late home who are often the ones who are
powerfully touched by God . . .

'Years ago, I saw people falling down when filled
with the Holy Spirit, and someone described the filling
as like riding a 1,000 cc motorbike for the first time.
If you're not used to being astride such a powerful
machine, you can easily come off it.'

Motorcycle be blowed! When I was learning to ride an
ordinary pushbike, I found it very difficult to stay on!
Even once I'd got the hang of riding the bike, getting
off it flummoxed me for several days. Whenever I
tried to dismount, I always landed on my bum in

the middle of the road! The best I could ever hope
for was that I'd managed to bring the bike to a halt
before I fell off; if I was unlucky, I came off when the
bike was still in motion and ended up with a bump on
my head.

Being filled with the Holy Spirit can often present
similar problems when you're not accustomed to it.
You don't know how to react to this amazing blessing
that is surging through you. Falling over, shaking,
laughing or crying can resolve deep problems and
hurts, but can also simply be part of the teething
problems – the equivalent of learning to stay on the
bicycle saddle, or struggling to stop before coming
unseated. Even when you've learned to ride with the
experience, coming safely down to earth afterwards can
take some additional learning.

'As you become more used to the Spirit, more accustomed to being in the presence of God in that way, you
learn to understand and to handle what is happening,'
Hawkes comments. 'In perfectly ordinary services, I've
seen people sob the whole way through, and they don't
know why. They feel something which they cannot
describe adequately.'

With my old pushbike, my dad and my brother
both greatly helped me to get the hang of it. Similarly, friends and experienced elders can often help a
novice to get used to the Spirit's anointing. Praying
with someone can be the equivalent of holding the
handlebars and saddle until the rider has steadied
himself. Reading what the Bible says about the gifts
of the Spirit is the equivalent of reading a maintenance
manual for practical tips and guidance.

Another analogy is the game of badminton. Getting
the hang of serving – by dropping the shuttlecock and
swinging the racquet at the right moment to hit it –
can be tricky at first. Until you've got the co-ordination

right, you may keep missing the shuttlecock with the racquet; yet once you've got the hang of it, it's difficult to see why it was ever a problem.

It became apparent to me, as I went about interviewing, discussing and consulting key figures in the 1994 outpouring – and visiting the services, meetings and conferences where the Holy Spirit's presence was powerfully demonstrated – that some leaders and clergymen were more adept than others at, as it were, serving the shuttlecock.

In Anglican churches in particular, the measures undertaken as a prelude to getting that spiritual shuttlecock over the net were often comical – though the Holy Spirit always responded with good grace. Clearly though, it was in the former house churches and the long-established Pentecostal congregations where the 'seeded players' could be found.

Kensington Temple

'This time of refreshing is exhausting!' quipped Colin Dye, senior pastor at Kensington Temple, to his congregation when I popped my head around the door one Sunday morning in September 1994. A friendly steward quickly found me a seat near the front – I figured he probably thought I was a pagan who needed converting!

The mainly black congregation, comprising people from more than 100 nations, laughed and cried as Dye's dynamic preaching – for the best part of an hour – kept them enthralled. I particularly liked the pithy and memorable asides:

'I'm not astonished that people fall down in the presence of God. I'm surprised they can stand up!'

'The time for niceness has gone. This is the time for power. There's no point in lying on the floor unless,

when you're down, the Holy Spirit gives you a divine
operation that changes your life.'

'If the Holy Spirit is a gentleman, he's not an English
gentleman. He threw someone off a horse and poked
them in the eye so that they couldn't see for three days!
That's how he called Saul. It's the only way God could
get his attention . . .'

'Gentle Jesus meek and mild? Come off it!'

When the Spirit dive-bombed Kensington Temple –
KT for short – around Easter 1994, he brought the
usual crew with him: holy laughter, sobbing, shaking
and other physical manifestations.

'KT is no stranger to these, as we have been
experiencing the power of the Holy Spirit for many
years now,' wrote Dye in the September issue of his
church magazine. 'We have learned some valuable
lessons through being in the middle of the floodtide
for so long. Above all, we have learned to seek God and
not phenomena; to keep our eyes on Jesus instead of
being sidetracked by unusual manifestations. Instead,
we have learned to test all things and, having found
them to be genuine, directed them towards their true
purpose – to lead us closer to the Lord.'

Accordingly, KT waited till September before running a month-long programme of 'receiving meetings'
six nights each week. A steady stream of people discovered Jesus for themselves, for the first time; while
others felt the Spirit's refreshing, like rain in the
wilderness. A trio of KT leaders were sent to Toronto,
where they became well acquainted with the Airport
Vineyard's carpet.

'We came into this in April, when we had Charles
and Francis Hunter with us. They had been with
Rodney Howard-Browne; in fact, most of what has
happened can be traced to what the Lord began to do
through Rodney,' Dye affirmed to me.

'On Good Friday, Francis Hunter prayed for me on the platform here at KT, and I went down in no uncertain terms. I felt this laughing phenomena. It was quite amazing; my mind was quite clear and rational about what was happening. I knew that at any moment, I could have got back up and been a proper dignified pastor, but I just didn't want to!'

It was an appropriate day for Dye to be a fool for God; in 1994, Good Friday fell on April 1st as he told me:

'I think I was *knocked* down by the Spirit – it was quite a powerful thing. I tried four or five times to get up, and each time the laughter caused me to collapse back. The experience brought about some quite profound changes in me, which for three months I never talked about. There was an experience of healing, like some burden being lifted – particularly the weight of responsibility. I think I had some anxiety related to leading the church, then I felt a deep and settled peace, though nothing I could really analyse.

'I've really found a freshness to my spiritual walk, with an increased revelation from Scripture. I am more passionate than ever to see people anointed, trained and released into the work of winning London and the world for Christ. That's not contrived, it's looking at the matter honestly. I can easily say that – since first being baptised with the Holy Spirit early in my Christian walk – *nothing has affected me more powerfully in terms of personal spiritual renewal*. And I wasn't feeling dry as bones before . . .

'Pentecost Sunday was the first time that the phenomena broke out spontaneously across the whole church. It broke out during the 9.00 am meeting, and the 11.00 am service was a high spot – we were interrupted by the Spirit. We've had a great time, but only within the context of clear leadership, and because this is for a season only. I can't think of

a more authentic way of God dealing with religious
pomposity than by throwing someone on the floor and
tickling them – but ultimately, the phenomena needs
to pass away, to produce spiritual gifts separate from
the effects.'

Each individual church may have its own season;
some will have ended by the time this book is published, but other churches may not reach their own season of refreshing rains for years to come. Church leadership needs to help people to keep their eyes on Jesus
when the spectacular is happening all around them.

The laughing, crying, shaking, and falling is not the
Holy Spirit's doing. It is a human reaction to the deeper
and more lasting activity of the Holy Spirit in that
person's life.

As Colin Dye drew his marathon exposition to a close,
he received a word of knowledge: God wanted forty-two
people to receive anointing for evangelism. One by
one, they trooped to the front as eight rows of chairs
were cleared to make room. Jabbering in tongues, and
without hesitation, Dye ran down the orderly lines like
an Old Testament prophet, his hand outstretched in
anointing – trying not to zap the ushers! – and like
synchronised rows of dominoes, everyone in correct
order fell backwards in ecstacy, each person caught
by an usher before they hit the carpeted floor!

I was sitting inches away, and I can vouch that this
time no one was faking. Each lay still for several
minutes, grinning beatifically as counsellors prayed
over him or her. I was sitting so close, I could feel a
sort of 'spiritual fall-out'. For the first time, I caught
an understanding of the shaking phenomena. Nothing
compelled me to shake, but a sensation like a cold draft
or a fresh breeze made me shudder slightly, while a
gentle itching sensation led me to move about to soothe
the not-unpleasant sensation. It lasted for only a few

moments, but I believe I experienced the early stages
of the shaking phenomenon.

All around, others were shaking frantically, many
were wailing and sobbing, still others were laughing
with the Spirit's joy. Yet I never doubted that Jesus
Christ was the true focus of the service. The choice of
worship material glorified him, and his name seemed
on everyone's lips in adoration. KT was a place of
transformation, of people stepping out in faith on some
bold new work for the extension of God's kingdom.

Chapter Seven

Resting in the Spirit

The powerful wind of the Spirit rose through the summer, sweeping into many fresh churches, and continued to blow through the autumn of 1994.

Amongst the lesser-known churches where the Holy Spirit had been blowing was St James-the-Less (if you'll excuse the pun), close to Victoria Station. The opening worship was awesome, with a splendid acoustic band leading several hundred people through a selection of choruses old and new, when I dropped in one warm September evening. Being a good Anglican church, a Confession, the Lord's Prayer and a closing prayer were all present and correct in the liturgy. Then the fun began!

Jeremy Crossley, leading the meeting, made it clear that people should feel free to leave, if they did not wish to stay for further ministry. Two or three minutes of chaos ensued, with people milling and chatting; but Crossley recovered the situation – moving into a prayer which hushed everyone, and the churning throngs exited quietly. The people who remained were asked to move to the first twelve rows. As he prayed for the Holy Spirit to come, the remaining stragglers cleared the room and the sixty to seventy committed to waiting on God began to softly pray.

The earlier anarchy had evaporated in such a re-markable way, and the meeting had suddenly regained

its focus with such clarity, that I felt a strong urge to
laugh joyfully. A woman began to sob quietly behind
me, and was later joined by a second woman weeping.
Only one person began to shake, and just one person, I
believe, was 'slain in the Spirit'. Beyond these outward
signs, it was clear from the peaceful smiles of the
others present, that the vast majority had received a
less dramatic – but no less valid and transforming –
anointing.

Deep in the inner city, at St Lukes, Hackney, services
took on a new dimension when the usual manifestations began in August 1994. An elder, John Roe,
told me too of a memorable time he had experienced
one Saturday at Magnus the Martyr, in the City of
London:

'It was the first time I had seen the Holy Spirit
knock people down in an Anglo-Catholic church, during quite a high Mass. I was surprised, too, than
many elderly people came forward and were overcome
by the Spirit, as the band played soft Taize-style
worship.'

In charismatic Catholic circles, the Cor Lumen Christi
community in south London, and the St Albans based
The Upper Room were amongst those to be touched.
When I visited the latter, I was impressed by the
devotion to Scripture, and the quality of worship. There
were opportunities for people to commit their life to
God, and to come forward for forgiveness, before the
Spirit was invited to come in power. These Catholics
put most evangelicals to shame with their authentically biblical faith.

Sal Solo – a Catholic singer with a Scripture-centred
ministry – discovered the Holy Spirit working alongside him in an unexpected way one night during a
concert tour of Ireland. Led by the Spirit, he called
forward people who wanted to be healed, prayed for

a man who had suffered from a slipped disk for eight years, and saw him healed.

Though Solo knocked up a total of nine UK chart hits – and became a major star in Europe, particularly in Poland – during his early career as a rock singer, he now has new criteria for judging his work:

'The most important aspect is the way the prayer and healing work has taken over; it's the only gauge I've got that I'm being effective. I can have as many as 40 per cent of a 1,000+ audience coming forward, particularly in Europe, for prayer at the conclusion of my concerts. One young man came forward and was "slain in the Spirit". When he got up, he felt that he had from the Lord everything for which he had been searching. I don't personally feel it's necessary to burst out in hysterics or to roar like lions.

'It's amusing for me as a Catholic when evangelicals make a big deal over the way many Catholics make pilgrimages; I personally discovered Christ on a pilgrimage to Italy, in 1983. Now, eleven years later, I'm amused to see so many evangelicals rushing off on a "pilgrimage" to Toronto!'

By September, many Baptist, Pentecostal and house churches were awash with signs and wonders. The Methodists have a long tradition of manifestations, dating back to Wesley's time. In 1994, many Methodist churches, particularly in the west country and the north-east were affected.

Strangely, only the Quaker movement reported that in none of its meetings had any shaking or quaking been observed!

The Fire Spreads

The September issue of *Renewal* revealed that the blessing had recently reached St-Michael-le-Belfrey in

York; the Christian Fellowship in Leigh, Manchester; two churches in Colchester; churches in Hazlemere and Slough; and St Thomas' Crookes, Sheffield. At a chapel in Bream, Gloustershire, too, the congregation fell like ninepins. It was reassuring that the Holy Spirit hadn't halted at Watford Gap, as the lack of reports from the north of England might have suggested – there was life 'up north', too.

At St Peters, Shipley, Rev Chris Edmondson was taken by surprise to hear laughter in the Spirit during one of his services, for three reasons: the man concerned was in his sixties, it was 8 am in the morning, and it was during the most staid of 1662 communions. This *had* to be the Holy Spirit!

'Our understanding of God is always going to be limited, because of his nature, and because of our nature. We find it hard to let God be God,' Edmondson told his congregation. He has been on the receiving of the Spirit's slaying in the past, and been startled to find others keeling over as he has prayed for them, finding afterwards that extraordinary healing work has been done to people's lives while they have been comatose under the Spirit's touch. He is cautious, though, of how the Church of England as a whole will react: 'Anglicans are past masters of nailing their colours to the fence . . .'

A conference at HTB attracted 800 people, with around twice that number flocking to Wembley Conference Centre for four nights of teaching and ministry, relating to the outpouring. Whilst hard figures were impossible to come by, estimates in September suggested that 1,500 churches – 3 per cent of the UK total – had experienced the erroneously-named Toronto Blessing. At a rally in the Royal Albert Hall on October 25th Gerald Coates suggested the figure was as high as 3,000 churches affected.

'Deep in the grounds of Blair castle, where the Duke of Atholl is empowered to keep Britain's only private army, the Holy Spirit sneaks past security each night and leaves them literally rolling in the aisles,' began John Prince's report in *The Daily Telegraph* (August 12th).

'For each of the past five evenings, Scotland has been witnessing mass religious hysteria, manifested in the 'charismata' reported as visited on the apostles at Pentecost. Hundreds of men, women and children line up before the stage of a large white marquee as the evangelism (*sic*) builds to a climax and at a signal, as the Spirit apparently swoops on the tent, they start to drop. Caught as they fall, laid gently on the wet grass, they lie shaking and shouting, either riven with gusts of laughter or weeping uncontrollably. Some have begun talking in tongues.'

The West Country was not excluded, either, on the Holy Spirit's whirlwind tour. In Plymouth, Northhill Community Church, and the Church of the Nations, both experienced the Spirit's powerful blessing. Methodist minister David King explained how the Blessing had also reached his own church: 'Some of our people went to the Community Church, and their lives were enriched in many ways. Young and old have been refreshed by God, finding inner healing, and a fresh enthusiasm for God. It has been incredibly gentle. I can't deny what I have seen happening in other people's lives, and in my own. A refreshed church will be more authentic, and better equipped for mission.'

At the 1994 Crossrhythms Festival, the Devon hillsides rang to laughter and tears. 'Many people fell under the powerful anointing of the Holy Spirit,' according to festival organiser Chris Cole. 'We've seen ongoing fruits in the lives of those affected. They are definitely growing as disciples in Christ.'

Martin Neil has played drums behind several Christian performers on European tours during the eighties and early nineties. He too noticed exciting signs during 1994. 'Symptoms at the Basilica Church in Switzerland were similar to those that later appeared at HTB, with people shaking for up to two weeks! The same thing is spreading all over Germany.

'I've spoken to several people about it all, and I've concluded that the blessing can be passed on from person to person. Someone has to go somewhere to "catch" it, and bring it back to his or her own congregation. They need to humble themselves, before another church leader; I think God is restoring the chain of Church leadership in this way.'

According to Phil Gazley, the blessing has also hit Vancouver, Nova Scotia, and other parts of Toronto. 'There has been very exciting prayer and intercession across the Church as a whole, which has sparked this off. I hope it spreads across the whole of Canada.'

The Flak Flies!

Not all the reports were positive, however. A reliable contact in West Yorkshire told me, 'If people have this experience this week, what are they going to want next week? Walking on water? They are behaving like fourteen-year-olds, with complete lack of maturity!

'Ladies have been seen adjusting their dresses as they fall; people lying on the floor have been caught looking around to see if anyone is still watching. I might be neurotic, but I think it's just another way of sneaking in the teachings of the Kansas City Prophets.'

In Matlock, Derbyshire, Baptist minister Alan Morrison published a leaflet condemning the Blessing: 'This phenomenon does not provide any evidence of genuine Christian revival. Thousands of professing Christians are being hoodwinked by a psycho-religious phenomenon that is completely unrelated to genuine Christian spirituality,' he told *The Sunday Telegraph*.

'Not only is this harmful to the emotional and spiritual health of those who fall under its compelling power, but the rampant encouragement of such experiences is bringing the Gospel and Church of Jesus Christ into disrepute.'

Barry Napier of the Swansea-based Bible Theology Ministries, described it as a 'cancer' in the Church. Quoted in a September 5th article in the *Western Mail*, under the headline, 'Holy Spirit "blessing" dismissed as demonic', Napier held forth at length: 'It's going around like wildfire and everyone is convinced that it's a great revival. It's going through the Church of England like a dose of salts and it's now hitting churches and chapels in Wales. They play lots of music and sing simple chants over and over again. They whip you up and call you out to the front and touch you on the head, and because you expect things to happen, they do.'

'The address reminded me of a sales pitch,' Napier's colleague, James Waddell said of one Swansea meeting. 'Some people twitched on the floor, others lay peacefully or they stretched out with their hands clenched by their sides. These are all familiar sights in hypnotism stage acts and the people affected include intelligent, professional medical people whom I respect.'

'The Toronto Blessing is demonic, with a covering of human psychological hysteria,' said Napier. 'It's so quick in its effect that people have no time to be defensive.'

Gerald Coates, naturally, took a very different view: 'We just have to face the fact that God is touching certain people, and they are travelling the world taking

that blessing with them. Some have put it all down to
the power of auto-suggestion, but if that were the case,
why are our churches not ten times the size they are?
If it's just auto-suggestion, we could have been seeing
this happen years ago.

'Trained psychotherapists have said that all the
symptoms of mass hysteria are missing from all the
meetings they have been to. One therapist, who is
not a Christian, said to a friend of mine that, "We
would give our right arms to see in our surgeries
what you are seeing in your church. It takes us two
or three years to bring someone to the point where
you bring them in two or three minutes. This is very
healthy".'

Just a mental problem? If you believe Napier, then
you have to explain why a large group of people, generally well-balanced individuals – often with good jobs
and no emotional problems, showing no other tendency
to react with overt emotion – should suddenly decide to
do something so dramatic and spontaneous.

At a Rainbow Church weekend away, one quiet and
reserved woman prayed quietly, 'Lord, there is no way
you are going to get me behaving like these other
people,' when she suddenly went out like a light.
Staggering to her feet, she exclaimed, 'Lord! How
could you!' before collapsing again. This is surely the
very opposite of someone being whipped up by so-called
mass hysteria.

Holy Spirit Therapy

Dismissing the manifestations as 'mass hysteria' is
quite meaningless, according to psychiatrist Richard
Laugharne, when I spoke to him at the close of a
sign-filled John Wimber conference. True hysteria is
actually a very rare phenomenon, and those who bandy

the word about in attempts to explain occurrences at Christian meetings are using the word in a loose coloquial sense, and not scientifically, to describe a verifiable clinical phenomenon.

'What matters is the consequences of the experience and the lasting benefits. In Christian terms, if the fruit of an experience is beneficial, subjectively and objectively, then who are we to try to destroy that person's experience – trying to explain it away – by giving it a label that is purely destructive? I'd much rather have the creative experience that these people have encountered,' said Dr Laugharne.

'For many people, it is very therapeutic. In my experience, most people find it beneficial. Many rationalist psychologists make the mistake of trying to explain something by sticking a label on it. At the end of the day, some of these experiences are simply unexplainable.'

It is essential for Christians to accept the unexplainable. If you try to explain everything, then you simply push God out of the picture.

'Praying in tongues brings relaxation and serenity,' psychologist Dan Montgomery has written positively in *New Covenant* magazine: 'Spontaneity and creativity are released by the baptism of the Holy Spirit. Personality dysfunction is fear-driven and results in exaggerated trends within the personality – being too angry, too loving, too withdrawn or too perfectionistic. But when we pray in the Holy Spirit, we are comforted. Our personality rigidities become more malleable in the hands of the Father.'

The current experience of the Holy Spirit seems to lead to the integration of mind and body, touching the whole person, according to mental health chaplain Nigel Copsey. The laughing and weeping reflects a willingness to express joy and sadness that is often

at odds with the traditional British 'stiff upper lip'
sentiments.

'Many who have been "locked in" by past experiences have been released by the Holy Spirit, healing
memories and feelings,' Copsey wrote in the *Baptist
Times*. 'For many, the "party" has been the discovery
of the healthy "child within" which has been lost for
many years, or has never been experienced before
because of a damaged childhood.'

Copsey is aware of the danger of hyped-up meetings,
where auto-suggestion can produce effects that mimic
the Holy Spirit, but which are not true spiritual
encounters. He calls for maturity and wise counsel,
care and pastoral leadership. 'Such support provides
the necessary psychological safety to God's people, so
that they can experience his love and power fully.'

Graham Cray is fundamentally in agreement: 'If
the work of the Holy Spirit takes place upon and
through our humanity, and if one dimension of our
humanity can be described through psychology – as I
believe it helpfully can – then to say of the Blessing
"it's psychological" is a truism. To go beyond it, as
reductionism, and to say "I can give it a psychological
explanation, therefore there is no other explanation,"
is actually to make an enormous logical jump, and to
claim something that you haven't proved!

'I am well aware of the power of suggestion, and
I am aware that people can learn responses, but –
even taking that as a worst-case scenario – what is
the difference between someone saying "Come Holy
Spirit" and it happening, and someone using the power
of suggestion? The Spirit of God has to come along
the same path. There's such a fine line, I think "it
can be God" even if the people up the front are not
very wise.'

Doctor's Orders

I say, I say, I say. A man goes to his GP and says,
'Doctor, doctor, I was at a church meeting last night.
I started talking in a strange language, shaking and
pogo-dancing in the Spirit. I fell over and started
crying. Then I got up and roared like a lion.' What is the
GP's 'punch line'? Would a referral to a psychiatrist be
in order? Would a strait-jacket be provided? I put the
questions to Christian doctor Paul Dakin, a member
of the Rainbow Church, who has both witnessed and
participated in such manifestations.

'I don't think a GP would call in a psychiatrist
in the first instance, unless there was some reason
from the person's background to be suspicious about
the person's mental health!' Dr Dakin laughed. 'It's
difficult to view the situation outside of the prejudices,
beliefs and background of the individual doctor, which
would colour his or her views.'

Anxiety and peer pressure might be regarded as
possible trigger causes. Only in former communist
Russia was the view taken that *God* doesn't exist,
so anyone who claims to speak with him must be
insane. Western medical experts are generally much
more broad minded.

Can any bodily harm come of the physical manifestations that occur at a charismatic meeting?

'I've never seen anybody come to any harm, which
surprises me when you think of a crowd of people
falling to the ground and not putting out their hands
to break their fall. You might assume that they would
be risking injury, but I've never even seen so much as
a bruise from someone being slain in the Spirit. I've
never heard of anyone complaining of any pain.'

If, like stunt men and trained martial arts enthu-
siasts, a person falls in a relaxed manner, the limbs

will be loose and the danger of injury minimalised. Only if someone attempts to *fake* such a spiritual manifestation are they apt to be in danger of injury if they fall in a tense state. Yet, even in the couple of times in my own life when I have fainted and *fallen relaxed*, I've still ended up with a bump on my head. When Paul Dakin fainted as a youngster, he ended up with a painfully bruised face. Perhaps there's more to this than meets the eye.

'Recently, I was slain in the Spirit myself,' says Dakin. 'I'd always assumed that it would never happen to me, but it did! I fell face forward onto a wooden floor. When my wife saw me, she thought I'd broken my glasses, broken my nose, or both. I went down with a colossal thud. I was conscious of a mild smarting, but suffered no injuries.

'If God is going to go to all the trouble of getting someone on the floor, he's quite gracious about the way he does it. In most meetings, the leader will try to have people standing by to catch those that fall. It's not always possible though; at one of our own meetings, a whole group of people fell across one another.

'There is certainly a danger, if you are face up on the ground – should someone fall directly over your face or pin your chest – of great discomfort or of suffocation. I'm sure, though, that someone else would see if this was occurring, and arrange the comatose forms in a more orderly fashion.' A responsible person should be appointed to oversee this function.

'It's important, if there are children present, or elderly and frail people, to keep them back from where prayer is taking place if there is a risk of someone falling. I've never heard of anyone injured when they fall under the influence of the Holy Spirit. I believe that God undertakes for their welfare.

'The Holy Spirit seems to move most comfortably in

what I would describe as "sanctified chaos", where there is freedom and flexibility both for God to do as he wills, and for people to respond to God in whatever way seems appropriate. There need to be people to keep order, and someone who is *taking responsibility*, so that nothing is left to chance. Someone who "hits the deck" should be prayed with, and not simply left. There need to be these safety nets,' says Dr Dakin.

But what if someone has a heart attack, a stroke, or an epileptic fit during a meeting? It would be tragic if people simply shouted, 'Alleluia, so-and-so has been touched by the Spirit!' when the person is actually dying.

Adrian Hawkes knows of one instance where a charismatic preacher prayed for the Holy Spirit to come down, and an elder immediately keeled over on the spot. Unfortunately the man was stone dead – which rather killed the enthusiasm of the meeting. This is not simply a problem for charismatics however; Paul Dakin knows of *two* instances of people having heart attacks during worship in non-charismatic churches!

It's fairly easy to spot when someone has 'hit the deck' under the influence of the Holy Spirit. They tend to move afterwards, even if it's only a matter of repositioning a limb. A beatific grin is also a dead giveaway.

The majority of people who suffer a heart attack have some sort of warning; it's uncommon for a heart failure to come 'out of the blue'. 'A person would look very uncomfortable, and would probably tell someone that they were in pain, or having breathing difficulties. An onlooker would see them breathing heavily, sweating and clutching their chest. They may have gone pale, or look grey, though they may simply look relaxed,' according to Dr Dakin.

'As a young Christian, I saw a woman having an

epileptic fit in church, which I mistook – not for a movement of the Spirit – but for a demonic manifestation! (If my memory serves me, the incident happened at Bryn Jones' Bradford church in the mid 1970s.) Fortunately, older and wiser Christians could tell the difference, even if I couldn't!

'Occasionally, someone might indeed keel over as a result of their own emotional state, or because of a psychological disorder which has nothing to do with God. With epilepsy, there may be an overlap with the demonic, but it would be very rare. Epilepsy usually has a history, a person would know that they are epileptic, and the church leaders should be made aware. The classic *grande mal* epilepsy leads to powerful jerking of the limbs, frothing at the mouth, and incontinence – that is very different from someone going down in the Spirit,' said Dr Dakin. I know of no instance of the Holy Spirit making someone incontinent.

Slain *in* the Spirit

For some, the problem is not whether the phenomena are spiritual or fleshly, but whether they are truly biblical.

Conservative evangelical Stephen Sizer, was particularly scathing about the lack of biblical support for the current crop of manifestations. With reference to the phenomenon of being 'slain in the Spirit', Sizer wrote, in a widely circulated response: 'This, we are told, is evidence of the "weight of the hand of the Lord" as apparently happened to prophets like Ezekiel. Unfortunately the text of Ezekiel refers to the "hand of the Lord" lifting Ezekiel *up*, not pushing him *down* (Ezekiel 3:14) and of Ezekiel being told to "get up and go" (Ezekiel 3:22). We are not specifically taught about these phenomena in Scripture, still less are we instructed to expect or seek them. It is therefore most unwise to place significance in them.'

Stephen Sizer is wise to recommend caution, where theological liberties seem to have been taken, and if the Church appears to be experiencing phenomena which goes beyond the clear parameters set down by Scripture.

Yet if it is the Spirit himself who is transcending those barriers, then what can the Church do? Can the clay tell the potter how to make his pot? If God is truly behind an outpouring of the Spirit, then who can argue back to the Almighty, and tell him that he's doing it all wrong? Is there a modern day Job? When Peter sought to reassure Jesus that he didn't have to die, the Lord answered, 'Get thee behind me, Satan!' Some who challenge the authenticity of God's works in the present day might find themselves on the receiving end of a similar rebuke for quenching the Spirit.

Falling to the floor under the Spirit's anointing is not explicitly mentioned in Scripture, yet there are many references to bodily strength becoming diminished during an encounter with God. The disciples 'fell face down to the ground, terrified' when they heard the voice of God (Matt 17:6). The soldiers coming to arrest Christ mysteriously 'fell to the ground' when he affirmed his identity (John 18:6). When John saw an apocalyptic vision of Christ, while on the island of Patmos: 'I fell at his feet as though dead' (Rev 1:17).

When Daniel received a powerful vision: 'I had no strength left, my face turned deathly pale and I was helpless ... I fell into a deep sleep, my face to the ground' (Dan 10:8–9). When an angel appeared to the guards at Christ's tomb, they seem similarly to have fallen to the ground: 'The guards were so afraid of him that they shook and became like dead men' (Matt 28:4).

Sizer's references to Ezekiel ignore the fact that the prophet observed the awesome manifestation of God that opens the book of Ezekiel (the four living creatures, and their mysterious wheels) *from on the ground*, for the prophet is told to get to his feet at the opening of the second chapter.

Slain *by* the Spirit

Ananias and Sapphira certainly quenched the Spirit. The early Christians shared all their possessions in common, but this couple held back some of their money while claiming to have given everything into a common pool. Peter received a word of knowledge from the Holy Spirit about the deception, and confronted Ananias: ''How is it that Satan has so filled your heart that you have lied to the Holy Spirit ... What made you think of doing such a thing? You have not lied to men but to God." When Ananias heard this, he fell down and died' (Acts 5:3–5).

Three hours later, his wife arrived and continued with the scam. 'Peter said to her, "How could you agree to test the Spirit of the Lord? Look! The feet of the men who buried your husband are at the door, and they will carry you out also." At that moment, she fell down at his feet and died' (Acts 5:9–10).

In these only two biblical instances of people *literally slain* in the Spirit – his holy presence revealed by a word of knowledge – it was again the manifestation of God's power that caused each initially to fall to the ground. (Personally, I believe that the terrible consequences – that neither person ever got up again! – in this case were more a reflection of Peter's impetuousness and lack of sensitivity, than the moral judgement of a righteous God.)

In recent times, some who have fallen to the floor

have done so from a sense of being smitten by God, but
for many others, slipping to the ground has been more
associated with the feelings of drunkenness making it
difficult for them to remain steady on their feet. Once
down, the vivid sense of communing with God removes
any desire to get up again – or, indeed, to do anything
which might disturb such a wonderful experience.

When I took part in a Christian Union camping
weekend in the 1970s, as we were preparing for bed,
it became apparent that something strange had happened to our president, John. Fully clothed within his
sleeping bag, he was lying strangely still, and making
no attempt to move. We shook him and inquired
whether he was feeling all right, but nothing we did
could revive him. Becoming alarmed, we considered
trying to find a doctor, then concluded that it would
be best to carry him to our nearby mini-bus, and whisk
him immediately for treatment at the nearest hospital.
Only upon loading him into the back, and turning on
the interior light, could we see the beatific smile on
his face! Like a little cherub, he was communing with
God in such a remarkable way that he had been totally
oblivious to his surroundings, and he enquired – when
he began to slip back into our own world – how he
came to be in the mini-bus! A spontaneous prayer
and praise meeting ensued – complete with tongues
and prophecy – with John speaking in tongues for the
first time.

Logistical problems meant that I had a tough time
serving on the Spring Harvest team at Minehead, 1987.
Feeling burnt out after only six days, I was slain in
the Spirit during a Clive Calver sermon – I still tease
him about it! Though I didn't fall to the ground – it
would have been dangerous sitting near the top of a
tall stand – I remained absolutely still, drained of all
strength, with no desire to move or speak. For about

half an hour I experienced such unutterable bliss, and a refreshing detachment from the everyday world, that you could probably have performed open-heart surgery on me without anesthetic, and I wouldn't have noticed!

In *Fourth Wave*, David Pawson writes: 'That it happened then and still happens now is indisputable as a matter of experience; it was acceptable by the inspired authors of Scripture and should be by us. But when a theological interpretation is put upon it, without biblical warrant, the result is confusion and even bondage ... Such distortions and abuses would never have occurred had the phenomenon been checked out with the Bible from the beginning. It would neither have been rejected nor encouraged, but simply accepted as a natural response to becoming the focus of divine attention.'

In his book *Overcome by the Spirit*, Francis MacNutt considers that there are two components to resting in the Spirit:

'The first element is *physical*, external, the falling phenomenon. To concentrate solely on bodies falling does an injustice to what we see happening in our prayer meetings.

'The second element is *internal*, the intense preoccupation of our spirit with the presence of God. Although this does not happen to everyone – nor perhaps even to most people who rest in the Spirit – it does happen to a significant percentage, who then experience great blessings. These include knowing Jesus better and loving God more; receiving an intense love of prayer and desire to study Scripture; receiving deep inner and physical healings; and being delivered from demonic bondage ...

'Dare we hope for a return to the time, two hundred years ago, when Methodist authorities suggested that if listeners fell to the ground while a Methodist evangelist was preaching, it was considered the best sign that he was called to be a bishop?'

Shakin' All Over

'The Vineyard Fellowship justify the "shaking" phenomenon by reference to Acts 4:31. The verse actually says no such thing. It was the "place" that was shaken, not the Christians. The Greek word implies something like an earthquake,' writes Stephen Sizer. 'Reference is also made to the experiences of the Quakers or "Shakers". This too is an unfortunate comparison, for the Quakers eventually preferred their experiences of the Spirit to the teaching of the Word of God.'

There is actually far greater biblical authority for trembling and shaking than Sizer seems to realise. From Jeremiah 5:22, it seems that trembling and shaking is a proper and valid activity when in the presence of almighty God: '"Should you not fear me?" declares the LORD. "Should you not tremble in my presence?"'

The apostle Paul was deeply affected with the shakes – associated with the work of the Holy Spirit – while he was visiting the Corinthian church: 'I came to you in weakness and fear, and with much trembling. My message and my preaching were not with wise and persuasive words, but with a demonstration of the Spirit's power, so that your faith might not rest on men's wisdom, but on God's power' (1 Cor 2:3–5).

When Paul wrote to the Philippian Church, he told its members: 'Continue to work out your salvation with fear and trembling, for it is God who works in you to will and to act according to his good purposes' (Phil 2:12–13). In context, Paul was urging the Philippians to imitate Christ's humility. Shaking of course, is a very humbling experience, entailing as it does loss of control of the body, with a corresponding loss of dignity and pride.

Trembling is associated with awesome revelations of God's power and strength, or divine visitation; at Sinai, for example: 'On the morning of the third day there was thunder and lightning, with a thick cloud over the mountain, and a very loud trumpet blast. Everyone in the camp trembled' (Ex 19:16). They literally had the fear of God in them. When an angel appeared to Daniel, in response to his prayers, the prophet experienced both loss of strength and trembling: 'I fell into a deep sleep, my face to the ground. A hand touched me and set me trembling on my hands and knees . . . I stood up trembling' (Dan 10:9–11).

Trembling is an indication that God is present in a situation in a remarkable way. It often reflects a fearsome awareness of God's awe and majesty. When the angels casually told the women at Christ's tomb that God had raised their master from the dead, 'Trembling and bewildered, the women went out and fled from the tomb. They said nothing to anyone, because they were afraid' (Mark 16:8). Demons too, quake in fear of God: 'You believe that there is one God. Good! Even the demons believe that – and shudder' (Jas 2:19). The Bible's historical and prophetic books are full of references to people shaking with fear at divine holiness – Job 37:1; Isa 66:2,5; Jer 5:22; Joel 2:1; Hab 3:16; Acts 7:32 and 19:17 will do for starters.

The psalms, too, affirm that trembling is an appropriate activity when confronted with the awesomeness of the Almighty's justice: 'My flesh trembles in fear of you; I stand in awe of your laws' (Psalm 119:120). 'Therefore, you kings, be wise; be warned, you rulers of the earth. Serve the LORD with fear and rejoice with trembling' (Psalm 2:10–11). How appropriate then,

that shaking should often be accompanied with rejoicing, joy and laughter.

Laughter and Tears

Clifford Hill has pointed out that 'throughout the
Bible, the great majority of references to laughter
are associated with scorn, derision or evil', and certainly *some* of the laughter that I have encountered
at 'Toronto Blessing' meetings has seemed mocking or
scornful. Mostly though, the laughter I have heard has
been a reflection of unbridled joy.

Laughter comes from heaven, and the psalms in
particular seem full of references to it. In Psalm 2,
when the nations rage and people plot against God,
'the One enthroned in heaven laughs' (Ps 2:4). Even
scornful laughter can be godly on the right occasion:
Of the deceitful person, 'the righteous will see and
fear; they will laugh at him, saying "Here now is the
man who did not make God his stronghold."' (Psalm
52:6–7). God laughs at the wicked, and he wants to
restore to the Christian the joy of salvation.

Gerald Coates: 'Jesus, giving prophetic kingdom
teaching declares "Blessed are you who weep now,
for you will laugh" (Luke 6:21). Is it possible our
Lord was thinking of Psalm 126, written as a song
of thanksgiving after the return from captivity, "When
the Lord brought back those who returned to Zion, we
were like those who dream. Then our mouth was filled
with laughter and our tongues with joyful shouting."

'The *Oxford Dictionary* describes joy as "vivid emotion of pleasure, gladness; a thing that causes delight."
The Bible has a great deal to say about joy in a wide
range of situations. The apostle Paul was not just
joyful in tribulation, but "overflowing with joy in all
our afflictions" (2 Cor 7:4). Being a Jew, he was of

course in good company. When David wrote a prayer
for rescue from his enemies, he said "let them shout
for joy and rejoice" (Psalm 35:27).

'Perhaps most interestingly, we have to ask, what
is "joy inexpressible"? (1 Peter 1:8). Indeed, the mark
of kingdom people is "righteousness and joy in the
Holy Spirit." What is laughter? A joy that cannot be
communicated with words.

'Interestingly, in our own church, Pioneer People
(situated between Guildford and Kingston), we have
had more weeping than laughing. In May 1990 it
was prophesied that our church would be marked by
weeping. This had not happened to any great extent
prior to that time. The scripture around which this
prophecy hung was: "Now while Ezra was praying and
making confession, weeping and prostrating himself
before the house of the Lord, a very large assembly,
men, women and children, gathered to him from Israel;
for the people wept bitterly" (Ezra 10:1).'

Joel invited God's people to return to God with
'fasting and weeping and mourning,' (Joel 2:12) while
Jeremiah wrote an entire book of Lamentations!

There are, of course, no undeniable 'proof texts' for
laughing, crying, shaking and falling specifically as
signs of the Spirit's current outpouring.

'There are things in the Bible that God approves of,
which we call "biblical", and things of which he disap-
proves, which we call "unbiblical", but there is also a
wide range of activities – saying grace before meals,
Sunday services, sitting around on Sundays having a
nip and a sip of bread and wine – for which you will
find no material in Scripture whatever. But Scripture
isn't meant to give us a proof text for everything.

'There are things which are simply "*non*-biblical" –
publishing houses, concerts, Marches for Jesus, Sunday schools, and a wide range of other things – for

which we should not be looking for proof texts. We should be asking, 'Does Scripture generally approve of love, worship, gathering and nurturing the body?' and, if so, we can as Paul said, use "all means" to do that.'

The Principal of Ridley Hall, one of the Anglican Church's most respectable training colleges, in Cambridge, has 'laughed in the Spirit'.

'Yes, it's happened to me!' Graham Cray was pleased to confirm. 'My wife and I regularly help out at David Pytches' New Wine event. Anne Watson had sent us some material from the Anaheim Vineyard too, but my wife and I were touched at New Wine.

'I found myself swaying, and I don't remember starting. After a while I began to laugh from the depths of my gut. The bit of me that is analytical was listening and looking, wondering what was happening; my emotions were the last part of me to be touched. I never felt that my sense of self-control was being over-ridden. I always felt that what was happening had not been initiated by myself, and that I could have stopped it had I wished, but I could find no reason to stop. There was a deep sense of personal liberation.

'The immediate aftermath is not that I have laughed more, but when I have found myself dealing with situations in a very broken world, I have found that tears have been nearer the surface. What was a releasing experience of the Holy Spirit has, I think, brought me nearer to a feeling of God's heart over his world. The laughter has served to make the tears easier.'

Both, of course, are ways of releasing the emotions.

'Here at Ridley Hall, we have an informal time to pray and debate these occurrences. The first time we met became a considerable encounter with the Holy Spirit. None of us invited it, or were aware of starting it, but there was some shaking, tears for one person, and a tremendous sense of the presence of God.'

Let the Fire Fall

When John Wimber came to Britain in September
1994, to speak at a conference at HTB, to preach at
Pioneer People, and to hold four-day Vineyard conferences in London and Manchester, some Christians
feared that he would 'take over' the move of the Spirit
as its figurehead. Others hoped that he would furnish
definite explanations of just what God was doing, and
why. As it happens, both parties were wrong.

During Let the Fire Fall, held in the half-full Wembley
Conference Centre, Wimber confessed affably that he
had been a little blasé when dramatic manifestations
of the Spirit had occurred at his own Anaheim church.
He'd seen it all before! When Clark and Arnott had
phoned him from Toronto for advice on how to handle
the situation at the Airport Vineyard, Wimber had told
them simply, 'Just enjoy it!'

Wimber stated 'The Sunday before Randy Clark
went to Toronto, I was due to preach twice. I had
both sermons ready, and was looking through the
evening sermon when the Holy Spirit said, "You won't
need that." He spoke in my head, and said the word
"Pentecost". I couldn't make head nor tail of it. I
went to church early that evening, and prayed. The
service started, and mid-way through, I received an
open vision. I saw a picture superimposed on the scene
in the church.'

In the vision, he saw sixty to eighty people come to
the front, and the Holy Spirit fall upon them. But he
still didn't have a text on which to preach when the
worship ended and he went into the pulpit. The young
people in the church were all seated near the back, and
Wimber's sight was so poor that he could see no young
people at all. He stood for a moment, then explained,
as the Lord led, that he was going to minister to young

people of nineteen to twenty-two years, who were living in sin. Sixty to eighty people came forward, exactly as in his vision. He prayed, and the Holy Spirit fell upon them. '*Then* the Lord gave me a text to preach upon!' And preach he did, while people were lying on the floor, shaking, and demonstrating all the charismatic gifts.

At Dallas, in April, powerful charismatic events had begun to take place at a Vineyard pastors' meeting. Then on a tour of Australia and New Zealand, Wimber continued 'At one meeting, the first three rows simply fell out of their seats. I thought, "Oh dear, here we go again. I'll have to explain what is happening." My explanation for the past seventeen years has been, "I don't *know* what's happening!" I decided several years ago that I would put up with things that I can't explain. I don't know, and I'm comfortable with that.'

Over summer 1994, Wimber went to see what was happening in Toronto, bringing some correction to certain aspects of the Toronto Vineyard's ministry. He was prayed for there, but didn't fall down. It was only when he was asked to speak to a group of 400 pastors there that he realised he had himself seen and done all the phenomena associated with the 'Toronto Blessing', but not in public. It had all happened at various times during his private devotions, or while praying with his wife.

Where did John Wimber think the situation was heading?

'Into revival, I hope; though it could easily go into less than that. We need to keep the engine on the tracks. The tracks are the word of God and the traditions of the Church. It's not biblical, or theologically justifiable, but it's not uncommon in revival.'

What about normal church life?

'Let it go on as it is, but convene special meetings,' was his recipe. He believed that phenomena and

experiences were an end in themselves, fuelling the act
of sharing God with others, witnessing on the highways
and byways. A phenomena could attract others to come
and hear the preaching of the Gospel.

How do all the diverse phenomena in different places
all fit together?

Wimber considered that the move of the Spirit would
probably be good for Christian unity – a way of calling
people back to God. He believed that revival is *needed*,
and hoped that it would result in God's glory being
imparted to every aspect of society. He preferred to
wait and judge the work by its fruit: 'If it leads people
to love Jesus more, then that's great.'

On the way to the conference I'd been surprised at
the large numbers of young people – particularly pre-
pubescent girls – milling around. I was amazed that
John Wimber could attract such a youthful following,
until I discovered the vast crowds were actually on
their way to Wembley Arena, for that evening's Take
That pop concert . . .

Clearly, the world was still much more attractive to
people than was the Church. There was still a long way
to go in remedying the situation, and John Wimber
didn't have any answers; though it was perhaps unrea-
sonable that so much anticipation and expectation
should have been heaped upon his broad shoulders,
when the Wimber groupies should really have been
looking to Jesus.

Chapter Eight

Spiritual Counterfeits?

'I was converted at Hildenborough Hall when I was fifteen, but I had a period of barrenness for about two years afterwards, because I was a member of a church that was not keyed into nurturing new Christians. I struggled a bit with my faith, and didn't read my Bible as much as I should have done,' David Hilborn, pastor of City Temple in central London admits.

'When I went to Nottingham University and joined the Christian Union, I met people who were renewed in the Spirit, through the charismatic movement. On Sunday evenings, I attended an Assemblies of God church in Talbot Street. Having heard people speaking in tongues for some time, I found myself with the overwhelming desire to sing – not in English, but in a tongue. So I received the tremendous filling of the Spirit – like Gerald Coates before me – through singing in tongues.'

Hilborn soon joined GEAR – Group for Evangelism And Renewal – connected with the United Reformed Church, and attended their overtly charismatic conferences. The spiritual gifts sustained him through some difficult times. Though he is first and foremost an evangelical – called to teach and preach the word of God – the gifts of the Spirit have become invaluable in his own devotional life.

When members of his congregation at City Temple
began to report to Hilborn their own experiences of the
new blessing that was sweeping the country, they suggested that City Temple should explore these blessings.

Hilborn said 'Some of us attended the leaders' meetings at Queen's Road Baptist Church, in Wimbledon.
Two went to a New Frontiers conference in the West
Country, and experienced the blessing profoundly.
Word also trickled through from former members
now based at a church in Sidcup where the Spirit
was moving.'

Hilborn went to a leaders' meeting at Wimbledon,
and was nonplussed. Though he had seen people slain
in the Spirit before, he had never experienced such
laughter and shaking as now confronted him. He had,
perhaps parochially, assumed that this was more of a
black Pentecostal experience – but was glad to have the
stereotype shattered.

'For myself, the first time I was prayed for – and it
took a long time to penetrate my intellectual reservations – I felt that I should allow God to minister to me.
I ended up on the floor, resting in the Spirit. I was
fully conscious and made a decision to allow myself to
go down, though I could have stayed on my feet. The
Spirit can profoundly surprise us, but I don't believe
he brainwashes us.'

Of the 100–150 ministers present, about 85 per cent
ended up on the floor, in spectacular fashion! Hilborn
believes, however, that mountain-top experiences like
this should always issue into prayer, revival and a
social impact by the Church upon secular culture.

'It has helped me to forge relations with people in my
congregation who had enjoyed the same experience and
found their faith immeasurably enhanced by it. People
are approaching the word of God, their personal devotions, and service in a tremendous new way. Several

people have found there is cost in such openness of
expression, so it has not all been plain sailing. But
on balance, people who needed to receive more of God
have received in abundance.

'I was impressed by the long and biblically-based
introduction given by Norman Moss at Queens Road
Baptist Church. He stressed that pastors should continue to preach in their services; there is sometimes
a tendency to lay aside exposition and preaching of
the word in favour of ministry in the Spirit. There
are many different ways to approach preaching, but I
was glad of the emphasis – word and Spirit together.'

Working Together

David Hilborn's colleague at City Temple is Tom
Houston, formerly pastor of a church in Nairobi,
before becoming Executive Director of the Bible Society
and then heading up World Vision International. Now
International Director of the Lausanne Committee
for World Evangelisation, Houston is renowned for
his dedication to Scripture, and he's the scourge of
unbiblical thinking. An outsider might consider that
he and Hilborn would be like chalk and cheese, and
expect the sparks to fly once the doors of City Temple
were firmly closed. This is not the case however!

'We're in this together,' Houston said supportively.
'I've attended the meetings, but I speak as some-
body who has not been "zapped", and who has been
described in print as a "post charismatic".'

Pastorally, Houston had noticed that immense release has come to one of his congregation through her
experience of the Spirit's touch; and the marriage of
two other church members was working better. Though
not glaringly obvious, the fruits of the experiences were
demonstrably present.

Hilborn counts himself fortunate to have the support of those who are not themselves charismatics – both in his church and his home, for his wife Mia is also not specifically charismatic, despite her own remarkable experience.

'In July, I went with my husband to Queen's Road Baptist Church, because I had been hearing so much about the "Toronto Blessing". I was going through a tough period in my ministry, and I needed some good teaching and a sense of closeness to God. I went there feeling very sceptical, and positioned myself behind some Salvation Army officers in full uniform; I was very surprised when they all fell on the floor! I was even more surprised when I ended up on the floor myself.

'I went back a couple more times, and took some friends with me, then we started a "receiving meeting" here at City Temple. I felt God was telling me that I should bring it here. I didn't feel it right that I should lead them, so I got my husband to take charge.

'Personally, the experience has led to total reinvigor-ation from top to toe. It's a process that has not yet been completed. It really is a feeling of blessing; of resting in the Lord with all batteries being recharged. There's a new freshness about everything, though I feel I'm still at the beginning.'

Many people have found it extremely difficult to speak of their extraordinary experiences of bless-ing. Houston recognises that 'communicating the un-communicable' can be problematic. Some experiences simply cannot be captured in words. He commented that he himself was finding it difficult, for example, to communicate with people about his own feelings over the situation in war-torn Rwanda:

'There's a powerful experience that I've been through, which I can't get people to understand. The trouble with life is that "you don't know what you don't know".

I've tried to explain what is going on, but no one can understand me, because they haven't been through the experiences that I've been through in Africa in the past. The same happened to me when I went to Russia.

'There are some things that can only happen when you've experienced them. My daughter has told me of an occasion where she didn't know what in the world I was talking about. "But *you* knew, and *we* were prepared to go along with you. And you were right," she said.' Sometimes the only option left is simply to trust, and to step out in faith.

'My deep concern is that all this shouldn't become a diversion. Our target in this church, is the City; and of *what* will all this be a sign to people in the City?'

Will it present an opportunity, or a threat?

In the Flesh

If people enjoy something, they sometimes like to call it worship. If they like rock music, they will play it in church and call it worship. If they like falling over, they will do that too, and stick the worship tag on it to sanctify it. Experiences can be very 'fleshly', and have nothing to do with God – nor the devil for that matter.

'Whether something is of God really depends on the person receiving it. It may be a human experience that can be carried into the heavenlies, or down to the depths below. When someone seeks physical evidence of God's presence, they are being fleshly,' Houston has concluded.

In any given meeting, there might be several people who are affected mainly by the psychological group experience, a couple who are 'fleshly' seeking physical evidence of God's presence, a person who is self-deceived, a touch of demonic activity, and very little that is purely of God.

'Any reflective person must understand that when the Holy Spirit touches a human spirit replete with psychological hangups, there are bound to be psychological accompaniments going hand in hand with the spiritual,' Roger Forster told me.

Personally, I feel that most of what I have seen *has* been of God. There are certain instances where I believe individuals have been faking, and occasions when a rational psychological process has been at work – albeit one that may have been directed by God. Here's my best example of what I mean by a psychological transformation:

In the days when *encounter groups* were very popular, I participated in several meetings. Led by experienced counsellors and/or therapists, the aim was to help the participants to understand themselves better, and to be in a better position to understand and help others. At the time, I was Vice-President of a student union, and I found the groups were invaluable training for my role as a counsellor – and subsequently as a writer and journalist.

Most of the participants were highly intelligent people, with responsible jobs, but they had often acquired hangups which prevented them from expressing themselves fully. During the psychologically-charged group sessions, people might be encouraged to beat cushions with baseball bats to release their emotions, and to unlock their inner self. I eventually stopped attending these meetings because – though it operated at a purely psychological level – others present were reading unwarranted spiritual significance, of the New Age variety, into the occurrences. It was getting cultic.

At one group, I found myself sitting next to Harry, a very tense and aggressive person with whom I'd had a few prickly meetings in the past. Within a matter of hours, Harry was totally transformed! He became better able to deal with his emotions, and to relate to people with greater confidence, compassion and tact. Unable to verbalise the wonderful transformation, the best description he could offer was, 'I've turned into a pumpkin!'

It was like an ugly caterpillar transformed into a fragrant butterfly. Though certainly not a religious experience in the traditional sense, a 'conversion' had taken place that changed his entire demeanour and outlook. Had this happened in any vaguely Christian context, people would have shouted 'Praise the Lord!' and attributed the changes to the Holy Spirit.

Some former drug users have said that being 'slain in the Spirit' is a very similar experience to the chemical 'high' they achieved with heroin or 'crack', says Dr Dakin. A tremendous sense of peace is perhaps the defining characteristic of any encounter with the Holy Spirit, but the same emotional release can come in other ways, too. There is a need for care and discernment.

'Meetings need to be well-ordered and led so that people can feel secure,' believes Roger Forster. 'Whether any particular manifestation is psychological, a reaction to God by the devil, or the genuine direct impact of the Spirit on their lives, we must believe that when we ask the Father for bread, we are not going to be given a scorpion or a stone, otherwise we cannot trust God. As long as a our hearts are clear before him, there is nothing to fear.

'The big danger, from the perspective of Church history, is that when people are mightily used by God, if God doesn't turn up according to their human expectations – shouldn't there have been more healings tonight? or whatever – there is a terrific danger that the man who has been used by God might want to acquire psychological or demonic power to keep being

a channel for manifestations. It's God's glory that
counts, we are there to use as God wishes.'

Which Spirit?

Ram Gidoomal is a trustee of Oasis Trust, and Chair
of both Christmas Cracker and South Asian Concern:

'As a child, when I was a Hindu, we went to a
temple in Nairobi – where my family had emigrated.
I have vivid memories of the priests shaking incredibly
violently. Some of them had very long hair, and I
remember the scene of hair waving backwards and
forwards. They performed demented dances – a little
like the cossack style of dancing – and shaking like
men possessed. Everyone else stepped back, taking the
attitude, "This guy is possessed; there is something
special going on with him, and he's specially blessed".
Everyone wanted to touch these people, in the hope of
catching part of the blessing.

'If you go around to Hindu temples, monuments and
shrines, you will find this kind of possession. In the
middle of a ceremony, someone will go into a frenzied
trance. It's just like you read about the prophets in
parts of the Old Testament. The point I'm trying to
make is that these things happen outside the Church;
so if someone says – when it happens in a church – that
it must be of God, it doesn't necessarily follow.

'I'm not saying that it isn't of God; just that it
happens elsewhere, so we shouldn't jump too hastily
to conclusions.

'Anyone claiming that signs and wonders are a
sure sign of God's glorious presence should look to
one of India's greatest gurus, Sathya Sai Baba. This
mystic with corkscrew hair is said to perform dozens of
miracles per day – mainly materialisations of trinkets
and *verbuti*, or holy ash. If you take the view that the

signs validate the message, or the theology, then you've got problems; Sai Baba's theology is virtually classical Hinduism. When I visited his Indian *ashram*, I discovered that he has millions of devotees across the globe, who believe that he is nothing less than God incarnate.

'Therefore we need to have a spirit of discernment. Wisdom is key. Prayer is key. We must pray and pray again for what is happening in the Church. We need to be aware that there is a supernatural world, and pray at all times for discernment and wisdom to check that everything that happens is of God. I'm finding a superficial reaction from Christians, "This is happening, so it must be of God", and I say, hang on, I've seen it in Hinduism! Let's be careful what spirit is at work here, and pray that it is God's Holy Spirit. We need to be on our guard.'

Gidoomal became a Christian in 1970, and in 1994 returned to his African birthplace to preach three sermons at Nairobi Pentecostal Church to 6,000 people at each service – and at Tom Houston's old church. In Kenya, the 'Toronto Blessing' was nowhere in sight. He returned refreshed to Britain in the late summer to discover that the Holy Spirit had been performing extraordinary actions while he had been away.

'One lady standing next to me at a service in Chiltern Church was visibly shaking. She commented to me that, had it continued, she felt she would have fallen down uncontrollably. My fellow elders have been open, but cautious. Barry, my brother, attends Harrow International Church, where he fell with a mighty thud after his minister prayed with him. "In normal circumstances, I would have been afraid that I had damaged my back," Barry told me.'

While he was away, Gidoomal also missed a captivating series of TV programmes about Sadhus – India's Holy Men.

The thought of Sadhu Lotan Baba on a pilgrimage to the sacred shrine of Vaishno Devi, rolling along the dusty road *on his side* for 4,000 kilometres, from the central plains of India to the foothills of the Himalayas, sounded like something from a Monty Python repeat.

And the sight of Jayendra Saraswati reverently pouring 300 kilograms of gold coins over his guru's head – it was his hundredth birthday – was so outlandish that I expected Noel Edmunds to pop out of the scenery with a 'Gotcha Oscar' at any moment!

In the third and final programme, however, India's rich hues took a darker turn. Ram Nath is a member of the *aghoris* sect, living on the burning *ghats* or cremation grounds. He has a bowl made from a human skull, which he uses for begging, eating from, and for ritual purposes. This was Asian spirituality in its most raw and grizzly.

But what is a Christian to make of such people? Whilst you would like them to become followers of Christ, you'd be appalled if they turned up at your church!

Austerities, or *tapas*, are believed by many Asians to bring them near to God, and to bestow extraordinary spiritual gifts. The idea was strongly present in Christianity in the Middle Ages, though it is really a distortion of the biblical notion that sacrifice is a good thing. Christ's atoning sacrifice was good for our souls, and selfless giving of oneself and one's possessions contributes to the Christ-like lifestyle that true followers should be living.

Happily, Ram Nath – whose regime includes eating both his own excreta and the burnt flesh of corpses – is about as typical of Asian spirituality as Jack the Ripper was of Victorian England. There are believed to be only about a dozen true *aghois* in the world. They believe that by polluting themselves, they actually destroy

their egos and purify themselves – a strange logic –
and that their gruesome meditations arm them with
occult powers. Your average Asian frowns upon such
practices in much the same way that Christians frown
upon satanists performing black masses in mockery of
the Eucharist . . .

Clearly, the Church is not the only place where extraordinary occurrences have been taking place. Christians need to be cautious that, in seeking spiritual
gifts, they are not merely pursuing the same selfish
desires as an Indian Sadhu, nor seeking the bizarre
simply for its novelty value.

Fear of the Demonic

What about the accusations from some Christians that
the 'Toronto Blessing' is demonic?

In spite of a profusion of books on spiritual warfare
since the early eighties, the Bible has precious little
to say on the subject of the demonic. Frank Perretti
probably had the best idea with his best-selling *This
Present Darkness*, confining unwarranted speculation
to the realm of fiction.

Many charismatic Christians live in a paranoid universe, with devils and demons lurking around every
corner, according to sociologist Andrew Walker – now
a lecturer in religion at King's College. He has traced
the origins of the Church's often unhealthy interest
in the demonic to the North American Latter Rain
movement, led by the heretical William Branham.
(Paul Cain was associated with Branham at one point,
but he has now dissociated himself from Branham's
eccentricities.)

Pentecostals Oral Roberts and Kathryn Kuhlman
both saw strong manifestations of slaying in the Spirit
at their meetings, and were not slow in preaching of

spiritual warfare. Derek Prince and Don Basham were keen on 'heavy shepherding' – a practice strongly connected with Latter Rains and the Manifest Sons of God – seeking to keep their flocks away from occult dangers. Basham even considered that the feminist movement was enpowered by the spirit of Jezebel!

At one of Basham's rallies, he decided on a mass exorcism of the 'spirit of masturbation', so he had all his ushers hand a paper hanky to all the men who were present. (Was he not aware that women masturbate, too?) At the word of deliverance, they were expected to cough up the demon!

Charms and talismans are believed by many Christians to have demonic power, and fetishes are thought to be the very homes of demons – though such a notion is totally unbiblical. In 1986, con-man Derry Knight took several charismatics for a ride to the tune of £200,000, which they coughed up for the purpose of buying some tatty old satanic regalia for them to destroy, believing that this opportunity would somehow strike a spiritual blow against the devil. It's a pity they didn't take a closer look at their Bibles first, or they would have known that there is no biblical precedence for such an unorthodox idea.

Christian paranoia about witchcraft, or *wicca*, often lends it greater credence than it deserves. Modern witchcraft is largely the invention of Gerald Gardner, in the 1940s, and scholars are sceptical about his sources. Alaistair Crowley may have had a hand in some of the rituals, but Alexander Sanders, the self-styled King of the Witches, was little more than an opportunist imitator of Gardner. Margaret Murray's *The Witch Cult in Western Europe*, which attempted to establish links between pre-Christian pagan religion and neo-paganism as practised today, has never carried much weight in academic circles. Though still a dangerous threat, modern witchcraft is a religious sham, with no historical basis earlier than this century.

The Bible is certainly not paranoid about the devil; he hardly rates a mention in the Old Testament. The Hebrew word for 'accuser', translated as Satan, occurs only ten times, and 'abaddon' or devil occurs not at all. In the New Testament, the devil – in his various guises as Satan or Apollyon – crops up about eighty times, mainly in the synoptic Gospels.

Walker has pointed out that his origins are never discussed. Christ says, 'I saw Satan fall like lightning from heaven,' (Luke 10:18) which *may* echo Isaiah 14:12 (though there is no agreement amongst scholars that the King of Babylon – the subject of the Isaiah passage – is actually the devil). The 'proof text' of the devil's origin is given as Revelation 12:7–9, but zealous commentators inconsistently treat this passage as history, while the rest of the book is said to refer to future events.

'In my opinion, the unsystematic and somewhat haphazard treatment of the devil in the Bible is a signal for us not to attempt to know more,' Walker concludes in *Charismatic Renewal*. 'We need to understand the dark powers as interpenetrating the power structures of society, so that we fight evil not in the realms of fantasy or the heavenlies, but in the public world of politics and economics.'

Self-fulfilling prophecies and the literalisation of parable and metaphor abound in the paranoid universe. It is this untheological sub-strata that has turned many conservative evangelicals against the charismatic movement.

Dr Richard Laugharne: 'In my own opinion, mental illness exists, and the effects of the demonic exist; sometimes they may co-exist. We must be careful about labelling something as demonic simply because it is

painful to us. Biblically, it is clear that many painful
things are a consequence of the Fall, or a consequence
of our own actions. We need to deal with that by
changing ourselves, and not by taking the easy option
of blaming an external force – a demon – for all our
problems.' It's no use 'delivering' someone when the
real problem lies in aspects of their own personality,
which they need to ask God to change.

Laugharne continued 'On the other hand, I strongly
believe that the demonic is a reality, which can affect
us in many ways. In some humans it affects them in a
very intense way, which I don't understand. I believe
in it, but I can't explain it. But we mustn't blame
all mental illness on the demonic. I've seen mentally
ill people severely traumatised because well-meaning
Christians have told them that they're demonised.
On the other hand, I know of people who have been
radically helped by being prayed for by Christians who
discerned that the demonic was genuinely involved.
Balance is the key.'

A move of the Holy Spirit releases the deep psyche
of a human being, Roger Forster believes, and sometimes there may genuinely be demonic manifestations:
'Within a large congregation, there will be people put
on the ground by God to rest – and to have dreams and
visions – and others who will be thrown violently to the
ground, as a work of the enemy reacting to the Holy
Spirit. It's difficult to discern which strand is which at
every stage with 100 per cent accuracy.'

A Question of Balance

Discernment is essential. Not all that passes for the
work of the Holy Spirit is genuine, but neither is it
all demonic, or all human according to David Hilborn.
'Simply because people are dancing – or because there

are shamanistic parallels – it's complete nonsense
to suggest that this must be of the devil. Speaking in tongues is manifest in all sorts of faiths –
and in people with psychiatric disorders as well –
so the outward sign is not crucial in judging the
significance. Discernment is the gift that needs to
be paramount.' The wheat must be separated from
the chaff.

Charismatics and evangelicals are in agreement, but
how does one know that the Spirit that appears to be
doing the discerning is itself the Spirit of God, and not
a counterfeit?

'You discern by applying the Bible to the experience.
You need to use hermeneutics, and apply the principles
of Scripture to situations that may not have an obvious
precedent in Scripture. It's a difficult task,' Hilborn
believes.

'Discernment is the most important gift necessary to
ensure that the charismatic movement doesn't go off
the rails,' says Walker, who himself is now a member of
the Orthodox Church: 'When something comes along,
in the nature of the fallen world in which we live, it will
be a mixture of the fallen, the depraved, the demonic,
and of God.

'I don't believe that discernment means instant
revelation. It's not a shortcut, another quick fix. One
shouldn't assume that good, sound theological training is irrelevant to discernment. Discernment is not
necessarily an instant "Oh, I know", it may well be
a careful and sober reflection. Good discernment is "a
true assessment."

'The press assume that there is a common phenomena called the Toronto Blessing, but my observation is
that it is all sorts of stuff. There are different types
of phenomena, and we need to discern one bit from
another.'

Walker cites Acts 15 as an example of good discernment. There, we read of a dispute which was only solved by a conference – a convocation of the elders of the early Church, meeting together. Only when the discussion was all over did the apostles say, 'It seemed good to the Holy Spirit and to us'. Walker fears that such careful, reflective and informed thinking – theological and prayerful – is absent from the charismatic movement.

You don't have to leave your brains on the seat when you stand up to be blessed.

Gifted with Discernment

Colin Dye, minister of Kensington Temple, was in basic agreement with the evangelical and orthodox positions: 'There is a charismatic gift of the discerning of spirits, which is not discernment *per se*. A discernment may involve the exercise of that gift, but alongside a whole range of other tests. For example, last night, someone began to laugh and – though technically it was no different from other laughter – I discerned instantly that there was something more behind it, so we straight away helped that person through their experience. This was a discernment of motivation, when we know whether an action is motivated by a human spirit, the Holy Spirit or a demonic spirit.

'But overall discernment is much broader. The simplest test is *root and fruit:* asking where is it coming from and where is it heading? What are its origin and destination? If the roots of a phenomenon are in a person hungry for the sensational, desiring to be the next church reported in newspapers, and self-promotion of personal ministry, then it may be no more unbiblical than anything that is happening in two-thirds of British churches, whether you're screaming

from the chandeliers or putting out expository sermons
– but it's not of God.

'Here in September 1994,' Dye told me, 'There is
little fruit. In many ways, what we are examining is
blossom and not fruit. The blossom is good, but when
the petals fall, that will be the real test. Everything
that is happening looks so beautiful, but even weeds
can blossom beautifully and people can enjoy it super-
ficially. All the time, we must be testing what is left
when the blossom falls.

'Here at KT we hand out a form, and then interview
people to find out how their experiences have affected
them. "Okay, so you fell to the floor laughing, and
you had a wonderfully great time, but how has the
experience changed you?" The major test of fruit is,
"Does this glorify Christ?" For myself, I'm so freshly
in love with Christ, I was recently invited to talk to
Elim's trainee ministers about the marks of the Holy
Spirit in the Church, and all I could do was talk about
Christ! Try as I might about talking directly about the
Spirit, I found myself talking all about Jesus. I could
do nothing else.

'The second test lies in the evangelistic fruits. If
this just remains some little move within the Church,
I don't want it. Who cares? A lot of charismatic stuff is
"all-rightish", but it doesn't lead to conviction of sin. I
have seen a very timid person witness powerfully as
a result of her recent experience. She had a "divine
appointment", a chance meeting with a Muslim woman
at the end of her tether, and that woman was powerfully converted.

'All September, we have had people drawn into our
nightly meetings. A Hari Krishna devotee came in,
manifested demons, and was ministered to; he was
set free and accepted Christ. I'm disappointed by the
generally low number of converts, but I am impressed

by the level of conviction and depth of conversion.
These were not nominal Christians deepening their
faith; every night for a month, we've had one or two
dramatic conversions, but it still doesn't represent
a revival.

'Other than in reformed publications that twist
history to fit a theology, revival is not neat and tidy.
There is so much of man's response involved; why not
let the human personality speak – we need to laugh
and cry – we are psychological beings. Is God going
to by-pass our psyche? It's pharasaical not to forgive
a little emotionalism within context. I'm not talking
about psychological manipulation, though. Emotionalism and intellectualism make the best psychological
conversions; Pentecostals are guilty of the one, and
evangelicals are guilty of the other!'

People who pray for revival often want it on their own
terms; but God will do it only on his terms, and he may
decide to re-write his own rule book as he goes along!

Norman Moss agrees that examining the fruit is the
strongest key to successful discernment. He has seen
marriages helped, and people who have found a great
sense of peace – as well as more profound spiritual
growth. Some people have abruptly fallen to the ground
when they had no expectation to do so. In September
1994, he was only too aware that it was too early to be
making a final judgement.

'A small amount of deliverance ministry has taken
place during this move,' said Moss. 'If the whole
phenomenon was of the evil one, I would find it very
odd if that was happening as a result. I don't think
it's demonic because it glorifies Jesus. There's no loss
of consciousness when people have been on the floor;
but the experience has led to resolution of problems,
and repentance. One theological student came up to
me afterwards to apologise: "I thought it was all

self-hypnosis, but now I have seen it for myself, I
know that it is not."'

Fruit and Veg

Graham Cray has been a member of theological panels
to discuss the 1994 moves of the Spirit at both New
Wine and Greenbelt. The general consensus at each
event seemed to be, 'I think this is broadly of God, but I
have some questions and reservations.' People wanted
to make distinctions between phenomena and fruit.

Cray cites a Christian therapist who commented: 'If
this is going on by an action of God, I can own it.
My key questions are not "Could God make someone
growl like a bear?" but "What are the pastoral support
networks that are needed to help people to whom this
is happening, for whom it can be initially a profoundly
disorientating experience, though ultimately a profound *integration* of themselves.'

Cray has been a charismatic evangelical since 1966,
and has learned a thing or two about discernment –
not least as a diocesan adviser on deliverance for ten
years. 'I am aware of the wide range of interpretation
that can be given to any particular phenomenon. It is
over-easy to label something demonic, just as it is easy
to attribute someone falling over to the influence of the
Holy Spirit.

'There are a number of other reasons for believing
this is of God. The core test is the fruit, and the fruit
of character does not grow overnight. We have to wait
and see, but we each owe a degree of stewardship to
God for anything he has given to us. We each have a
responsibility for whether or not there is fruit in our
own lives.

'On the tentative evidence of what I have seen, for
example in my wife's life: yes, there is an equipping for

ministry. Yes, there is a growing closer to the heart and mind of God.

'We need to ask: Does the thing, in itself, have a Christ-like character. I'm glad the Toronto Vineyard is in the wrong end of town, and not out in affluent California. There is nothing flashy or ostentatious about that Vineyard – it is seeking to grow and live in the love of God, and to give that love away. Without seeking any reputation for itself, it has simply made itself available six days a week to bless whoever goes there, and that character of servanthood is profoundly Christ-like.

'I believe the pastor was previously in a situation where there was an outpouring of the Spirit, where he decided that he couldn't cope with it, and closed the whole thing down. A time of repentance followed, where he said, "God, if you ever let me see anything like this again, I will keep my hands off it".'

Cray believes there are strong parallels with the genesis of the Pentecostal movement in Azusa Street, Los Angeles, in 1906. That outpouring occurred in an unimpressive store front church with a black pastor and an uneducated congregation, and Pentecostals see it as the birth of their tradition. What is happening now is not totally new.

Cray continued: 'One of my students came back from Zimbabwe, and it's been happening over there; it started, I believe, from an Alpha course.

'If something pops up from nowhere – is recognisably comparable to something you've seen before, but which has an intensity about it – and of which there is a selfless giving away, it has to be a character of the work of God. If that work results in a significant encounter with Christ – Jesus being honoured, Scripture being loved, and the outworking of godly practice – those are other promising signs.

'I know of a curate who had a powerful encounter with God at an Alpha conference. He told me, "Since then, I have led people to Christ, my preaching has taken off, I have prayed for sick people and they have got better, and just don't ask me how much I love Jesus." I have to say there, that the Holy Spirit has been at work.

'Theologically, the Spirit is the foretaste of God's future – the first fruits, and the down payment on what is to come. We are told in Romans 8 that part of the future – of which we only have the first fruits – is the redemption of our bodies. If there is then an *intensification* of the presence of that Spirit, would you not expect some physical reaction? Shaking and falling can have a theological explanation.'

'If we only have the anticipation, however, we can never have 100 per cent pure experience which is entirely of God without your sin getting in the way, so we always need to be discerning.'

The *roots* of the Blessing, its connection with the Faith Movement and the cultish Latter Rains, is unpromising weak evidence of its authenticity. But – just as a person from a non-Christian family can transcend his roots and become an anointed Christian teacher – the *fruit* that is still to come may genuinely be heaven-sent, and be strong evidence that we are seeing a real work of God.

Cray believes that 'What is transpiring in the present is never just for the present, it is to equip you for God's work in the future. Therefore an experience is never for its own sake. You should never separate a touch of the Spirit from the transformation of character that makes you more like Christ. One day – no matter how much last minute surgery needs to be done – you're going to see Christ face-to-face and be like him!

'A full-blooded Trinitarian theology tells us that, all the time, the Holy Spirit is taking us to the Father, through the Son. You might laugh, cry, fall down, or just be deeply aware of the Holy Spirit, but the whole point is not about the Holy Spirit – the point is about Christ!'.

Jonathan Edwards was a major theological brain working overtime, and he said if we acknowledge that, though we are in Christ, we have but a glimpse of the full reality that is the glory of God, we should not wonder if our strength fails us when our vision of that glory is intensified.

We have conformed to a rationalist culture that is now disintegrating. We are not balanced and integrated people. Cray considers that the dynamic Spirit is putting people in touch with their bodies and emotions. In such a situation, pastoral care is essential.

He concludes that 'A lot of charismatics, without understanding the filters that the culture has put on them, reduce the sovereign work of the Spirit to a banal, "something happened to me which felt good, so Christianity must be true." We are reductionists who reduce things to the narrow field of our world view. When God acts by the Spirit, instead of engaging with it all, we put it through our filters and end up with a narrower view than God ever intended.

'I believe we are experiencing an initiative of the Holy Spirit, but there's a danger of it becoming simply "the latest charismatic thing" – the sequel to the Kansas City Prophets, the "Signs and Wimbers" or the Vineyard – the "latest thing" that we will be into until the next "latest thing" happens, till it becomes a commodity culture, a trip for its own sake.'

We mustn't major on the phenomena, but on the outworking: healing the sick, feeding the poor and winning the lost – translating the move into a ministry

outwards, or a golden opportunity may be lost. There
have been impressive testimonies, but Cray still fears
that charismatics are prone to keeping these things
for their own blessing, instead of giving it away –
they become religious vegetables instead of producing
spiritual fruit. We will be accountable to God for how
we use what he gives.

Sign Language

Tom Houston: 'My basic view of the gifts of the Spirit is
that they are programmed in us from birth. I take very
seriously what Jeremiah says about being a prophet
from his mother's womb. The gifts, whatever they are
– and all are paralleled outside Scripture – can be
used neutrally, evily (in sorcery and witchcraft) or
spiritually, taken up by the Holy Spirit and used in
the context of the Church. God uses everything that
he has programmed into us as human beings, but
we are looking at phenomena that are common in
human experience in different places. They are *signs*,
but who are they signs *to*, and what are they signs
from,' Houston wondered, as we drank coffee in his
City Temple office.

In Scripture, signs are mostly not for the person who
is part of it, but for someone else.

Unlike Roger Forster, he does not believe that the
signs have important intrinsic worth, until they are
channelled. They are not threats, but they could be
opportunities. One woman at City Temple had an
experience that she considered to be a sign – that God
is alive, loving and communicates. It has led her back
to the Bible, to receive his communications through
the written word. The sign spoke eloquently of the
availability of God, and led to an ongoing communion.

For evidence that unusual events can have a diverse

range of causes, one need look no further than the first
king of Israel, Saul. When the prophet Samuel (they
were called 'seers' in those days) anointed Saul as king,
he prophesied over him, with a word of knowledge:
'You will meet a procession of prophets coming down
from the high place with lyres, tambourines, flutes
and harps being played before them, and they will
be prophesying. The Spirit of the LORD will come
upon you in power, and you will prophesy with them;
and you will be changed into a different person.' (1
Sam 10:5–6)

So it came to pass that Saul had a life-transforming
experience under the Holy Spirit's anointing.

The Spirit came upon him again (1 Sam 11:6) and he
defeated the Ammonites. But Saul disobeyed God: 'The
Spirit of the LORD had departed from Saul, and *an evil
spirit* from the LORD tormented him' (1 Sam 16:14, my
italics). When Saul had David play his harp, the Bible
simply reports that 'he felt better'. Nothing was done to
deliver him from the evil spirit, but the *psychological
effect* – the 'feelgood' factor – was there!

The second time we read of Saul prophesying (1 Sam
18:10) it is the same phenomenon as before, but even as
he is in the very act of exhibiting the spiritual gift in a
godly way, a second spiritual influence – the evil spirit
– causes him to throw a spear at David (1 Sam 18:10).
Here we have evil and godly phenomena exhibited in
the same person at the same time.

The second time he throws a spear at David, possessed by *an injurious spirit*, there are no prophetic
manifestations, and the spiritual influence is purely
malevolent (1 Sam 19:10). But he later throws a spear
at Jonathan, without any spiritual causes whatsoever,
in a *purely human* rage (1 Sam 20:33). The next
spiritual phenomenon is triggered by the *Spirit of God*
again, causing him to strip off his robes and prophesy (1

Sam 19:24). The final spiritual manifestation in Saul's life – perhaps the most amazing of them all! – is the ghost of Samuel, conjured up through *necromancy* by the Witch of Endor.

In Saul's life then, the Holy Spirit, psychological influences, necromancy and an evil spirit all produced extraordinary behaviour patterns, in an unpredictable and volatile mixture. There were plenty of signs, but from a variety of sources, and Saul hadn't a clue what they meant, or how to respond properly to any of them!

'The production of religious phenomena, as in the case of Saul, is no necessary indicator of spirituality. Here, true discernment is needed in the channelling of religious experience,' Andrew Walker has written. 'Psychic of religious phenomena may become divorced or dislocated from the Spirit of God. Once triggered into life, they are apt to assume a life of their own and become self-generating.' Stereotyped ritual behaviour can result. Emotions are contagious, particularly in groups, and any attempt to whip up hysteria must be considered highly suspect.

Charismatic experiences often play down 'understanding'. The laughter can make people speak unwisely, in an offhand manner, because the mirth has reduced the experience to something very casual. The Blessing can become a threat.

We need to look at the issues of knowledge and wisdom – which happen to be the last two gifts of the Spirit that we have still to cover.

Chapter Nine

Gifted with Knowledge

In November 1992, my mother died after a long and painful illness. She'd been partially paralysed and unable to speak for twelve years following a stroke, but the last agonising months of her life were spent in hospital with painful circulatory problems, that resulted in her losing a leg.

The last time I saw her, she hardly recognised me. In my teen years, she'd been terrified (aren't all mothers?) that *I* might become a drug addict; now, here *she* was, medicated to the eyeballs with diamorphine – about as close to pure heroin as you can get.

My mum, a junky! I'm sure she'd have appreciated the irony, and laughed heartily about it, had she not been comatose.

For her, death came as a welcome friend, I'm sure. She wasn't a Christian, in the evangelical sense – she had never invited Christ into her life – and she never attended church. Yet my mother said a prayer every night; she was always generous with her own time and possessions – and often with mine!

God worked in a curious way to show me that she was now safe in his hands, and that it would be appropriate – not simply to bury her with moribund reminiscences and predictable eulogies – but, as I believed the Holy Spirit was prompting, for me to use the evangelistic opportunity presented by my mother's funeral.

I don't remember the topic at the Bible study a week later, but there were a selection of Bible references in the notes, and we were each given one at random to look up and read to the group. I read: 'Let the dead bury their own dead, but you go and proclaim the kingdom of God'! (Luke 9:60).

When I preached at her funeral, I was careful to speak of God's mercy and to stress that death is not the end. Strangely, the most traumatic moment of the whole bereavement came during the singing of her favourite hymn *The Old Rugged Cross*, immediately before my talk. It was the thought of Christ's death that filled me with sorrow, and it was difficult to compose myself.

It was astonishing the way God had spoken eloquently to me through Scripture, affirming with an objective word the subjective experience I had already felt. Here was a classic example of word and Spirit working together, in a prophetic manner.

Words of Knowledge

A few weeks later, my dad was taken into hospital with a minor heart problem. The day before he was due to return home, he too suffered a stroke. Rather than immediately make the six hour journey to join the many relatives at his bedside, I reluctantly agreed with my brother that *he* would first make his much shorter trip to ascertain our father's condition.

The next morning, as I prayed, God told me to go immediately and pray with my father. It was as simple as that! I don't often hear God's voice so clearly, but on this occasion I had no doubts. The timing was impossibly inconvenient, I was far too busy working on a book, but the Holy Spirit would brook no denial.

Without waiting to hear from my brother, I caught the very next train.

I held my old dad's hand and prayed for him as he slipped into unconsciousness for the last time. His breathing was raspy and painful, with a chilling rattle in his throat, and his condition was certainly life-threatening – but I believed that God might heal him.

When the hospital phoned at 5.00 am to say that he'd passed away in his sleep, I broke down in tears. My first thought was: 'How could I have been so stupid to think I could do some deal with God? A deal with God! My task is simply to follow and obey.'

I felt comforted that God had spoken supernaturally with a word of knowledge, telling me to go to my father's bedside.

I knew a strange serenity through my grief. My dad had always been a popular figure in all the local pubs and clubs. I'll never forget the surprise I felt when I rose nervously to speak at the crematorium. Every seat was filled, and forty or so of his old drinking mates stood at the back, non-churchgoers to a man. In ten short minutes, they got a tribute to my dad, and the full glorious Gospel message into the bargain. One of his coffin bearers, a young drinking companion, put me straight: 'I've no time for any religious nonsense, but what you said meant a lot to me.' It was the highest compliment he could have offered!

A few weeks later, at the end of a prayer meeting, I sensed an image popping into my mind. I mentioned it to the other people present, then promptly forgot about it. It certainly wasn't a spectacular vision, nor much of a picture; just an impression really – of a woman about to give birth.

I was amazed to be congratulated, a few weeks later, on the alleged accuracy of my 'word of knowledge'! It seems that the woman sitting next to me at the prayer meeting had believed herself to be pregnant. She'd consulted her doctor, but had still been awaiting final confirmation of her happy condition.

A year later, after she and her husband had become the proud parents of a bouncing baby girl, I remained sceptical whether the Holy Spirit had really implanted the picture in my mind. As a sign, it had no importance or significance for myself – yet it had clearly been received as a welcome sign by the expectant mother at a time of uncertainty.

God has given me no further words of knowledge since then; though I am open to him, I have neither sought nor expected them, so I feel no disappointment. I don't believe that God communicates supernaturally about mundane matters; but I'm sure he speaks powerfully through the Holy Spirit at crisis points, and at the defining moments in the lives and ministries of his followers. And who could doubt that the death of a parent or the birth of a child should cause God to move compassionately in miraculous ways?

But many pundits believe that such remarkable occurrences will become much more common in days to come.

Gifts of Revelation

The outworkings of the three final gifts of the Spirit are often almost indistinguishable from one another. These gifts, discernment, knowledge and wisdom, are sometimes called the gifts of revelation because they consist, apparently, of the supernatural receipt of information.

Discernment lies in knowing what motivates a person, and who or what exerts an influence over him or her; the word of knowledge is the supernatural revelation of information, past present and future, which is not acquired through the five senses; while the word of wisdom is the supernatural application of knowledge – knowing what to do with the information received.

Again, many Christians believe that these phenomena essentially involve the use of latent *natural* gifts which have been drawn from dormancy by the Holy Spirit. A contemporary and non-religious example of knowledge being supernaturally received is cited by Stuart Holroyd, in his book *Psi and the Unconsciousness Explosion*: 'Peter Hurkos was a Dutch house painter who became clairvoyant after an accident which left him in a coma for three days. 'You're a bad man,' he blurted out to the man in the next bed while recovering in hospital. 'When your father died, he left you with a large gold watch. He died only a short time ago, and you have already sold the watch.'

Shades of Ananias and Sapphira! The man was dumbfounded. Hurkos' denouncement was true, though he had never met the man before.

Morton Kelsey lists sixteen instances in the book of Acts where knowledge, wisdom or instruction were received in 'clairvoyant, precognitive or telepathic experiences'; with nearly twenty further examples from the Gospels. In many instances – Acts 1:9–11; 8:26; 10:1–8, 30–33 – the experience involved the apparent materialisation of angels, or of visionary manifestations – one of which we will encounter at the end of this chapter.

Evangelicals prefer to derive theological discernment, knowledge and wisdom purely from Scripture – using intellectual reasoning, and the logical principles of hermeneutics – but there are philosophical problems with this approach.

Modern philosophers, like Descartes and Locke, also began with the premise that man can and has to know the truth purely by applying his own logical reasoning and empirical experience. But the British philosopher

Berkeley pointed out eruditely that, by these alone, *we cannot even prove that the world exists*. It could just be a product of your imagination!

Scottish philosopher David Hume went a step further and argued that – not only can you never know for certain that the world around you is really there – you cannot even know that *you yourself* really exist!

It's intellectually dishonest to use intellectual reasoning alone to interpret Scripture, and then blithely to dismiss that same reasoning faculty when it produces results that tend to deny your very existence. Logic and reason alone will not lead you into all truth.

In the West, the youth revolution of the 1960s and 1970s which sought vainly to build a counter-culture – a viable alternative to the Western mechanistic society – searched for truth through non-rational means. Suzuki taught Zen Buddhism, Huxley added *soma*, and Leary advocated LSD as the transcendental path to knowledge.

The Pentecostal or charismatic often chooses a similar non-rational route, blandly dismissing intellectual knowledge and reasoning, in favour of a direct mystic experience of the Holy Spirit through prayer and worship. Here, they say, the Spirit fortifies them with knowledge and discernment, and empowers them with signs and wonders.

It is undeniable that profound mystical experiences are usually so vivid that they carry their own inimitable authority with them. A person who has experienced them cannot doubt their genuineness. However, though mystical incidents are often so life-transforming that the person to whom they have happened cannot doubt their validity, it does not follow that the *interpretations* given to the experiences are also true.

The twin dilemmas are: If a person begins purely with *reason*, he or she will end up, not with knowledge, but with uncertainty. The mystic offers an escape, teaching a non-rational *experience,* but the non-rational cannot be objectively verified or understood.

What a drag!

There is a third way: *Divine revelation.* Though the evangelical may claim to gain knowledge by using reason to discern the Scriptures, and the charismatic may lay claim to dynamic experience, truly both are equally dependent upon divine revelation in one of its two forms.

Generally, revelation is considered to be *propositional* (contained in the words of scriptures) or *personal* (given directly through a divine supernatural agency). Mystic experience is *non-rational and subjective,* whereas revelation is *rational and objective* – something which all people can read or hear, and understand.

When the Holy Spirit graciously communicates direct, this personal *rhema* (the 'present' word of God) should be compared with the Scriptures, the *logos* (the 'past' word of God) in discerning whether it is truly of God. Charismatics are prone regrettably to considering the *rhema* to be an addition, alternative or advance on the *logos,* when it is subservient to the written word, and has a purely local or personal application.

The Bible is authoritative for the Christian, not because of its intellectual brilliance, or because it was inspired by the Holy Spirit. Its authority comes from its unique status as *the only divine revelation (other than the perfect revelation in the person of Christ) which has universal application* – it's true for everyone, for all time. Evangelicals are prone to deluding themselves that their own interpretations (*exegesis*) or applications (*hermeneutics*) carry equal authority.

The same Holy Spirit that inspired Scripture, also

directly inspires and guides the charismatic. The best discernment, knowledge and wisdom comes when Spirit and Scripture are brought into use together, and the Spirit is allowed to lead us into the true interpretation and contemporary application of Scripture.

We will do well to remember this as a strength when we try to analyse the implications of any piece of Scripture, or any move of the Holy Spirit particularly in baptism, renewal and revival.

Hawkes-eye Overview

In 1994, Adrian Hawkes observed the fresh blessings in several different contexts. Does he believe that revival is on the way?

'When you talk about *revival*, Christians expect people to come to God, but I think that is *awakening*. You can't revive something that has never been alive! You revive the Church and that might lead to an awakening where Christians go out and reach the unconverted.

'In the last ten years I've seen a gradual increase in the Church's effectiveness. There is a new awareness in the country that Christianity is acceptable, in a way which wasn't there twenty-five years ago. Many Afro-Carribbean immigrants are more God conscious than whites, and maybe that has had a positive effect. They sense that there is another dimension to life over and above the physical.

'I think prophecy has become more real. At each stage in the fulfilment of a biblical prophecy, it gets more intense. Just as Peter could stand up in Acts 2, and claim that Pentecost was the fulfilment of Joel's prophecy, so can I in the present generation. It's the same prophecy fulfilled two thousand years apart.' Here, the word and the Spirit work together.

Though many have seen the Spirit move tantalisingly in waves through this century, Hawkes prefers to see its locus as peaks and troughs – climbing mountains and dipping a bit into valleys, until the valleys are eventually higher than the original peaks.

He also believes strongly that he is seeing the reconciliation of differing theologies. Instead of churches saying, 'Oh, but we have a different interpretation from you of this obscure word in Leviticus, so we can't join with you in your global mission endeavours,' there is more co-operation between different fellowships, all serving the one Lord.

Hawkes's theology of the Holy Spirit has developed substantially in recent years. Some of the ideas he was taught as a Pentecostal he would now find amusing, though the changes are sometimes just a question of interpretations and definitions.

Gary Kinnaman, writing in *And Signs Shall Follow*, now believes that 'doctrinally, charismatic and non-charismatic evangelicals differ only on one major issue: the ministry of the Holy Spirit, specifically Spirit baptism.'

We've come back to the issue raised in Chapter Three: If one receives the Spirit of Christ at conversion, how can you receive the Spirit separately, without doing an injustice to the concept of the trinity? Yet baptism in the Holy Spirit is biblical terminology.

Baptism Revisited

Hawkes believes that baptism is subtly different from merely receiving. 'Upon baptism in the Holy Spirit, the Holy Spirit floods out of the spirit of man where he dwells, into the soul and body. The only exception was at Pentecost, when the Spirit first came.'

Colin Dye considers that perhaps we all receive the

Holy Spirit *unconsciously* at conversion (in the traditional evangelical way) but we then need the *conscious* release of his power for service (the charismatic view): 'In Acts, the reception of the Spirit is always experiential and phenomenological; there is no conservative evangelical doctrine that can handle that fact. There is clearly still a bit of reconciling to do, and creative ways of doing it. I reconcile it through conscious and unconscious reception of the Spirit. You cannot believe in Jesus without some very powerful move of the Spirit. I believe that unconscious reception is *indwelling*, and conscious reception is *empowering*.'

It's likely that, whatever the exact solution, both evangelicals and charismatics are essentially right, but each is only seeing a part of the picture. Two-stage theology is not popular with evangelicals, Andrew Walker believes. 'Wimber plays it down, because basically it's not an issue for him. Only classical Pentecostals liked the two-stage model, because it fitted their experience. Not all Pentecostals these days are sold on the two-stage blessing being axiomatic.'

Perhaps the Holy Spirit is like a swimming pool: Do we enter with a toe in the shallow end, and with exacting slowness move ever deeper, so that there will never be one sudden moment when we can say we were immersed (the evangelical way), or do we enter with a triple somersault diving from the highest board in the baths (the charismatic way)? At the end of the day, whichever way you get in, you still end up with a good soaking!

Plunging in will give you a kick – the manifestation of singing in tongues, laughing, falling over, etc – while the slower approach might mean no sudden sense of immersion, no rush of exhilaration, but at the end of the day, you're still swimming powerfully in the deep water.

To return to a previous metaphor: If the Holy Spirit
could be likened to a vast ocean, then many Christians
like to live their spiritual lives as though they were
a yacht, cruising elegantly and serenely on the calm
surface. But their life is intended to be lived like a submarine – plain, stubby and downright ugly, eschewing
the surface and plunging into the turbulent and unex-
plored depths – totally submerged and surrounded by
the Holy Spirit.

'Too often we want to have everything explained
logically. I find it amusing that God uses tongues which
we don't understand as the means of confirming that
he has acted in baptising in the Spirit. It confounds the
human pride which says, "I can work everything out
intelligently with my brain power",' Hawkes believes.

Theology of the Spirit

My own conceptions of the Holy Spirit have changed
gradually, beyond all expectation, in recent years. As a
radical charismatic evangelical moving in conservative
evangelical circles, I've had to redefine and redescribe
my own relationship with the Holy Spirit – in order
to avoid giving offence by appearing to advocate the
notion of first and second class Christians – but also
because my own devotional and intellectual experiences have compelled me to adjust.

One thing is for certain: You can't have 'a little
bit' of Holy Spirit, then get a bit more. He is God,
and God is infinite; a little bit of the infinite is still
infinite. The New Testament refers instead to the idea
of *being filled* with the Spirit – a continual process.
The Spirit doesn't change, but the Christian does,
according to the incremental graduation of the filling
– with a constant need to be 'topped up'. The Bible
also refers to the notion of *baptism* in Holy Spirit –

being so full of the Spirit, that one is completely submerged.

How does one become literally immersed or baptised in the Holy Spirit? It's literally impossible – we are flesh and blood and the Holy Spirit, logically enough, is spirit! The expression is clearly a metaphor that makes no physical sense.

But for what illusive reality does the metaphor stand? Both the idea of being *filled*, and of being *immersed* carry the notion of levels and gradations. Surely we are speaking of the process of our own spirit being incrementally immersed in the Holy Spirit, which can be a very gradual or relatively sudden procedure. There is, of course, more than one way of becoming immersed.

I remember a school trip which ended with a dip in a mountain tarn. It was extremely cold, and most of the class inched their way in gingerly, first a toe, then a foot, in up to the knees, then the waist, tentatively up to the chest and duck under quick. Most of us never got beyond a quick paddle, then out again! A brave handful simply plunged straight into the freezing water and began swimming – the shock of the sudden immersion, I'm told, gives a euphoric 'buzz' – a zestful 'high' that you don't get if you immerse gradually.

It's a little like drug abuse – the bigger the dose taken at once, the greater the 'high'; but take a few milligrammes spread over several weeks, and the body will adjust so gradually that you'll feel no buzz at all. Take heroin at the rate of one grain a day, and you will never know you've taken it.

The Holy Spirit is responsible for *sanctification*. That's usually a *gradual* process and, like lowering oneself cautiously into the cold tarn, there may be no sudden 'rush', but incremental discomfort. With the tarn, the distress came from the cold; with the Holy Spirit, malaise can come from conviction of sin, and hesitant changes in life style – which may mean giving up attitudes and/or activities that are no longer appropriate for a Christian. This discomfort may discourage many believers from proceeding further.

In the West, the gradual sanctification is most common, since there are a plethora of areas of life for the Holy Spirit to address, and often no urgent need for radical change. That's why conservative evangelicals cannot state a specific time when they were suddenly submerged in Holy Spirit; it happened slowly. The charismatic, on the other hand, remembers vividly when it happened; it was the equivalent of being thrown in the freezing tarn fully clothed!

Some would argue that a sudden filling subsequent to conversion is the old pentecostal two-stage theology in a different guise. My response is to point to water baptism, which is always subsequent to repentance, conversion and justification. The submission to water baptism, in all its multi-layered significance, comes subsequent to the act of repentance – yet no one complains that this is a two-stage theology of justification. Anglicans certainly have a nominal two-stage theology of conversion, with water baptism generally followed years later by confirmation, and the invitation for the Holy Spirit to come upon someone who may have been a Christian for many years, spoken by the confirming bishop.

Water baptism is something that people do for God; Spirit baptism is something that God does for people.

The incremental filling is not the 'normative' New Testament pattern, where the Holy Spirit often seems to have filled a young Christian so rapidly that the resulting 'kick' manifested euphorically in tongues or other clear signs of the Spirit's sudden infilling to the point of total immersion or baptism. Yet the New Testament pattern has probably been normative for most of the Church through most of its history, because the pattern is one appropriate to a persecuted Church. In Europe and North America, the Church is *abnormal*, because it is clearly not being persecuted — when's the last time a member of your home group was dragged off and fed to the lions?

Abroad, the Church has been under extreme persecution for most of this century in China and the former Iron Curtain countries. In the Middle East, the pressure has come from Islam; in India from Hinduism and Asian culture; and in South America from spiritism. I have met Asian Christians whose families disowned them on the spot when they came to Christ. In 1993, a Christian woman in Pakistan was abducted and forced to divorce her husband, leaving her children, to marry a Muslim against her will.

Desperate times require drastic measures. With Europe and North America witnessing a change of emphasis, and dramatic fillings of the Holy Spirit becoming more common, perhaps God is tacitly preparing the Church in the West for a period of persecution – or perhaps for an unprecedented time of renewal and revival.

Transformation

In any strange new situation, initially it's easy to make the most absurd mistakes. I've always been amused by the 'Football Pools' mentality in Acts 1, when the disciples decided to choose a replacement for Judas by drawing lots! There's no evidence that God told them to do anything of the sort; their only justification was a somewhat dubious interpretation brought to an Old Testament Scripture, taken out of context. Of course there needed to be a replacement for Judas, but God already had one lined up: Paul.

God's choice was eloquently revealed in the fulness of time, and had God told his Church in advance that the maniac Saul who was going around persecuting them was going to become one of their most important members, they'd have thought God was pulling their leg!

Many people expected what happened in 1994 to happen in 1982. But it seems as though the Church needed to get its act in order administratively first. People want to abandon what they are doing because God is doing something else, as though it's an either/or situation, and that's a weakness. The churches need to give plenty of time to what God is doing, but it doesn't mean that they need immediately to abandon anything else they are doing. It might mean putting programmes on one side, but not always. We don't have to leave everything to go and be refreshed.

I often feel that Christians are more at home on a genteel roundabout or a swing than on a fast helter-skelter or a ferocious white-knuckle ride; we often seek the same weak and routine experience over and over again. Or we desire something that God is doing for someone else. God is always wanting to move us on, whilst we often crave a repeat of something we've enjoyed previously.

Peter, James and John certainly felt that way at the Transfiguration. In a literal mountain-top experience, they witnessed Jesus transformed: 'His face shone like the sun, and his clothes became as white as the light. Just then there appeared before them Moses and Elijah, talking with Jesus' (Matt 17:2–3). Peter's naive response was to suggest building shelters, so that they could stay on top of the mountain with Jesus and the patriarchs for ever and ever!

God responded with an audible voice, proclaiming

that Jesus was his Son: 'When the disciples heard this, they fell face down to the ground, terrified' (Matt 17:6). In the face of unbridled divinity, the very presence of God, the disciples were slain in the Spirit! But in spite of their experiences, a cross awaited Christ at Calvary, and the time came for them to come down from the mountain-top experience. They had been refreshed in order to go out and help the suffering world in which they lived; not to stay in their cosy little private world, tucked away with Elijah and Moses, languidly playing their harps for all eternity.

New experiences should not be feared; discernment is needed, but fresh opportunity should be welcomed warmly as a potential friend and ally.

Ever-fresh religious *experience* in dynamic interaction with the authentic teachings of Christ, was the living matrix of New Testament theology, according to James Dunn in *Jesus and the Spirit*. 'Without the latter, faith all too easily becomes fanaticism and burns itself out. But without the former, without God as a living reality in religious experience, faith never comes to life and theology remains sterile and dead.'

Chapter Ten

Revival Culture

God's actions in the past can help us to understand his activities in the present.

Through 1994, many attempts were made to legitimise the 'new' phenomena through copious reference to Church history. The stunning revival in Indonesia in the sixties, for example, was fired by amazing miracles. Latin America has had an invigorating taste, too.

All through history, revivals have stemmed from the energetic prayers of the committed few. Each revival has seen one person, or a handful at most, becoming mightily used by God. George Whitefield, John and Charles Wesley, John Calvin, John Bunyan, George Fox, Charles Spurgeon and William Booth. Who knows if one day the name of Rodney Howard-Browne may not be added to the list?

Charles Finney, who led many of the great revival meetings of the nineteenth century, wrote evocatively in his memoirs: 'I returned to the front office and found that the fire that I had made of large wood was nearly burned out. But as I turned and was about to take a seat by the fire, I received a mighty baptism of the Holy Ghost. Without any expectation of it, without any recollection that I had ever heard the thing mentioned by any person in the world, the Holy Spirit descended upon me in a manner that seemed to go through me, body and soul.

'I could feel the impression like a wave of electricity, going through me. Indeed, it seemed to come in waves and waves of liquid love, for I could not express it in any other way. It seemed like the very breath of God. I can recall distinctly that it seemed to fan me, like immense wings.'

Here, God was starting a revival simply by touching one person, just as the Awakening came to North America in 1735 through one man sanctified by God – Jonathan Edwards. Later, it would be the turn of D.L. Moody to be an instrument in God's hands for revival.

A second common feature of revival is a dynamic move of the Holy Spirit – both invigorating the prayer life of the believer, and convicting the unbeliever of sin and the need for repentance. Spurgeon has recorded how he attended prayer meetings 'during which we could not speak because we felt so much the presence of God. We just had to sit still and pour out our supplications in tears and sobs and groanings that could not be uttered.' At open meetings, people cried out in anguish because the Spirit had revealed to them in vivid detail the judgement of God that hung over their heads, convicting them of their desperate plight.

During the last major revival to hit the UK – the 1904 Welsh Revival – these opportune features were strongly present. Evan John Roberts was God's man, beginning revival work following his filling with the Holy Spirit under the ministry of evangelist Seth Joshua, at Blaenannerch in October 1904. Within months, thousands were thronging to his meetings at chapels across Wales. 100,000 came into church membership during this short period – some churches doubled their membership – and the strong side effects included a drastic drop in crime, and prayer meetings held at the coal faces of Welsh mines.

At Moriah, Roberts found it difficult to halt the

exuberant singing for long enough to preach. Uncontrolled emotion and disorder characterised the revival in many places: a weakness. Prayers, singing and joyful shouting rang through the hills and villages: a strength. Bizarrely, one church leader regularly performed handstands and somersaults during his meetings 'to keep the flesh under subjugation'!

In South Carolina, around 1801, during an Awakening, William Henry Foote noted, 'loss of strength, swoons, outcries, sobs and groans, and violent spasmodic jerkings of the body. Some serious men who scorned the phenomena when present at these meetings ... subsequently were subject to them themselves, to their consternation.' Preachers exhorted people to pray, for prayer is not simply the *cause* of revival, but also its *effect*. Strong conviction of sin, and repentance, are the fruits of prayer and the action of the Spirit.

Revival Today?

'All across the globe where you have revival happening, it's all charismatic,' Gerald Coates told me. 'The people involved have not heard of Benny Hinn or John Arnott – they've not heard of Luther or Calvin for that matter – I don't know how God's doing it, but there you are! I'm quite sure that there are many ministers in those places who have not presented themselves well, and who believe things that I don't.

'Go to Latin America and you will find a theologically-illiterate love for people, and a sacrificial spirit that puts us to shame. We think our theology is so very important, but we're not seeing revival – and they are! Paul didn't write people off, he encouraged them in the things of God.'

Roger Forster: 'In Church history where these manifestations have appeared – Wesley, Salvation Army,

Welsh Revival, early Pentecostal movement – it's usually been just a few people who have been affected dramatically. The majority observe it and are brought to a sense of awe. At the moment, perhaps underlining the priesthood of all believers, it is a very large number of ordinary people who have received some kind of manifestation, instead of just a small number. God is speaking to us saying it's our sons and our daughters, the old and the young, all are to be blessed in the Spirit, in different ways.'

Andrew Walker was amused that evangelicals should so uncharacteristically have developed such a thirst for history! He identifies difficulties, though, in assessing such material: 'You weren't there, so you cannot in any real sense assess what really happened, say, in Jonathan Edwards day. Secondly, the phenomena that were around in the eighteenth and nineteenth century were all secondary issues in what was clearly a revival movement,' he told me, in his college office close to Waterloo Bridge.

'In October 1994, as we speak, we do not yet have a revival – and the phenomena we are seeing are precisely the phenomena that were peripheral then. It might be of God, but we can't say at this stage. It has not been around long enough. We need to see still more evidence of changed lives, a love for Scripture, an integration of Christians coming together, and a desire for social justice. Converts can fall away in a few months . . .

'If the Blessing goes quickly without leaving fruits, will it mean we have become too experiential? If, on the other hand, it heralds a revivalistic dawn, will we get carried away with millenialism? Will we think "This is the final big push, we no longer need to give to charities, or take a missionary approach because Jesus is coming soon"?'

'I don't want to be cynical, but the charismatic movement has had a long history of hype. This is a natural excess of enthusiasm for Jesus. The enthusiasm for God's good things can lead to untampered exaggeration. The charismatic movement sometimes falls short of the Gospel.'

Tom Houston accepts that the pilgrimage mentality – 'we're all off to Toronto' – is not biblical, but historically it has happened before in revivals: 'Revival can spread in many ways, but it often spreads through someone who has been at one revival being present at the next one. Revival spread with Finney, wherever he went.

'Regarding the Church growth implications, no one can say. Peter Wagner taught Church growth theory, but then he realised that churches were growing without following his sound principles at all, and went over to Wimber's signs and wonders ideas. Church life may be enriched, but the numbers of converts are not keeping up with those who are dying. We need a revival *and* an awakening.'

Blessings in Context

I don't believe that the 1994 outpouring of the Holy Spirit occurred as an isolated event. I think it happened, in God's perfect timing, because the Church was ready for it.

Over the previous twenty years or so, small Bible study groups, fellowship groups or home groups had sprung up from virtually every church, providing a vibrant sense of community and integration. Devotion to the written word had produced a seemingly endless stream of conferences and teaching events. Evangelicals and charismatics had grown closer than ever before in the preceding ten years. In the previous six or seven years, the walls had come off the churches, as praise marches have seen millions of Christians taking to the streets. I believe that God poured out his Spirit in a powerful new way because the time was right.

Many conservative Christians though, have been alarmed in recent years about the marches and triumphalistic songs which characterise the cutting edge of Church renewal. What of the people who are not ready for such radical and innovative changes in Church life, and who are desperately searching for the brakes?

'My response is that I take no notice of them whatever!' is Gerald Coates' blunt response. 'People who make those comments are not living in either renewal or revival. Praise, worship, prayer unity and making Jesus attractive is what the New Testament is about.

'Those who criticise the March for Jesus have no biblical precedent for having clergymen walking around in strange clothes; having an altar in their church; church buildings; holding Sunday schools, women's meetings, and youth groups; and a wide range of other things for which there is no biblical material whatever. Suddenly, because they're invited to come out onto the streets they don't want to do it because "it isn't biblical". That isn't the real reason; they don't want to do it because of issues of pride, and of being identified with other Christians.'

A non-participant commented that 'It's wonderful for them,' to which Coates retorted, 'Why is it "wonderful for *them*", and not "wonderful for *us*"? Why should black, whites and browns take to the streets in Africa and not in London? It's sheer lunacy, which only exposes prejudices and lack of understanding.' No doubt the same attitudes will prevail in many churches regarding God's new blessing.

I'm sure though that many churches take the view,

'Oh that's someone else's idea, we don't want to get
involved with that because we didn't think of it. The
Toronto Blessing came from the Vineyard, we'll wait
around till God gives us one of our own.'

Coates believes that many Christians often lack a
present-day experience of the Holy Spirit. They have
almost become dispensationalists through their 'post-
charismatic depression'. They say, 'God did all these
things, and I suppose he could do them again today,
but the bottom line is that he isn't doing them.'

Is too much stress being placed on the Holy Spirit
and not enough on Christ? The whole Gospel is surely
more than just John 3:16, but aren't charismatics
just a little unbalanced with their emphasis on the
Holy Spirit?

'I can't remember the last time I was at a charismatic convention and heard a talk about the work of
the Holy Spirit,' Coates told me. 'I've heard talks
on Christ, evangelism, the Church, Scripture, prayer,
intercession, fresh vision, and compassion for the lost
– but not about the Holy Spirit as such.

'Paul didn't have a narrow-minded approach to
Scripture. On Mars Hill, he didn't read any Scripture
at all in his talk; and at the end, he quoted a poem
about the god Zeus!

'Evangelism can go on without prophecy, healing,
signs and wonders. Most of it is friendship evangelism
and seeker-sensitive meetings, supper parties with
talks at the end, and the legendary Alpha course.'

Is there any real danger in receiving prayer from
someone who once said something that is not scripturally
accurate?

Coates replied: 'I think it's completely barmy! I have
not been to Toronto, and I have not been prayed for by
any of these people, but these signs are happening all
over the Pioneer network. I'm grateful to God. I would

like to see the current signs and wonders lasting for the rest of my life.'

Come off it, Gerald! Do we really want to become old codgers who come home from church saying, 'I had a wonderful time; I don't know what happened because I fell over in the first five minutes, but I'm sure it was wonderful!' Isn't it like the drunk who downs ten pints of Guinness and a quick vindaloo, stops for a puke in the gutter, and can't remember anything about it the next morning, but is convinced he had a wonderful time?

But Coates remained unmoved.

He simply referred me to a tale told by Baptist pastor David Obbard in his autobiography *Ploughboy to Pastor*. One day in 1954, Obbard was studying Ezekiel 37 – the story of the dry bones. 'It came to me in this way', he wrote, explaining what seemed to be a revelation of the Holy Spirit that over a twenty-year period from that date, there would be a 'revival of interest in the doctrines of grace' as the bones came together; a twenty-year revival of biblical order and spiritual life, as the flesh and sinews came on the bones; then twenty years of revival 'as there would be a mighty movement of the Holy Spirit, the breath of God, and the church would be raised from its lifeless state to that of an exceeding great army.'

Early in the 1990s, Obbard reflected that the first stage had come about through the ministry of people like Martyn Lloyd-Jones. For the second stage, he pointed to the growth of the charismatic movement, and expressed his hope of revival beginning in 1994.

Was this indeed the Spirit and the word working together, the Spirit giving a word of knowledge, or *rhema*, regarding a valid interpretation and application of Ezekiel's prophecy? Is revival really at hand? Perhaps time will tell . . .

Leaders Forum

'This is a wonderful day to be alive. It is a day in which God has allowed us to live to see a new dawning for evangelism,' Dr Billy Graham told an American evangelists' conference, on June 28th 1994. 'Seldom has the soil of the human heart and mind been better prepared than today . . . I've never seen so many people come to salvation in such a short period of time.'

He was speaking in Louisville – Rodney Howard-Browne's base – which has witnessed widespread revival.

'I'm staggered by the lack of opposition,' David Holden told me. 'I'm enjoying what is happening now, and living in the present. But if this move doesn't turn into something outward, affecting the nation, it will all fade away.'

The Evangelical Alliance appointed Joel Edwards to keep a beady eye on developments. His concern has been to test the phenomena and to look for fruit, while maintaining Church unity. 'At the end of the day, we need to be theologically discerning. There needs to be a relationship between our experience and God's word. When something manifests itself, we have to ask whether it is diametrically opposed to Scripture; if it is, we have to be very doubtful about it. But if it appears to co-exist with the word, then we need to judge it by its fruit.'

Many Christian leaders have taken a 'Gamalielan' approach. In the book of Acts, Gamaliel was a wise Pharisee who told the Sanhedrin that they should allow the apostles to continue to preach their controversial message: 'For if their purpose or activity is of human origin, it will fail. But if it is from God, you will not be able to stop these men; you will only find yourselves fighting against God' (Acts 5:38–39).

This, of course, does not make it right to simply 'sit on the fence'. Assessing fruit is an active learning process, not a passive experience. Wise shoppers do not simply wait for good fruit to jump into their basket – you have to pick it up, test it with a squeeze, and bag it yourself!

'Parents know that mistakes are part of the learning process,' believes David Pytches. 'We must include the freedom to *step out in faith* (or what is sincerely believed to be faith) even if the immediate end is apparent failure and temporary disorder. The end-product for God the Father is not an object for mass-production. It is rather the shaping up of each precious individual child into the image of Christ.'

It was very radical for such a reformed bastion of Calvinism as Westminster Chapel to invite Sandy Millar to speak. But this step in faith was swiftly rewarded:

'I was prayed for by Sandy and his team during the evening. I saw two or three people fall to the floor, out of about 125 present, and one of our deacons wept aloud – he was just full of it,' Kentucky-born R. T. Kendall told me, during our second meeting. 'At about 10.20 pm, Sandy asked if he could pray for me again. "Sure" I said, with minimal expectancy. Now I once had an operation and was given sodium pentathol to put me to sleep. As Sandy prayed over me, I felt the same sensation of relaxation. Though I didn't go to sleep, I found myself slumping forwards and I was helped to the floor. It was very humbling.

'That hadn't happened before at Westminster Chapel, and it hasn't happened since.' Kendall didn't feel that he had received a mandate from God to continue with these experiences. 'One thing that my church will not abide is "working something up".'

If he had seen dozens of people anointed, he would

have cancelled his holiday plans, but he felt it right to head off on vacation in the Florida Keys, keeping in touch with his church and ready to return at the drop of a hat. But the manifestations of the Holy Spirit proved to be a one-off event as far as Westminster Chapel was concerned.

'I believe that what is happening is of God – though I don't understand it. I'm a little "hurt" at God, if I may say this, that he hasn't done much here, because I *know* we are open.'

Perhaps God is working as mightily at Westminster Chapel as he is in so many other churches – but without the signs and manifestations which, after all, are only peripheral – I suggested.

'I would like to believe that is the case, but there is no *identifiable evidence* of the "Toronto Blessing" in Westminster Chapel, as at October 11th 1994, as we speak. But just before you arrived this morning, a very "proper" lady in the congregation took time off work to come and see me. She told me that she has never before known such blessings in her life as she has experienced recently, and she wanted to add her name to the list of people who have prophesied great things to come for us.

'I would eventually want to see an increasing number of conversions, and a fear of God in society. In Jonathan Edwards' day, he said that "the whole town was filled with talk of God"; that is not yet happening in London. So far so good, but a new phase is needed – a sense of God himself acting upon the community.'

Something which produces rich changes in people's lives, making them vigorously 'on fire' for God, must surely be welcomed for the opportunities it brings. When God offers us spiritual food, there is only one proper response.

Take and Eat

'[The apostle] Peter became hungry and wanted something to eat, and while it was being prepared, he fell into a trance. He saw heaven opened and something like a large sheet being let down to earth by its four corners. It contained all kinds of four-footed animals, as well as reptiles of the earth and birds of the air. Then a voice told him, "Get up, Peter. Kill and eat."

"Surely not, Lord!" Peter replied. "I have never eaten anything impure or unclean."

The voice spoke to him a second time, "Do not call anything impure that God has made clean."'

(Acts 10:10–15)

It was neither the first nor the last time that Peter said 'No' to God!

Terry Virgo, speaking eloquently on Acts 10 and 11 at the Stoneleigh International Bible Week 1994, wedded Spirit and word to show that the worries and misgivings of the early disciples are mirrored by the feelings of many Christians at the end of the twentieth century.

When the Holy Spirit makes a new breakthrough, the only acceptable attitude is one of *obedience*; even though, often, a fresh move of the Spirit clashes with previous experience. Like Peter in Acts 10:10–15, portions of today's Church have experienced a transforming encounter with God, and are facing the uphill task of sensitively convincing those who have not shared in the experience that God is seeking to do a new work – while maintaining unity.

Peter and the Jerusalem Church were like a wonky old gramophone with the needle stuck in a groove, thinking that Christ's message was intended simply to transform Judaism. God repeatedly had to nudge the record and let them hear that Christ's message was broader. It had to be taken to the Gentiles, too. It was not a revival of Judaism but a powerful awakening intended to transform the whole earth.

God was trying to tell them, 'Bung the wind-up gramophone in the attic, and buy a CD player!' The apostles remonstrated, 'But what will we play our scratchy old LP records on?'

Has the Holy Spirit said, similarly, in 1994, that the gifts of the Spirit are to come to conservative evangelicals as well as pentecostals and charismatics? There is certainly no biblical basis for believing that the gifts should be the exclusive property of one part of the Church; yet a significant number of Christians leave charismatic gifts at the back of their wardrobes, like unopened and unwanted Christmas presents. Is God moving his historic purpose forward with a new style and a fresh urgency, at a time pregnant with opportunity for revival and anointing? Has he given us the same music on a shiny set of spanking new CDs?

'If you are to understand Church history, you have to understand that it is wrapped up in the sovereignty of God, and in the Christ who rules and governs his Church,' said Virgo. 'God says "Now I will work, now is my season, now I will do a new thing!" Even in this nation, when days of terrible evil preceded the great Wesleyan Awakening, when Whitefield, Wesley and others were mightily raised up, the nation was in a terrible condition. Then again, in another period of dullness in the Church, God suddenly moved again in the time of the early Salvation Army, with William Booth. In one generation, those early works from Booth circled the globe. Church history has always had these floodtides.'

The Puritans believed optimistically that the kingdom of Christ would spread and triumph through powerful operations of the Holy Spirit, poured out upon the Church in revivals, at the command of Christ. They rejected the weak naturalistic view of inevitable process, and sought to flow with God in each fresh breathing of the Spirit and each strong new move – for a while anyway.

'Every new move of God always has its roots back into the authentic,' Virgo explained. 'Look at John the Baptist. He was a threatening new word from God, but his stock went back into the roots of Judaism.'

To continue the analogy, it was exactly the same music, in a different format.

'Peter, in just the tenth chapter of Acts, experienced: prayer, a trance, a vision, an audable voice, the Spirit leading, angels, and the Spirit falling on people so that they are overwhelmed. This is Church life, folks!'

Divine Invasion

Heaven invades our lives. Christianity was never intended to be simply a static 'bookish' religion, but an evolving one of experiential relationship with the Creator of the universe.

Peter's sermon in Acts 10:34–48 has solid Gospel content, but it's full of references to the supernatural. People interrupted Peter's sermon to respond to the Holy Spirit, in Acts 10:44. The apostle was perplexed by it all, in spite of the signs and wonders performed by Christ, which he had personally witnessed.

Yet there was also a rational response to God's acts of power.

When Peter reported back to his 'parochial church council' or his 'deacons' meeting', he 'began and explained everything to them precisely as it had happened' (Acts 11:4). He offered no theological explanation; he simply said what had occurred, in orderly sequence!

'You can be in a totally strange, supernatural, other-worldly phenomenon – but you can still, in an orderly way, explain what happened,' said Virgo. It's not good enough to simply say in an offhand way: 'Oh, you have to experience it, then you'll know!' Or 'I can't communicate it. It was just wonderful, but I can't tell you what happened. *I kissed my brains goodbye!*' Neither approach is very helpful to the rest of the body of Christ. Virgo believes 'we owe it to our brothers and sisters to explain as far as we are able', otherwise an opportunity will be lost.

When presented with an awesome trance-vision by God, why didn't Peter take the acceptable animals to eat? The close association of what was acceptable with what was not acceptable, perhaps, made it hard for him to distinguish and to take any of it, Virgo believes. We can sometimes see God do something new, something fresh, but there are things connected with it that we don't like, so we mistake an opportunity for a threat.

Peter could have said, "All right, I'll have a bit of that. I know some of these animals are unacceptable, but there are some here that I can have for my supper!" It was a mix. He could have taken some, but the association made him refuse it all – even though God had now declared all of it clean.

The parallel with our own time is not exact. God has categorically *not* now declared that the heresies of the Faith Movement, the Latter Rains, and the Manifest Sons of God are now acceptable to him! *Doctrinal error will always remain doctrinal error*. We must still discern the good from the bad, the healthy from the heretical, using the strong combination of the Spirit and the word.

A tree with weak roots may produce *less* fruit than a tree with strong roots, but it may still be good fruit. Wheat and tares may grow side by side, but the wise farmer does not risk his good crop by pulling out the tares prematurely. A day of reckoning will come, but in God's good time.

At charismatic meetings and during moves of the Spirit, where some mistakes are made – a bit of teaching may be awry, or the leadership may be a little lax – there will still be much that is of God that we can safely take and eat. But, often, we miss the opportunity to seize the good that is offered because we don't like the way God has presented it to us. Our own weak prejudices threaten to overcome us. What God has called clean, we still call unclean.

We want to put God into a little box and tell him what he's permitted to do. We want to send him to bed without any supper if he steps out of line.

Chapter Eleven

Gifted with Wisdom

Perhaps the greatest criticism which the 1994 outpouring attracted from the more staid evangelical churches was the accusation that many churches had taken their eyes off Christ, and were being carried along by emotional euphoria.

Some church leaders have belatedly admitted that – perhaps for a while – they were indeed carried away with the novelty of it all. But those were probably exceptional cases, where the situation has now been redressed. Most churches that experienced the blessing held firmly to their traditional message.

You would never have guessed that Pioneer's two-week tent crusade – the wittily titled 'Event in a Tent' – held in Surrey in September 1994, was organised and run by a church staggering under the weight of a tremendous Spirit outpouring. On the night that I visited, a more conventional and traditional tent crusade would have been hard to imagine.

The lucid preaching scarcely touched upon signs and wonders, firmly focusing instead on the need to come to Christ. 'It's not about laughter, it's not about falling down. It's about changed lives,' explained the preacher. Afterwards, there was prayer for people to be freed from superstition, but very little shaking – though I saw a handful 'slain in the Spirit', including a girl of about eight.

In the L-shaped chapel at Queen's Road Baptist Church, Norman Moss continued to preach expositionally throughout the year, unperturbed by the magnificent visitation of the Holy Spirit.

At one Sunday service, a visitor who had just returned hot-foot from Toronto described how he had felt God's awesome presence so strongly and powerfully there that he had wished he could lie not merely *on* the carpet but *under* it, so overpowering was the manifestation. Another person returned vivaciously bearing stories of how the influence of the Holy Spirit had caused him first to march on the spot, then to canter around the room, leaping over the prone bodies like a steeplechaser!

As 1994 drew near to a close, more and more churches were affected. Early autumn saw the Holy Spirit's whistlestop UK tour reach Tyneside, reproducing phenomena that had last occurred there in 1907. For six nights a week, at the Sunderland New Life church, 400–600 people a night crammed in for a touch of the Spirit's blessing:

'Some of my church members have been, and the experience has refuelled their energy and enthusiasm for God,' explained local Methodist minister John Attwood, late in October. 'One of the folk I took along had a slipped disk in her neck; she was "slain in the Spirit" there, and when she came round, her neck was better. Myself, I feel very peaceful about what has been happening. Denominational background no longer matters – the Holy Spirit is bringing Christians closer together.'

In the Croydon Vineyard, 'an older man who received prayer went down on the floor and was down for forty-five minutes. When he got up, he explained that he'd never before received such a revelation of the peace of God, and the love of the Father,' said Phil Gazley.

'It's easy to think that everything going on is a massive release of joy, but there is also a tremendous *squeezing* going on as sin is being dealt with, and brokenness is occurring. I've heard more people speak about "the dark night of the soul" in the last six months than in the last eight years. Part of the process is ministering holiness and sanctification, and it can be painful.'

Considerable wisdom has been shown in most churches and fellowships I visited where the Spirit's anointing has been manifest; but the two dozen or so meetings I attended during the weeks of preparation for this book probably covered less than 1 per cent of the churches affected. New churches affected have generally been quick to dispatch members of their ministry team to Queens Road, to HTB – or even to Toronto – to pick up tips on how the phenomena are best handled. Discernment has been vital, but perhaps something more than discernment is needed.

Go To the Ant!

One of my favourite phrases from the T.S. Eliot oeuvre is found in the *Four Quartets*:

Where is the wisdom we have lost in knowledge?
Where is the knowledge we have lost in information?

It is one matter to know when and where the Spirit of God is moving, and quite another to discern any overall plan. Even if such a general plan could be detected – and we have had scarcely a glimmer – knowing what it all signifies and *means* is a tougher exercise altogether.

We desperately need wisdom, because discernment

and knowledge are not enough. We have to discover how to apply and use knowledge. Whatever the Church has learned from the unusual outpouring – which still continues as I write in October 1994 – should be used wisely for the furtherance of God's kingdom, and to keep the Church together.

Charismatic gifts may be welcomed with open arms by the Pentecostals and the Charismatics, but they are *deeply disturbing* to many ordinary evangelicals, who feel that the Church should simply stick with preaching the New Testament. I have spoken with many devout Christians whose devotion to the Bible and the ministry of God's holy word is beyond reproach; and many have been quite traumatised in their passionate concern that their fellow Christians might inadvertently get 'carried away' and lose sight of the Church's main mission. Many charismatics are equally distraught that their brothers in Christ may tragically miss out on God's tremendous blessing.

Tom Houston believes that charismatic and non-charismatic models of the Church are both equally valid. He carefully deduces from Scripture that about half of the early churches were charismatic and half were not: 'Half the places described in Acts and half the epistles have no reference to charismatic gifts.' He has been striving to hold together the charismatic and the non-charismatic.

'I'm determined that this is not going to be divisive for City Temple, and my colleague David Hilborn feels the same. With the Lausanne Committee, I've been trying for years to put my arms around charismatics and non-charismatics alike – because I believe that both positions are authentic to the New Testament Church.

'Some churches have been split down the middle by diverse responses to this outpouring – but churches split anyway, for all sorts of reasons.

'There's no question that the British Church in 1994 was smaller than in 1975, but the proportion who have received a first hand experience of Christ is much larger now. We are a much more vibrant Church.' He didn't recognise the early signs as being a *revival*, but he was optimistic: 'This may simply be my age and my cynicism coming out, but I take heart when I hear people say that "this is just the first phase"!'

What will happen next? If revival and awakening are to follow, then the enrichment of Church life experienced in the seventies and eighties will need to lead inexorably to numerical growth before the nineties are out. If the 1981 Bible Society survey still holds up, then charismatic evangelical churches are experiencing five times the numerical growth of evangelical churches that are not charismatic. Think what will happen as more and more evangelical churches are visited by the power of the Holy Spirit.

The Fourth Wave

David Pawson, in his 1992 book, *Fourth Wave*, noted that since the late 1960s, charismatics and evangelicals have been drawing closer to each other, and suggested that, 'the time is ripe for the two fastest-growing streams in Christendom to be fully integrated.'

The Church could be likened to a television set. The one-eyed monster that most of us have in the corner of our living room produces a picture by means of four 'electron guns'. One of those guns produces a black and white picture (monochrome television sets have only this one gun) while the other three guns produce the primary colours of red, blue and green – which, in various combinations and tints, produce all the other colours.

With just the first gun functioning, you get a pristine black and white picture, with excellent definition and contrast; but it's a bit dull without the bright colours to excite the eye. You never know what colours are represented by the various tones of grey; and, if you've ever tried to watch a snooker match in B&W, it can be quite infuriating at times!

On the other hand, to have three colours without the black to give sharpness, the picture can look blurred and the shapes may appear abstract, psychedelic and ill-defined. All four electron guns need to be functioning correctly to produce a good sharp picture, vibrant and natural.

Similarly, excessive concentration on the Bible can lead to sharply defined theological ideas – and a good sense of the doctrinal principles derived from Scripture – but a certain dynamism is lacking, which can only come from a direct experience of God to validate the theoretical knowledge gleened from the study. Overemphasis on the experiential works of the Spirit can produce a vibrant and living faith, but one that lacks precision and direction, emotionally grounded and prone to sharp fluctuations and temperaments. *Both the word **and** the Spirit are needed for a balanced Christian life.*

That Pentecostal giant Smith Wigglesworth predicted two important developments that would set the Church alight with revival fire: the restoration of the gifts of the Spirit into normal Church life, and a revived emphasis on the Bible's teachings. 'When these two moves of the Spirit combine, we shall see the greatest move the Church of Jesus Christ has ever seen.'

The arrival of the fresh Blessing could feasibly result in the fulfilment of that great vision – or it could set back both unity and revival for at least a generation. The choice, I think, is ours. It's no use taking a back

seat and hoping that the decision will be taken out of
our hands. God is not going to force unity upon us
against our collective will; it is a relational matter, and
I don't believe that God forces 'arranged marriages'.
We have to take an active decision as to which way the
Church is going to go.

Back in 1992, Pawson was aware that: 'The solution
to the gap between the evangelical thesis and the charismatic antithesis will not be found at some mid-point
of "balance" *between* them, but in a new synthesis
above them.'

The charismatic needs to learn that tongues are
not everything; whilst the conservative evangelical
must discover that tongues are *not nothing*. The 'Holy
Spirit Fan Club' must learn that making a service
more spontaneous does not necessarily make it more
spiritual; and the 'Devotees of Scripture' need to learn
that a service can be orderly and Spirit-organised,
without needing everything to be written down on a
printed order of service. Many of the points of con-
flict between charismatics and evangelicals are based
distressingly on misunderstandings of each others'
viewpoints. Hopefully, the fresh outpouring of the
Spirit will result in people carefully questioning their
own closely-fought positions, and perhaps seeing the
sense in the other person's argument.

I believe that the Holy Spirit is saying to the Church
today: 'You can't have your own way all the time. You
cannot have unity and/or revival on your own terms,
but only on your heavenly Father's terms.'

Pawson pleads: 'It is for the sake of the world, and
not just the Church, that we need to combine forces.
It is ultimately for the lost that we need to sanctify
ourselves for the task of uniting our two streams. God's
purpose in giving the Spirit and the Scripture was
that we might be equipped to bring the good news of

salvation to a sad and sinful society that does not know why it is here or where it is going. That is why he needs a people who are both charismatic and evangelical.'

Love Thy Neighbour

Clearly there are equal dangers from people sticking unswervingly to their traditions and letting the wind of the Spirit blow past them, as there are in people ignoring the cerebral aspect and flamboyantly seeking the experience. Polarisation is not only bad in itself, it also produces a peculiar form of myopia which makes the sufferer earnestly believe that his own and the opposing position are all that exist, when there is at least one other view worthy to take into account.

Since the outcome of the 1994 outpouring is uncertain, Tom Houston considers that *loving God and helping your neighbour* are more important than either the cerebral *or* the emotional aspects: 'I don't need people to be cerebral, but I do need them to love their neighbour and to keep the commandments. The outcome that *is* measurable is the realm of the ethical and the neighbourly.'

Pentecost took place around AD 30 and the Jerusalem church had a whale of a time, but it 'bit the dust' around AD 70. The early Church failed lamentably to make any social or political impact on the city in which it was founded. Without a sincere concern for the welfare of others, its effectiveness in its own birthplace tragically fizzled out completely. That's a salutary lesson for those who ignore Christ's commands to take up the cross and follow in his footsteps, visiting the sick, comforting the afflicted, and healing the broken hearted – out of pure and selfless love.

'I don't want to be negative about the signs of the Spirit, but the Great Commission sends us into the world to teach, baptise and disciple; not necessarily to fire up revival everywhere – that's the responsibility of the Holy Spirit,' Roger Forster told me. 'We've been told to get on with the job. In Ichthus, we are maintaining a Church programme that contains a lot of political and social action. A couple of our leading lights employ twenty-four people on a lifeskills course for people out of work. They were a couple of the first to get blessed and to return with great zeal to their work!'

A Christian, in his or her walk with Jesus, intrinsically needs a heart for God, desiring to do whatever God wants to do, and to receive whatever the Holy Spirit wants to give. In relation to our neighbours, we shouldn't be asking 'How can I be blessed?' but 'How can I bless other people?'

'It all really started for us on Pentecost Sunday 1994,' explained Oasis' National Director Steve Chalke. 'It happened in our staff and training meetings; it's not been an engineered thing, our leaders didn't sit down and debate, "should or shouldn't we let it happen".

'I think, in itself, it is wholly good. God has the sovereign right to do what he wants, when he wants. Those who are taking a negative attitude are being destructive and judgemental. The Church has been very introverted about Pentecost, when the Holy Spirit was given to the Church for the benefit of the world.

'But there are dangers with such a great gift if it is not used properly. I'm worried about church programmes being stepped up, when the Church has too many meetings already. There's a danger of navel gazing; the Blessing is only good if it equips people to move out into society. We need to get out into the world to be salt and light. We must be more committed to seeing a *world* that can laugh and rejoice.'

Graham Cray affirms that we have the privilege of

engaging with a *broken* world: 'If the Spirit of God
has touched you, that is the kind of world in which
we have to work it out. Romans 8 helps us to make
sense of it. The groaning in the world is met by the
groaning in the heart of God. But also God the Spirit
within us is *interceding* with groans that are too deep
for words.

'We become the meeting place between the pain in
the heart of God over his world, and the pain of the
world over its brokenness. We are given security by
the Spirit that we can be in there feeling the pain, but
without becoming bereft of hope.

'Stickability in the most hopeless of situations is the
fruit of the anointing of the Spirit.'

Cray suggests that we shouldn't be asking 'Is God
in this Blessing?' but asking instead: 'Are we geared
up to showing people what this Blessing *means*, and
showing them the way to where they can live it out?'
We need to be able to move people on from simply
returning to 'receiving meetings' and to find them a
place in a mission field. We need to help people to find
places where they can serve God.

The Spirit's outpouring is for people to receive and
to take away to their own church and their own
community – it's wrong to keep coming back. It's not
for them to keep, it's for them to give away. You're
shopping in a religious supermarket, when you should
be serving in a spiritual soup kitchen!

As St Paul said pithily, 'If I have the gift of prophecy
and can fathom all mysteries and all knowledge, and if
I have a faith that can move mountains, but have not
love, I am nothing. If I give all I possess to the poor and
surrender my body to the flames, but have not love, I
gain nothing' (1 Cor 13:2–4).

This, of course, should not be used as an excuse not to
give to the poor.

Jesus Christ, naturally, was more controversial about the matter. The people to whom he will eventually say, 'Come, you who are blessed by my Father; take your inheritance, the kingdom prepared for you since the creation of the world,' will be the same ones to whom he can also say, 'I was hungry and you gave me something to eat, I was thirsty and you gave me something to drink, I was a stranger and you invited me in, I needed clothes and you clothed me, I was sick and you looked after me, I was in prison and you came to visit me ... whatever you did for one of the least of these brothers of mine, you did for me.'
(Matt 25:34–36, 40).

If we are truly wise, these are the true fruits we should essentially look for in discerning whether any manifestation is truly of God: committed concern for neighbours and friends, with effective friendship evangelism, on the part of the individual Christian; and co-ordinated social action and relief on the part of fellowships of believers.

Into All Nations

In the Third World, dedicated missionaries and indigenous churches toil together joyfully to improve the lot of the destitute and the dispossessed, upholding social justice in a way related to the praxis of Scripture through carefully argued liberation theologies – word and action going hand in hand. Often, this occurs in countries where the Church is inherently charismatic and thriving numerically. Compassionate community care is always a wonderful example of Christian love, and a powerful magnet which attracts the unchurched into a personal relationship with Christ himself.

In the East and West alike, Christians have been

the pioneers behind many AIDS hospices, just as they were behind leprosy missions a century earlier. On the streets of London, Christians hold a virtual monopoly on soup runs for the homeless. In Soho, Ichthus Fellowship have a living ministry to prostitutes. Across America, and now Europe, Victory Outreach International reach out compassionately to street people, prostitutes, drug addicts and the homeless, showing them Christ's love through practical care; and, in consequence, many are coming to God and turning their lives around. These are all measurable fruits of the Holy Spirit in Christian lives.

The most striking example of Christ-like caring that I have ever personally encountered was in Mother Theresa's Calcutta hospice. There, all the patients have terminal diseases – commonly tuberculosis, malnutrition, meningitis or cancer. Some have AIDS.

'We had one man in here,' said my guide, 'who had been in some sort of accident and had injured his leg. He left it untreated and the flesh began to rot. Soon the wound infested with maggots. We cleaned out the maggots and bathed the wound. He'll die of gangrene, but in a caring environment which is kept clean and hygienic.' As I was being shown around, my guide paused to help a dying man off his bedpan, wiped his rusty bottom for him, and then cheerfully cleaned out the bedpan.

If those who claim to have received the 'Toronto Blessing' have really been touched by God, then this is the kind of selfless behaviour that ought naturally to follow!

'God bless you,' said the world's most famous nun, as she greeted me on her way to supper later that evening. 'Keep growing in Jesus,' she counselled, her rice and dall growing cold. It's difficult to argue with that piece of advice.

Christ was all around me in that place of the dying. You could see him in every face, hear his words 'I thirst' from those forsaken by the world. But you would never hear them whisper, 'Father, into your hands I commend my spirit,' with their terminal breath, and they will not be with him in paradise today, unless someone shares with them the love of a dying Saviour who came – not so that people can fall on the church floor – but so that they can stand up transformed and follow their Master faithfully wherever he leads.

Now that would indeed be spiritual fruit!

Spirituality Unpacked

The essential connection between (i) Scripture, (ii) signs & wonders, and (iii) loving your neighbour, is much simpler than it appears – and the Holy Spirit is the key to them all – once you can grasp the various strands of spirituality in their correct context:

The first spiritual fruit that we read about in the Bible is the one that Adam and Eve ate when they were disobedient, and which led to their spiritual death! They didn't realise that God meant what he said. (That's what happens if you don't have discernment.)

God's compassionate response was to inaugurate the *sacrificial* tradition. The death of an animal, killed to provide the first two humans with clothing, was the prototype of God's own atoning death to eradicate the penalty of sin. This tradition is universal in early cultures the world over, though its true significance was seldom grasped. We are familiar with the Jewish sacrificial system, given at Sinai, enshrined in the Old Testament. As I have outlined in detail in my book *Karma'N'Chips*, similar traditions exist in South Asia – the *karma yoga* tradition, where it was believed that only a perfect high priest making a perfect sacrifice

would suffice to rescue a person from physical and
spiritual death.

In its modern form, Christians, Jews and Hindus
alike practise sacrificial giving of their time and tithes,
giving to others as they have been given to by their
deity. It's the *fruit* of faith, a practical outworking of
a tradition which believes it is better to give than to
receive. It can be good or bad, depending on whether
charitable acts are performed grudgingly out of a sense
of duty and legalistic obligation, or from a heart filled
with grace and love.

A second tradition ran alongside the sacrificial tradition from very early on in human history. This is a
signs and wonders *mystic* tradition, apparently derived
from an inquisitiveness about the spiritual world. In
many places, priests distorted the sacrificial tradition,
becoming sorcerors – turning their rituals into rites,
and their holy books into *grimoires* – intending to cajole
spiritual forces into doing their bidding.

It was a grotesque parody of prayer; instead of
asking God to act, these sorcerer priests sought to
manipulate demonic gods into doing their bidding. Just
as God acts supernaturally through signs and wonders
– particularly around the time of the Exodus, through
Elijah and Elisha, and during the lives of Christ and
the apostles – others sought unwisely to control the
supernatural for their own ends. Signs and wonders
themselves are neutral; it is the motivation and the
power behind them that can make them good or evil.

Around 700 BC, a third strand of spirituality emerged.
It was a bookish tradition, appealing to the intellect,
which gave rise to Theravada Buddhism, jnana yoga
and Greek gnosticism. This *intellectual* spirituality is
based upon the study of various scriptures, seeking
to derive knowledge of God from them. An essential
characteristic is the need for a sound and reliable

teacher, who does not simply exposit the scriptures, but faithfully passes on the deepest secrets of their meaning – to lead the reader into all truth.

The fruit of this tradition can be sweet or sour – good or bad – depending on which scriptures you use, and who you choose for a teacher. Pick the Bible for your Scriptures and Christ for your teacher and you've got an unbeatable combination. But other combinations can lead to uncertainty, superstition and oppression.

The fourth strand is suggested in the ancient texts of many faiths, but found its fulfilment in the historical person of Jesus Christ – whose death we could accurately term *The Calvary Blessing!*

This *devotional* tradition – giving wholehearted worship and commitment to one's chosen deity – is the principle behind Mahayana Buddhism and bhakti yoga. With legalistic trappings, it is the foundation of Islam, but its purest form is found in biblical Christianity.

These four strands of spirituality, all of which have survived to the present day, are essentially neutral. You can place yourself in the centre of each and become a selfish humanist. You can put an idolatrous figure or object of devotion – it can be money, sex, television, drugs or anything else open to misuse – at the heart of any of the four traditions and become a 'religious' nut besotted by ideals and lifestyles that are ultimately unfulfilling. Or you can place the almighty and eternal God at the centre, and harvest spiritual fruit – not religion, but the fulfilment and culmination of all religions, a living relationship with the Creator of the universe.

Clearly, evangelicals draw strongest from *intellectual* and *devotional* spirituality, while charismatics drink their water from the wells of the *devotional* and *mystic* traditions. The *sacrificial* strand is also prevalent in both – though not as strongly as it may

be found in either Anglo-Catholicism or the Orthodox
Church.

It is rare to find in any one church – or any one
individual for that matter – a balanced blend drawing
the best from all four traditions. Yet a rope braded from
all four strands of spirituality would be unbreakable;
it would be a worthy cord to bind the church together
in an unbreakable bond. If the Church would allow
itself to produce such a four-fold spiritual cord – from
a uniting of evangelicals and charismatics (perhaps the
sacramental traditions too) with a desire to sacrificially
serve God and their fellows – then I believe that revival
and awakening would swiftly follow.

And that would be a breath of fresh air.

4D Man

Songwriter Howard Werth once recorded a tune containing the line, 'I'm a 4D man, living in a 3D plan'.
It's no fun being confined to a world where a part of
yourself is cramped and unfulfilled.

We are all mental, emotional, physical and spiritual
creatures. We desire and need fulfilment in all four
areas of our lives. The Bible reading and study so
beloved by evangelicals is mentally stimulating, and
fulfils intellectual cravings to know more of God. Worship fulfils the emotional need to give expression to
our feelings about God – and charismatic worship has
filtered into many non-charismatic churches, I believe,
because of the way it is capable of satisfying our
deepest emotional desires. A merging of the evangelical
and charismatic wings of the Church could lead to cross
fertilisation – and a restoration of the intellectual and
emotional balance that the Church desperately needs.

But there are still two aspects of life, the relational
and the spiritual, where many people still fall down.

– Evangelicals are often lacking a truly mystical dimension to their spirituality. For them, signs and wonders are something they often read about in Scripture, but are not part of their everyday lives. The charismatic Christian has regular experience of the supernatural workings of God, but often with little understanding. Generally, the mystical is a great mystery – a world that they glimpse but dimly through signs and wonders, prophecy and words of knowledge, but fail fully to understand.

– In the world of physical human interactions, many evangelicals are often generous to the poor and zealous for friendship evangelism, out of a well-developed sense of duty. They love their neighbours because the Bible tells them so to do, rather than because they empathetically feel genuine love for their neighbour. The charismatic, on the other hand, may love insensitively, overpowering people with a claustrophobic and smothering sentiment that cloyingly lacks the disciplined concern and forethought that would come with a more analytical mindset. In the pragmatics of day-by-day existence, the charismatic needs to be more thoughtful, and the evangelical needs to be become more passionate. Each has much to learn from the other.

Just as the four braids of spirituality need to interweave to produce an unbreakable cord to bind Christ's followers together, so all the aspects of human life and experience must be adequately catered for by the Church (both locally and worldwide) if mature and balanced Christians are to be nurtured within the bond.

Not all Christians are intellectuals, anymore than all are worship leaders, but the local church needs a balance of people with strengths in the appropriate areas that will enable it to fulfil its work in its particular locality.

If one of those important aspects is neglected, then the result is like a chair where the legs are all different lengths – discomfort is guaranteed. If the *intellectual, emotional, relational* and *spiritual* needs are all adequately met, then the Church as a whole can become a stable and balanced body through which God's Spirit and grace can smoothly be outpoured without hindrance.

'This grace is not poured out simply to brighten up dull services, to make us better members of our churches, or to excite people with signs and wonders,' maintains Peter Hocken of charismatic renewal. 'It is poured out to restore God's Church to be a Church after his own mind,' he writes in *One Lord, One Spirit, One Body*.

'It is poured out so that whoever looks upon the Church will give praise and glory to the Son of God. It is poured out so that the lives of Christians may declare the truth of the Gospel by the way they live as fully reconciled sisters and brothers. It is poured out so that the Church can proclaim to a dying world the full richness of the Gospel with unmistakable clarity and manifest power. It is poured out so that a believing people may once again cry out with faith, "Come, Lord Jesus" (Rev 22:20). To him be glory for ever and ever!'

Chapter Twelve

Gifted with Grace

The Holy Spirit adroitly draws attention to Christ, making his presence both attractive and desirable to non-believer and Christian alike, though clearly the responses of those in each category will differ:

To the non-Christian. Perhaps the biggest lie that anyone has ever told me is that salvation – a relationship with the living God – comes *without a price tag*. It is actually the most precious commodity in the universe, because it cost the sinless Lord Jesus an agonising death. To receive the justification that comes from Christ's atoning death can be costly too.

Becoming a follower of Christ, being 'born again' or any of the other euphemisms that stand for adoption into God's family, is usually achieved by saying the 'sinner's prayer' which runs along the lines of: 'Jesus, I confess my sinful nature, and I recognise my need of your forgiveness, so please come into my life as Saviour and Lord.' But at what point during that prayer does salvation become effective? When is the instant of conversion?

I suggest that the point at which a person becomes a member of God's family is actually *before* the prayer is spoken!

It is the role of the Holy Spirit to make someone aware of their sin; it is not the Christian's job to make people feel guilty! The stirrings of conviction about sin, righteousness and judgement – an essential part of revival – are due to the Holy Spirit's presence. He makes the truths about Jesus convincing, and makes possible repentance and faith. It's a rather more serious role than simply making people fall over.

I believe that the Holy Spirit makes a walk with Christ seem so desirable that the convicted person then makes a commitment *within his or her own heart,* before the public confession is made with words. Most people have little or no grasp of the theological niceties of the steps they are taking when they 'come to Christ'.

I believe that once you come to desire God more than anything else, the nature of the silent commitment you make is one of total self-giving. You shamefully admit that nothing you have can equal the precious bounty that is offered, you confess your unworthiness and throw yourself at God's mercy. Like the man who found a pearl of great price and sold everything he had to purchase it, at the moment of receiving Christ, the inarticulate prayer of our hearts is: 'God, I want and need you so badly! I'll do *whatever it takes* to come to you!'

'Whatever it takes' is *inclusive* of the prayer of commitment that will eventually be made, and salvation is sealed from that inner commitment to self-sacrifice. You become a Christian by putting yourself – all your hopes and aspirations, all your possessions, your whole life, your past, present and future – on the altar of sacrifice.

And God says, 'No! That lot is not good enough. It nowhere near meets the asking price!'

That's the painful reality of the human condition.

Only then does Jesus Christ take your place, substituting his own righteousness for *your* sinfulness, and giving *you* his perfect holiness into the bargain, as an act of unmerited favour. You can shop around, but you won't get a better deal anywhere else!

Yet the transaction takes place only once you yourself – like Abraham with Isaac – have been prepared to sacrifice everything that is dear to you! From that moment on, you are adopted into his family. The fabulous treasure which you couldn't possibly afford to purchase becomes yours as the most costly gift in the universe. It's the most expensive present anyone could ever give you, because it required the sinless Christ to *pay* for those sins he traded from you – cash on the nail – during his agonising crucifixion.

His grace is not cheap.

But that's only the beginning. Anyone who has not made that first step ought to know that living your life with Christ is very rewarding, but also very demanding. Jesus is not a very tidy person to have in your life. In biblical times, if Christ was with you, people were apt to tear holes in your roof and lower cripples to be healed in your front room! He leaves his ugly and blood-splattered cross in your hallway; it doesn't go with the wallpaper, and it clashes with the curtains. Even worse, he expects you to carry it for him.

You should also be aware that Christ will want to change your life, through his Holy Spirit. He takes you as you are, and makes you like him. You'll like the change; but it's the Holy Spirit that has to convince you, not any articulate words of mine. Once you've accepted him, you'll wonder why you held out against his gracious approach for so long. Without him, there's no way worth travelling; no truth worth knowing; and no life worth living.

Salvation has past, present and future tenses. It begins with justification. As William Brown describes it in *Who Are You Holy Spirit?*: 'Justification describes how the Lord Jesus Christ paid the penalty for our own sins by dying upon the cross for us. By our repentance and faith, God calls us personally to lay hold of his gift of forgiveness and eternal life.'

Justification is the past-tense part. The future-tense is the *glorification* which will come at the end of your life, when you go to be with God forever. In the middle is the present-tense bit, with a terribly religious-sounding name – *sanctification*. Sanctification is the main task of the Holy Spirit. Making people laugh, cry, shake, fall and speak in tongues are only his sidelines. Brown says:

'It is God's gracious process of cleaning us up. We may be forgiven sinners, but we are still sinners. If we are in a road accident and the Royal Infirmary staff get our heart restarted and reset our broken bones, it would be a poor job if, having saved our lives, they sent us home without also cleaning off the oil and mud and matted blood to make us fit for society. So it is with God. Having saved our souls through the Lord Jesus Christ, he has to go on and clean up some pretty murky parts of us.'

Every human religion teaches that you have to become perfect under your own steam, before God will accept you. Some chance! In Christianity, God takes the initiative. It is the only world faith that places sanctification *after* justification; God accepts you as you are, and then makes you into the perfect person you could never otherwise become.

For the non-Christian reader, if you have felt the Holy Spirit moving you to conviction while reading this book, and particularly the last few pages, then perhaps it's time to think about saying the 'sinner's prayer' for yourself. You cannot receive the Holy Spirit until you are prepared to lay yourself on the altar.

A Time for Choices

For the Christian who desires to receive some of the blessing that God has poured out particularly during 1994 – and its reception may not be as dramatic as the experiences you've read about in the pages of this book – then you need to ask him for it. Simply pray: 'Heavenly Father, in the name of your precious Son, Jesus Christ, please send your Holy Spirit now! Come, Holy Spirit!' (There is no biblical warrant for praying directly to the Holy Spirit.)

- If you would prefer to receive whatever blessing God wants to give you within the fellowship of other Christians, then you would do best to speak firstly with your own pastor.

- If a leadership team is not moving charismatically in the Spirit, what should a member of the congregation do? 'I would encourage people to pray for their leadership, and to love them,' Sandy Millar suggested. 'All sorts of things can happen when we pray in love. I can think of many people who have been enormously helped.'

- If your church leader is not prepared to run a 'receiving meeting', or feels too uncomfortable doing so, then you need to find the nearest church to you where such meetings are held. After prayer and consideration, if you still feel led to seek the Blessing, then go along to be prayed over by a responsible person who has a ministry for it.

- If you are a church leader yourself, and would like to commence 'receiving meetings', Millar's advice to pastors is: 'Eliminate eccentricity, to allow the Spirit to do what he wants to do without people being affected by our oddness.' HTB, of course, pioneered the evangelistic Alpha course; and Millar still believes that evangelism and any move of the Spirit should go together. A church needs to respond to any move of the Spirit with humility and faith.

If you are responsible for facilitating a 'receiving meeting', ensure that you don't seek personal gain, prominence or benefit from a divine visitation. In Acts 8 we read of Simon the sorceror who wanted to facilitate the Spirit's anointing for thoroughly tarnished motives, and was roundly denounced by the apostle Peter. Remember that God looks into our hearts and knows our true motives.

Gerald Coates and others have produced guidelines for churches experiencing 'times of refreshing'. Briefly: Do not develop a ministry of manifestations when God wants something deeper; do not hype meetings; focus on Christ, and not methodology; create a worshipful environment; refer to Scripture to retain subjectivity; wait on God; encourage a continual response; encourage people to release their emotions; and ensure you have trusted people to minister to those responding.

Do not, in any way, manipulate the activity of the Holy Spirit.

Encourage people to be open to God, not looking for manifestations, but a work of the Spirit seen or unseen. Explain any unusual activity, with reference to the Bible. Be prepared for criticism. While not discouraging people from visiting other churches to see what is happening, be wary of competitiveness and comparisons, and also of people running around like headless chickens simply to 'get blessed' without that blessing being allowed to bring about a radical change in their lives. Encourage people always, but find time for yourself to receive, rest, pray and study Scripture.

Don't feel either, that there is any compulsion to seek blessing, much less to desire manifestations and phenomena. Blessing comes in God's own good time.

In Luke 10, we read that when Jesus and the disciples stayed with Mary and Martha, Mary made sure that she was in the best place to receive a rich blessing – listening to the words of Jesus, and sitting at his feet, the same feet over which she would later pour perfume and dry with her hair. But Martha was not best pleased. She went to Jesus to complain: 'Lord, don't you care that my sister has left me to do the work by myself? Tell her to help me' (Luke 10:40).

Jesus *could* have responded by indicating to Mary that sitting in the presence of God Incarnate, and being blessed with his teaching, was less important than sacrificially helping Martha to make God's supper: 'Get into that kitchen and rattle those pots and pans!' But instead, he told Martha not to worry so much: 'Mary has chosen what is better, and it will not be taken away from her' (Luke 10:42).

I'm struck by what Jesus *doesn't* say. If it was better to be blessed with Jesus' presence than to be concerned with all the preparations, why did Jesus not say sternly to Martha: 'Come off it! You should be in here with Mary, sitting and listening, not messing about with other matters!'

It seems that Christ was content for one sister to be active behind the scenes, and the other to be receiving the blessing of his divine presence. I suggest that not all need to receive the so-called 'Toronto Blessing' in dramatic circumstances, with accompanying signs. Like Martha's, there are administrative tasks to be undertaken which do not necessitate the more dynamic touch of God; though those working selflessly behind the scenes should be wary of criticising others who are queueing to be blessed.

Different parts of the body of Christ possess different needs, and each Christian needs to receive whatever he or she needs at any given time – without feeling guilty or greedy, and without criticising others whose requirements differ from their own.

Not all need to shake or fall, but *all need to produce the fruit of the Spirit* in a powerful way. Laughter and/or tears will be essential, too, in many cases, to free the blocked emotions and to open up new areas of the personality to God's healing and empowering touch. If the fruit can be produced without the dramatic manifestations, then well and good. As Forster has pointed out, in previous revivals, only a small percentage experienced the phenomena, and this demonstration of the sovereign moves of God served to convict others.

You can legitimately be a Mary or a Martha, but you mustn't be a Lazarus – waiting for a miracle to raise you from your complacent oblivion. Some Christians have been sitting docile in the same pew for forty years, when there was work to be done.

The Bottom Line

Those who have expressed concern that the recent outpouring of the Holy Spirit is 'not part of the normative Christian experience' are probably correct; the undeniable fact that it occurred so often in 1994 suggests that these are not 'normal' times.

The Blessing either *is* or it *isn't* a powerful outpouring of God's Spirit. If it *is*, and the manifestations *appear* to be contrary to God's received word in the Scriptures, then either God is wrong, or the critic's theology is wrong, and needs urgently to be reassessed. I know which I believe to be the case, but I'll let the reader make up his or her own mind!

If the Church has experienced occurrences in 1994 that are *not* genuine outpourings of God's Spirit, then this does not justify or validate the critics' theology. Their theology generally is not framed in such a way that it is capable of authentication or falsification. It has nothing much to say about renewal.

Those who have grown closer to God through their prayers, their reading of Scripture, and their exercise of spiritual gifts – and who have produced spiritual fruit – will not care that they were premature in identifying a move of the Spirit. They will be moving blissfully on with God. Indeed, their spiritual progress may itself be the yardstick by which any future estimation of the importance of the 1994th year of the Christian era will be judged. Their optimistic enthusiasm, prayerful pleading for revival and awakening, and outspoken commitment to renewal at the present time, may be self-fulfilling prophecy.

Theology ought rightly to explain systematically how God thinks and operates, but it cannot be a rule book which chains the Omnipotent into petty bureaucracy. He's not an errand boy who has to obey the office rules; he's God!

The Bible contains sufficient for salvation and good conduct, but it is not exhaustive; the world could not contain all the books that could be written to present such an extensive decription of the mystery of God's workings. He does not merely contain himself to repeating everything he's said and done before. Anyone who seeks to dictate to the Almighty the ways in which he is allowed to work should perhaps heed the lesson of Job.

We each need to choose individually whatever will move us forward collectively into the next stage of God's plan; we need to look for his leading. Whether the immediate future will bring renewal, revival, awakening or a spiritual recession, ultimately is known only to God. The evidence suggests persuasively that the 1994 'wave' will fuel the renewal movement, but it's too early to judge whether the whole Church will be affected – much less whether society will feel the reverberations.

But one day we *will* know. Perhaps, in the next century, people will re-read these words from the vantage point of a major Awakening, and wonder with amusement why so many Christian leaders were so cautious at the beginning of a revival!

One glorious day, Christ's followers will see the whole panorama of redemptive history laid tantalisingly before them, and understand fully the purpose of God at each stage. We see poor reflections now, but one day we will see face to face. Now we know in part, but in heaven, we will know in full.

> All shall be well and
> All manner of things shall be well
> When the tongues of flame are in-folded
> Into the crowned knot of fire
> And the fire and the rose are one.

T.S. Eliot's words are more eloquent than mine in evoking the mystery of God's redemptive purpose. But no words can adequately describe the wonder that will one day be laid before our eyes.

Selected Bibliography

Angel, G. *Delusion or Dynamite? Reflections on a Quarter Century of Charismatic Renewal* (MARC: 1989)

Babcox, N. *My Search for Charismatic Reality* (Multnomah Press: 1985)

Barnhart, J.E. *Jim and Tammy: Charismatic Intrigue Inside PTL* (Prometheus Books: 1988)

Basham, D. *Face Up With a Miracle* (Whitaker: 1967)

Bennett, D.J. *Nine O'Clock in the Morning* (Kingsway: 1970)

Bennett, D.J. and R. *The Holy Spirit and You* (Kingsway: 1971)

Brown, W. *Who Are You Holy Spirit?* (Handsel Press: 1992)

Buchanan, C. *Encountering Charismatic Worship* (Grove: 1977)

Budgen, V. *The Charismatics and the Word of God* (Evangelical Press: 1985)

Butler, C.S. *Test the Spirits* (Evangelical Press: 1985)

Cassidy, M. *Bursting the Wineskins* (Hodder: 1983)

Cerullo, M. with Pain, T, *Forgiven!* (Kingsway: 1993)

Chevreau, G. *Catch the Fire* (Marshall Pickering: 1994)

Christenson, L. (ed) *Come Holy Spirit: A Study of Charismatic Renewal in the Church* (Augsburg: 1987)

Dayton, D.W. *Theological Roots of Pentecostalism* (Scarecrow Press Inc: 1987)

Dunn, J.D.G. *Jesus and the Spirit* (SCM: 1975)

Eliot, T.S. *Four Quartets* (Faber and Faber: 1944)

Fearon, M. *Through a Glass Clearly* (unpublished manuscript)

Finney, C.G. *Power from on High* (Victory Press: 1944)

Gidoomal, R. and Fearon, M. *Karma'N'Chips: The New Age of Asian Spirituality* (Wimbledon Publishing Company: 1994)

Gordon, B. *Explaining the Holy Spirit* (Sovereign World: 1991)

Harper, M. *These Wonderful Gifts* (Hodder: 1989)

Higton, T. *That the World May Believe* (Marshalls: 1985)

Hinn, B. *The Anointing* (NelsonWord: 1991)

Hocken, P. *One Lord, One Spirit, One Body* (Paternoster: 1987)

Holroyd, S. *Psi and the Consciousness Explosion* (Bodley Head: 1977)

Johnian, M. *Fresh Blessings* (1994)

Kelsey, M. *The Christian and the Supernatural* (Augsberg: 1976)

Kinnaman, G.D. *And Signs Shall Follow* (Sovereign World: 1992)

Kissell, B. *Walking on Water* (Hodder: 1986)

Larcombe, J.R. *Unexpected Healing* (Hodder: 1991)

Masters, P. and Whitcomb, J. *The Charismatic Phenomena* (Wakeman Trust: 1982)

McConnell, D. *The Promise of Health and Wealth* (Hodder: 1992)

MacNutt, F. *Overcome by the Spirit* (Eagle: 1991)

Neitz, M.J. *Charisma and Community* (Transaction Books: 1987)

Noble, J and C. *Everyman's Guide to the Holy Spirit, the End of the World and You* (Kingsway: 1991)

O'Neill, A. *Charismatic Healing in Everyday Life* (Mercer Press: 1991)

Pain, T. *Baptism in Holy Spirit* (Kingsway: 1987)

Pawson, D. *Fourth Wave* (Hodder: 1992)

Pytches, D. *Some Said it Thundered* (Hodder: 1990)

Sizer, S. *Rector's Reflections* (privately published pamphlet)

Smail, T. Walker, A. and Wright, N. *Charismatic Renewal: The Search for a Theology* (SPCK: 1993)

Symonds, M. *The Coming Revival* (Highland: 1993)

Tari, M. *Like a Mighty Wind* (Kingsway: 1971)

Walker, A. *Restoring the Kingdom: The Radical Christianity of the House Church Movement* (Hodder: 1985)

Watson, D. *One in the Spirit* (Hodder: 1973)

Wimber, J. and Springer, K. *The Dynamics of Spiritual Growth* (Hodder: 1990)

Wimber, J. and Springer, K. *Power Evangelism* (Hodder: 2nd ed. 1992)

Worsfold, J.E. *A History of the Charismatic Movement in New Zealand* (Julian Literature Trust: 1974)

The Interlinear Greek-English New Testament (Bagster: 1958)

For background material, I am grateful to the authors of the above books, and to other authors too numerous to mention here. (However, inclusion does not necessarily indicate endorsement of their individual scholarship or theology.)

Acknowledgements

Thanks to the writers of the various magazine and newspaper articles, named individually in the text, who wrote in: *Alpha, Baptist Times, Charisma, Christian Herald, Church of England Newspaper, The Daily Mail, The Daily Telegraph, Evangelical Now, Evangelism Today, Focus on HTB, Good News, The Independent, Media Spotlight, New Covenant, Prophecy Today, Redemption, Renewal, Sunday Times, Sunday Telegraph, The Times*, and *The Western Mail*.

I am grateful to the following, who graciously consented to be interviewed face-to-face for this book, all at extremely short notice: *Gerald Coates, Graham Cray, Paul Dakin, Colin Dye, Joel Edwards, Roger Forster, Phil Gazley, Ram Gidoomal, Adrian Hawkes, David and Mia Hilborn, Tom Houston, R.T. Kendall, Richard Laugharne, Sandy Millar, Norman Moss*, and *Andrew Walker*.

Thanks to the following, for agreeing to be interviewed by telephone: *John Atwood, Steve Chalke, Chris Cole, Chris Edmondson, Glyn Ellis, David Holden, David King, Martin Neil, David Roberts, John Roe*, and *Peter Watherston*.

The interviews with Paul Cain and Sal Solo were originally conducted by me for the *Baptist Times*. Interviews with Clive Calver and Dave Tomlinson were conducted by me for the *Church Times*. The interview with Peter Singh was conducted by me while in India, under the auspice of South Asian Concern, originally with no specific purpose in mind. The interview with David Pytches was conducted by David Wavre, originally for the Foreword to *Overcome by the Spirit*.

John Wimber is quoted from (amongst other sources) his talks at Let the Fire Fall held in Wembley Conference Centre in September 1994. The Billy Graham quote is from *Alpha* magazine. The Mary Pytches quotes are from *Focus on HTB*. Terry Virgo is quoted from a talk given at Stoneleigh International Bible Week 1994. Eleanor Mumford is quoted from two talks given at Holy Trinity Brompton in May 1994.

Special thanks to Ed Chatelier, Joel Edwards, Mark Elsdon-Dew, Keith Ewing, Nazar Georgis and Adrian Hawkes for alerting me to essential background material, facilitating interviews, and serving as sounding boards. Thanks, too, to the press office at Westminster Central Hall, and to Paul Smith, for facilitating certain telephone interviews.

I am deeply grateful to David Wavre and all at Eagle, not simply for commissioning this book, but for getting it out so quickly and painlessly.

Finally, belated thanks to members past and present of: Huddersfield Polytechnic Christian Union; Kirkheaton Parish Church; The Risen Christ and All Souls, Clapton Park; Arts Centre Group; All Souls, Langham Place; ASLAN: and last, but (not) least, the motley mavericks at 'Thursdays'.

You have all influenced this book in more ways than you can possibly imagine. My heartfelt thanks!